Photoshop® cs2
Top 100

Simplified®

TIPS & TRICKS

by Lynette Kent

Visual

WILEY

Photoshop® cs2: Top 100 Simplified® Tips & Tricks

Published by
Wiley Publishing, Inc.
111 River Street
Hoboken, NJ 07030-5774

Published simultaneously in Canada

Copyright © 2006 by Wiley Publishing, Inc., Indianapolis, Indiana

Library of Congress Control Number: 2005923200

ISBN-13: 978-0-7645-8841-9

ISBN-10: 0-7645-8841-9

Manufactured in the United States of America

10 9 8 7 6 5 4 3 2 1

1K/QY/RR/QV/IN

Trademark Acknowledgments

Contact Us

For general information on our other products and services contact our Customer Care Department within the U.S. at 800-762-2974, outside the U.S. at 317-572-3993 or fax 317-572-4002.

For technical support, please visit www.wiley.com/techsupport.

Permissions

Permissions Granted

Wiley Publishing, Inc.

U.S. Sales

Contact Wiley at (800) 762-2974 or fax (317) 572-4002.

PRAISE FOR VISUAL BOOKS

"I have to praise you and your company on the fine products you turn out. I have twelve Visual books in my house. They were instrumental in helping me pass a difficult computer course. Thank you for creating books that are easy to follow. Keep turning out those quality books."
Gordon Justin (Brielle, NJ)

"What fantastic teaching books you have produced! Congratulations to you and your staff. You deserve the Nobel prize in Education. Thanks for helping me understand computers."
Bruno Tonon (Melbourne, Australia)

"A Picture Is Worth a Thousand Words! If your learning method is by observing or hands-on training, this is the book for you!"
Lorri Pegan-Durastante (Wickliffe, OH)

"Over time, I have bought a number of your 'Read Less - Learn More' books. For me, they are THE way to learn anything easily. I learn easiest using your method of teaching."
José A. Mazón (Cuba, NY)

"You've got a fan for life!! Thanks so much!!"
Kevin P. Quinn (Oakland, CA)

"I have several books from the Visual series and have always found them to be valuable resources."
Stephen P. Miller (Ballston Spa, NY)

"I have several of your Visual books and they are the best I have ever used."
Stanley Clark (Crawfordville, FL)

"Like a lot of other people, I understand things best when I see them visually. Your books really make learning easy and life more fun."
John T. Frey (Cadillac, MI)

"I have quite a few of your Visual books and have been very pleased with all of them. I love the way the lessons are presented!"
Mary Jane Newman (Yorba Linda, CA)

"Thank you, thank you, thank you...for making it so easy for me to break into this high-tech world."
Gay O'Donnell (Calgary, Alberta, Canada)

"I write to extend my thanks and appreciation for your books. They are clear, easy to follow, and straight to the point. Keep up the good work! I bought several of your books and they are just right! No regrets! I will always buy your books because they are the best."
Seward Kollie (Dakar, Senegal)

"I would like to take this time to thank you and your company for producing great and easy-to-learn products. I bought two of your books from a local bookstore, and it was the best investment I've ever made! Thank you for thinking of us ordinary people."
Jeff Eastman (West Des Moines, IA)

"Compliments to the chef!! Your books are extraordinary! Or, simply put, extra-ordinary, meaning way above the rest! THANKYOU THANKYOU THANKYOU! I buy them for friends, family, and colleagues."
Christine J. Manfrin (Castle Rock, CO)

CREDITS

Project Editor
Jade L. Williams

Acquisitions Editor
Jody Lefevere

Product Development Manager
Lindsay Sandman

Copy Editor
Kim Heusel

Technical Editor
Rick Redfern

Editorial Manager
Robyn Siesky

Permissions Editor
Laura Moss

Editorial Assistant
Adrienne Porter

Manufacturing
Allan Conley
Linda Cook
Paul Gilchrist
Jennifer Guynn

Screen Artist
Jill Proll

Illustrators
Ronda David-Burroughs

Book Design
Kathie Rickard

Production Coordinator
Maridee Ennis

Layout
Jennifer Heleine
Amanda Spagnuolo

Cover Design
Anthony Bunyan

Proofreader
Christine Pingleton

Quality Control
Amanda Briggs
John Greenough

Indexer
Johnna VanHoose

Special Help
Adobe Systems, Inc.

Vice President and Executive Group Publisher
Richard Swadley

Vice President and Publisher
Barry Pruett

Composition Director
Debbie Stailey

ABOUT THE AUTHOR

Lynette Kent is a split nationality. A native Californian and Parisian, both by birthright and having lived in California and Paris, she speaks both French and English fluently. After completing her master's degree at Stanford University, she taught art at the high school and community college levels. Lynette is a demo artist at trade shows for computer graphics companies, and helps lead the Adobe Technology Exchange of Southern California, a professional organization for designers, photographers, and artists.

HOW TO USE THIS BOOK

Photoshop® cs2: Top 100 Simplified® Tips & Tricks includes 100 tasks that reveal cool secrets, teach timesaving tricks, and explain great tips guaranteed to make you more productive with Photoshop. The easy-to-use layout lets you work through all the tasks from beginning to end or jump in at random.

Who Is This Book For?

You already know Photoshop basics. Now you'd like to go beyond, with shortcuts, tricks and tips that let you work smarter and faster. And because you learn more easily when someone *shows* you how, this is the book for you.

Conventions Used In This Book

❶ Steps
This book uses step-by-step instructions to guide you easily through each task. Numbered callouts on every screen shot show you exactly how to perform each task, step by step.

❷ Tips
Practical tips provide insights to save you time and trouble, caution you about hazards to avoid, and reveal how to do things in Photoshop that you never thought possible!

❸ Task Numbers
Task numbers from 1 to 100 indicate which lesson you are working on.

❹ Difficulty Levels
For quick reference, these symbols mark the difficulty level of each task.

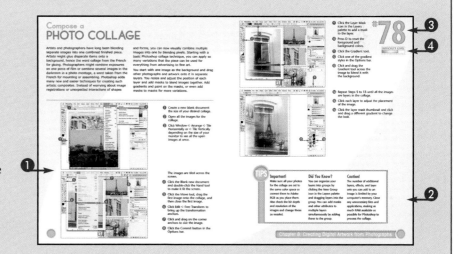

DIFFICULTY LEVEL	Demonstrates a new spin on a common task
DIFFICULTY LEVEL	Introduces a new skill or a new task
DIFFICULTY LEVEL	Combines multiple skills requiring in-depth knowledge
DIFFICULTY LEVEL	Requires extensive skill and may involve other technologies

Table of Contents

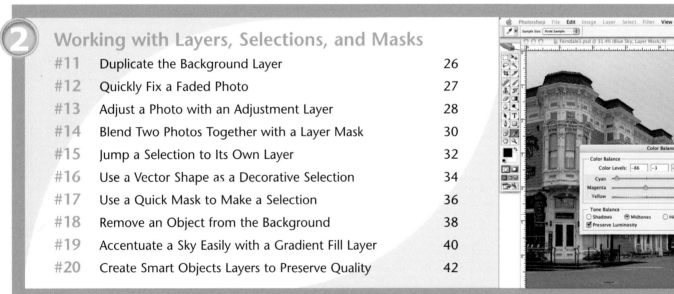

Table of Contents

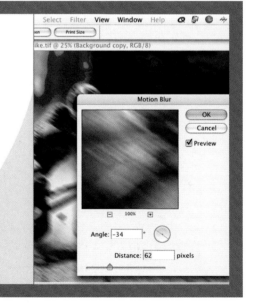

7 Designing with Text Effects

8 Creating Digital Artwork from Photographs

Table of Contents

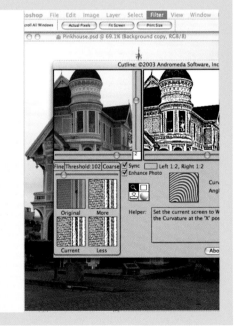

Customizing Photoshop for Your Projects

Photoshop is a wonderfully powerful program. Not only can you do so many things with Photoshop, there are always a number of ways to accomplish each project. By setting Photoshop to work for you, you can develop your own techniques and find ways to adapt the standard tools to those techniques.

Using Photoshop is really learning to customize the application for your own personal projects and your own personal style. When you work on an image, you may prefer to see some palettes and not others. You may also prefer certain tool settings to others. Setting up Photoshop to work your way makes you more productive, the program more useful, and everything you do with Photoshop much more fun.

With Photoshop CS2, Adobe has taken customization to a new level. You can now modify your settings and preferences in more ways than ever before by adjusting the workspace, the palettes, and the tools to fit the requirements of specific projects or just for your own preferences. These may seem like boring steps, yet setting up Photoshop's preferences and the workspace, knowing how to make your own gradients, customizing some shortcuts and tools, and designing templates and brushes can save you time as you work on images, and free you to become more creative. By customizing Photoshop and setting the application your way, you gain familiarity with the program and become more comfortable as you try different projects.

Top 100

CHANGE THE COLOR SETTINGS
to fit your projects

Using Adobe Photoshop CS2 is an image-altering experience! You can work on images for print or for the Web. You can improve photographs, repurpose them, or create original designs. Because printed images and Web images have different limits on the range of colors they can represent, you need to set the working color space for your project.

The first time you open Photoshop, you are asked to choose your color settings. Photoshop's default color space is set to sRGB, the correct color space for preparing Web images. However, sRGB is a very

limited color space, much smaller than what printers can actually produce. Most photographers and designers prefer the larger color space called Adobe RGB (1998), a good color space for working with photographs and projects you plan to print.

In Photoshop CS2, you can easily choose your color space and even use the new predesigned color space settings. Try the North America Prepress 2 settings with the Adobe RGB (1998) color space for images that you plan to print. Your printed colors will look much better.

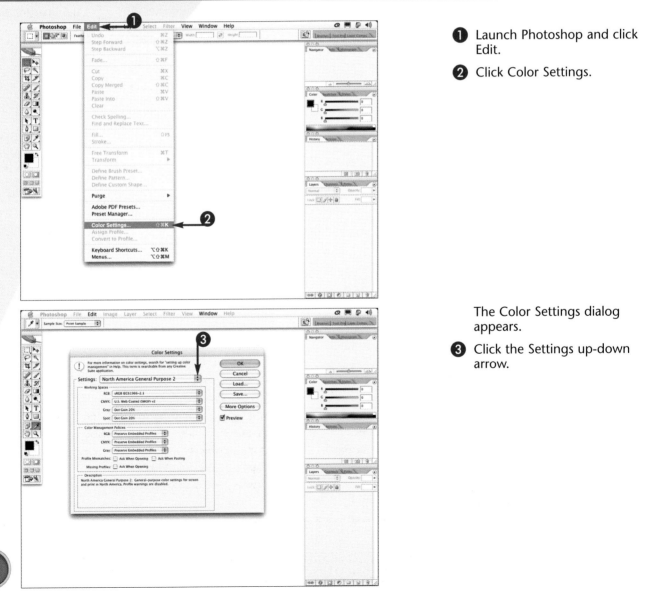

① Launch Photoshop and click Edit.

② Click Color Settings.

The Color Settings dialog appears.

③ Click the Settings up-down arrow.

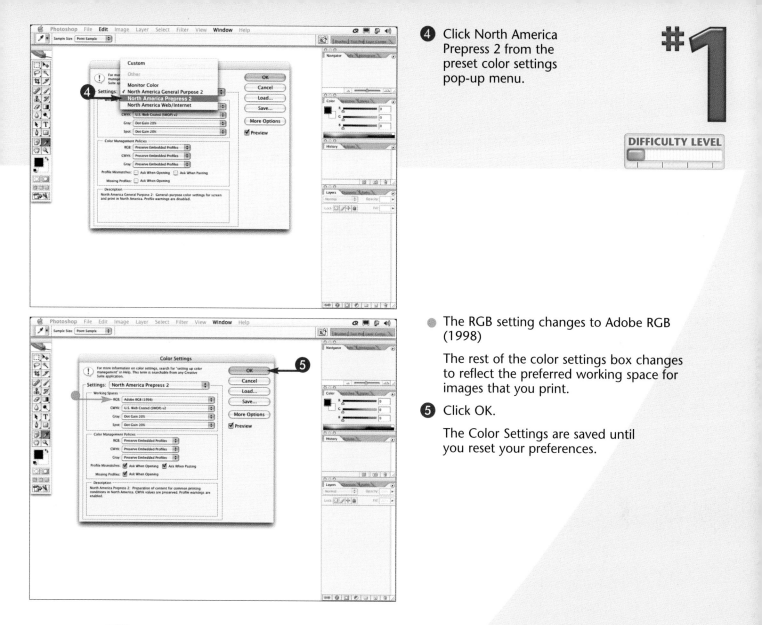

④ Click North America Prepress 2 from the preset color settings pop-up menu.

● The RGB setting changes to Adobe RGB (1998)

The rest of the color settings box changes to reflect the preferred working space for images that you print.

⑤ Click OK.

The Color Settings are saved until you reset your preferences.

TIPS

Try This!

Click More Options to show Conversion Options. Click the Engine up-down arrow and click Adobe ACE. The Adobe Color Engine is considered the best all-around choice for conversions. The selections for the Intent depend upon the type of project. Click the Intent up-down arrows. Click Relative Colorimetric for a graphic design project. Click Perceptual for photography.

Customize It!

You can save your own Color Settings preset. The name of the preset changes to Custom when you deselect any check box ( ) or make any other changes. Click Save after customizing your settings. Type a name in the Save dialog and click Save in that dialog. Your customized preset appears in the Settings pop-up menu, ready for you to choose.

Chapter 1: Customizing Photoshop for Your Projects

SET THE PREFERENCES
for the way you work

Photoshop includes nine different preferences dialogs in addition to the Color Settings. Although you can work with the default settings, changing some of these can make your computer run more efficiently and changing others can make it easier to work with your projects. For example, by default, Photoshop is set to use more than half of the available RAM. You can lower this default setting to 15 percent or 25 percent depending on how much RAM you have installed in the computer, especially if you have several other applications open at the same time. You can change the default colors for the guides and

grid when they are too similar to those in your image. Other personalized options, such as asking Photoshop to automatically launch the Bridge, can help you use Photoshop the way you want.

Read through each preference dialog to familiarize yourself with the choices. Select the settings that correspond to your computer's memory and hard drive space, the types of files you work on, and your personal preferences. Preparing Photoshop to work for you can enhance Photoshop's speed and your productivity.

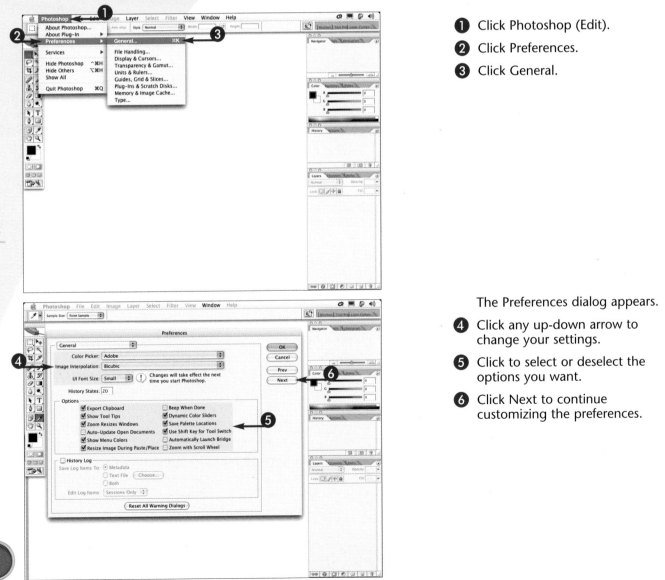

① Click Photoshop (Edit).

② Click Preferences.

③ Click General.

The Preferences dialog appears.

④ Click any up-down arrow to change your settings.

⑤ Click to select or deselect the options you want.

⑥ Click Next to continue customizing the preferences.

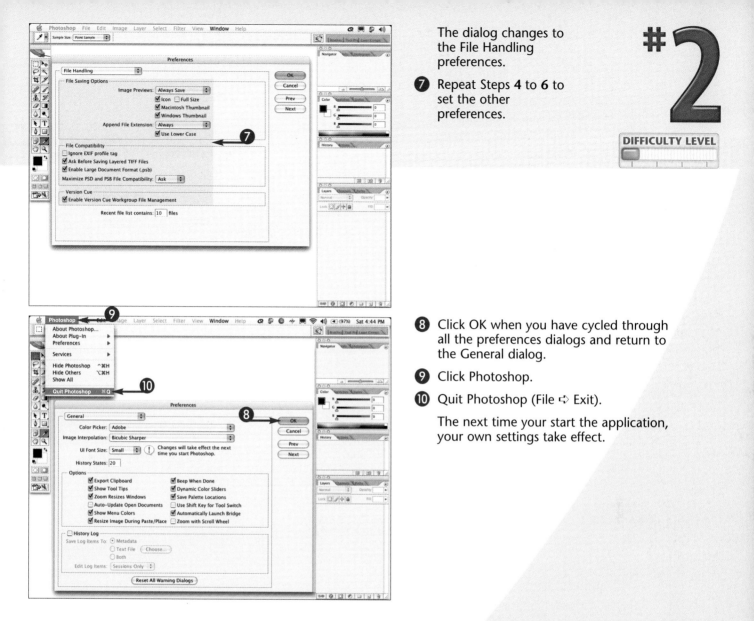

The dialog changes to the File Handling preferences.

7 Repeat Steps **4** to **6** to set the other preferences.

8 Click OK when you have cycled through all the preferences dialogs and return to the General dialog.

9 Click Photoshop.

10 Quit Photoshop (File ➪ Exit).

The next time your start the application, your own settings take effect.

TIPS

Desktop Trick!

You can use keyboard shortcuts to set the Preferences. Press ⌘-K (Ctrl+K). Set your options for General preferences. Then press ⌘-2 (Ctrl+2), and set your choices for File Handling. Press ⌘-3 (Ctrl+3), and so on, for each of the nine Preferences dialogs.

Try This!

Pressing the Shift key and an appropriate letter toggles the tools in the toolbar. Streamline this shortcut by changing a setting in the General Preferences dialog. Deselect the Use Shift Key for Tool Switch check box (☐). Now you can just press the appropriate letter to toggle the tools.

Did You Know?

You can restore the Preferences any time by holding the ⌘-Option-Shift (Ctrl+Alt+Shift) keys as you launch the application. A dialog appears asking if you want to delete the Adobe Photoshop Settings File. Click Yes, and the preferences are reset to the defaults.

Customize your
PERSONAL WORKSPACE

The workspace in Photoshop refers to the layout of all the different palettes and tools on your monitor screen. Because your productivity depends on how easily you can access palettes or find the tools you need, Photoshop allows you to design your own workspace and save it.

You can place the palettes you use most in front and hide others. You can separate the palettes, lengthen one and shorten another, and move your toolbar where it is more convenient for you. You can customize keyboard shortcuts and menus and save the current palette locations with your keyboard

shortcuts and menu changes. If you move or close a palette, you can easily return to your saved workspace.

You can even set up more than one workspace to accommodate different tasks, such as one for color-correcting photographs and one for working with type.

You can also set up different workspaces for others who may share the computer. Each person can quickly access the tools he or she uses most often by selecting his or her personal workspace from the menu.

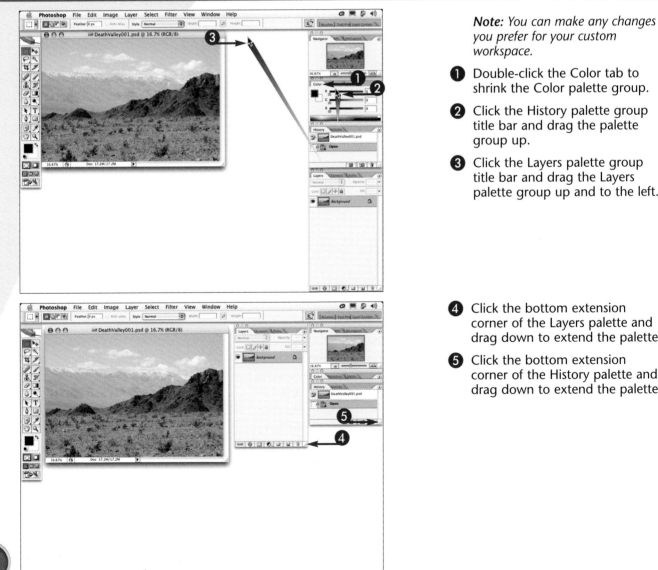

Note: You can make any changes you prefer for your custom workspace.

① Double-click the Color tab to shrink the Color palette group.

② Click the History palette group title bar and drag the palette group up.

③ Click the Layers palette group title bar and drag the Layers palette group up and to the left.

④ Click the bottom extension corner of the Layers palette and drag down to extend the palette.

⑤ Click the bottom extension corner of the History palette and drag down to extend the palette.

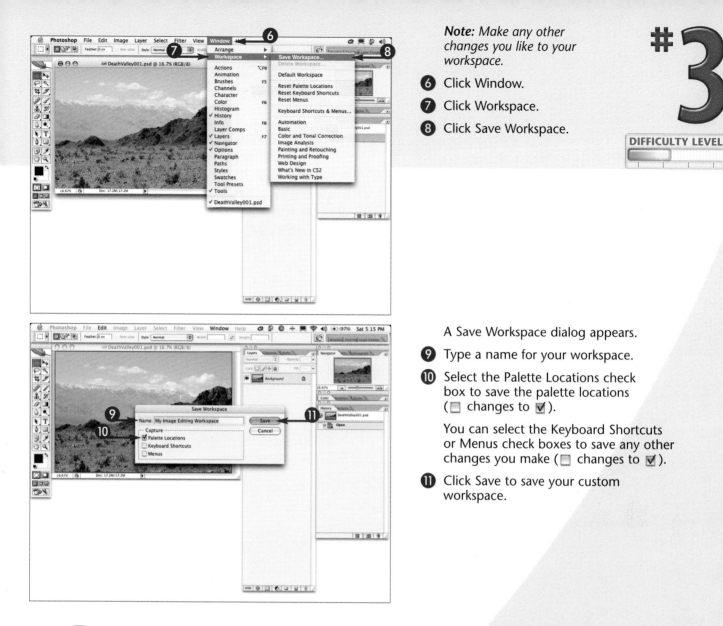

#3

DIFFICULTY LEVEL

Note: *Make any other changes you like to your workspace.*

6 Click Window.

7 Click Workspace.

8 Click Save Workspace.

A Save Workspace dialog appears.

9 Type a name for your workspace.

10 Select the Palette Locations check box to save the palette locations (☐ changes to ☑).

You can select the Keyboard Shortcuts or Menus check boxes to save any other changes you make (☐ changes to ☑).

11 Click Save to save your custom workspace.

TIPS

Did You Know?

You can return to the original workspace any time by clicking Window ➪ Workspace ➪ Default Workspace. You can also delete unused workspaces by clicking Window ➪ Workspace ➪ Delete Workspace and selecting the one you want to delete.

More Options!

Photoshop CS2 includes a number of predesigned workspaces for particular projects, such as Color and Tonal Correction and Painting and Retouching. Click Window ➪ Workspace and select a workspace from the lower section of the pull-down menu.

More Options!

You can color code the menu items you use most often. Click Edit ➪ Menus. In the dialog that appears, click the expand triangle next to a menu name. Click None, and select a color from the pull-down menu.

PERSONALIZE YOUR VIEW
of the Bridge

In Photoshop CS2, Adobe replaced the Browser with a power browser called the Bridge. The Bridge is actually the central hub for all the Creative Suite 2 applications and functions as an application on its own.

As with the original browser, you can view and search for images in various folders with the Bridge. The Bridge shows all files and folders that are available. You can even see thumbnails of documents and files from other applications, such as Word or Acrobat files. When you double-click such a thumbnail from the Bridge, the other application launches.

The Bridge offers more automation, more ways to search and categorize your files, new options for adding information, and many ways to view your images. You can now customize and save your Bridge workspace. Searching and reviewing your images is not only more efficient, but more fun.

You can launch the Bridge by choosing Browse from the File menu, by clicking the Go to Bridge icon in the Options bar, or by using the keyboard shortcut ⌘-Option-O (Ctrl+Alt+O). The default workspace appears with information palettes on the left and thumbnails on the right.

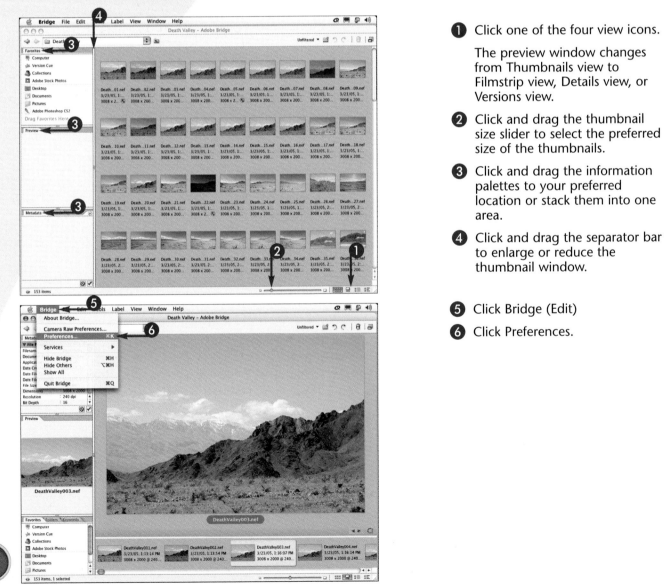

① Click one of the four view icons.

The preview window changes from Thumbnails view to Filmstrip view, Details view, or Versions view.

② Click and drag the thumbnail size slider to select the preferred size of the thumbnails.

③ Click and drag the information palettes to your preferred location or stack them into one area.

④ Click and drag the separator bar to enlarge or reduce the thumbnail window.

⑤ Click Bridge (Edit)

⑥ Click Preferences.

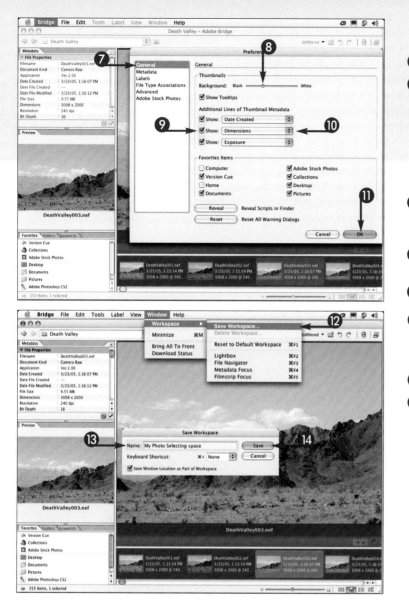

The Bridge Preferences dialog appears.

⑦ Click General.

⑧ Click and drag the Background slider to select the background viewing color.

The color behind the thumbnails changes from white to gray to black.

⑨ Select the check boxes to show the Thumbnail Metadata you want to add (☐ changes to ☑).

⑩ Click the up-down arrow and select the type of information you want to display.

⑪ Click OK.

⑫ Click Window ➪ Workspace ➪ Save Workspace.

A Save Workspace dialog appears.

⑬ Type a name for your workspace.

⑭ Click Save to save your custom workspace.

You can now find your customized Bridge workspace by clicking Window ➪ Workspace.

DIFFICULTY LEVEL

TIPS

Did You Know?
You can sort your photos in different ways. The default is set to Ascending Order, but you can choose a different order. Click the View menu, select Sort, and then choose from the list of options for sorting.

More Options!
You can assign a keyboard shortcut to your customized view of the Bridge. When you are in the Save Workspace dialog, click the up-down arrow next to the word None. Select one of the Keyboard shortcuts listed and click Save.

Try This!
You can hide all the information palettes in the panels on the left and enlarge your thumbnail window even more. Each time you click the double-headed arrow in the bottom-left corner of the Bridge, the panels toggle on and off.

Chapter 1: Customizing Photoshop for Your Projects

CREATE A KEYBOARD SHORTCUT
for a favorite filter

Photoshop includes a number of keyboard shortcuts for a variety of tasks. You can work more efficiently if you use shortcuts for the tools you use most often. Many of the tools in the toolbar already have keyboard shortcuts assigned. Still, you may find yourself going to the menu to select an item, such as the Gaussian Blur filter, so often that a personalized keyboard shortcut is very useful and a huge timesaver.

You can easily create your own custom keyboard shortcuts to fit your workflow. You can even change

the ones that Photoshop has already assigned to something you can remember better. If the Keyboard Shortcut you choose is already in use, Photoshop warns you when you type the text. You can change Photoshop's default shortcuts or you can try a different set of keystrokes that are not already assigned.

Learning and using custom keyboard shortcuts can streamline your workflow, leaving you more time for designing and photo editing.

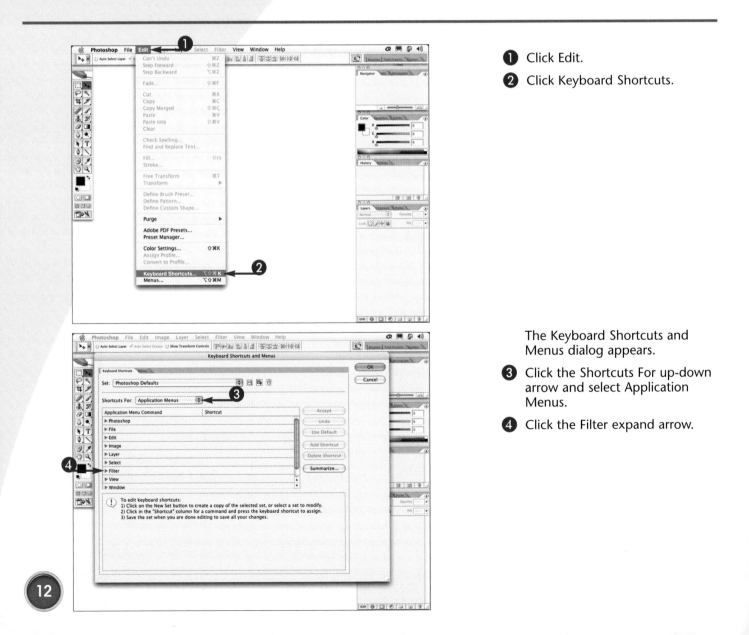

① Click Edit.

② Click Keyboard Shortcuts.

The Keyboard Shortcuts and Menus dialog appears.

③ Click the Shortcuts For up-down arrow and select Application Menus.

④ Click the Filter expand arrow.

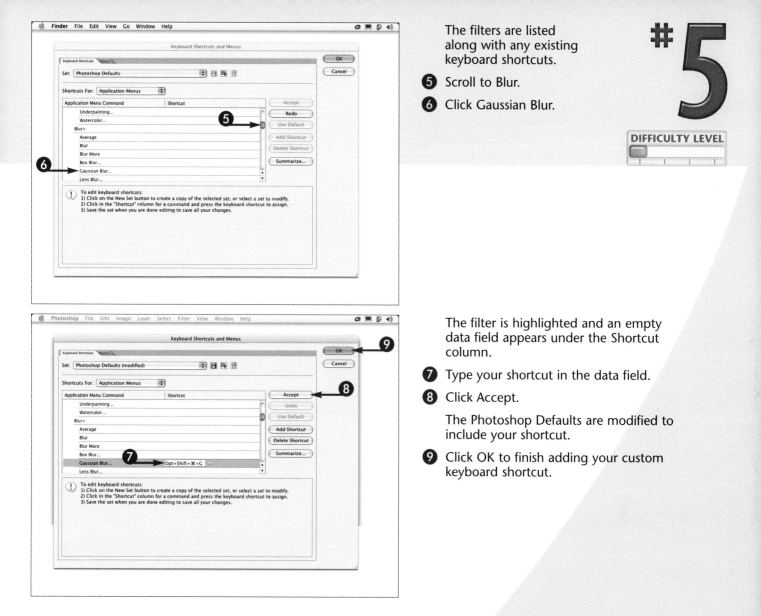

The filters are listed along with any existing keyboard shortcuts.

⑤ Scroll to Blur.

⑥ Click Gaussian Blur.

#5

DIFFICULTY LEVEL

The filter is highlighted and an empty data field appears under the Shortcut column.

⑦ Type your shortcut in the data field.

⑧ Click Accept.

The Photoshop Defaults are modified to include your shortcut.

⑨ Click OK to finish adding your custom keyboard shortcut.

Did You Know?
The Keyboard Shortcuts and Menus dialog is found under both the Edit menu and the Window ➪ Workspace menu. You can also access the Keyboard Shortcuts and Menus dialog by using a keyboard shortcut. Press ⌘-Shift-Option-K (Ctrl+Shift+Alt+K).

Try This!
You can save a list of the default Photoshop keyboard shortcuts or your customized shortcuts. Click Summarize in the Keyboard Shortcuts and Menus dialog and save the file as Photoshop Defaults.htm. Open the file and print the list for reference.

More Options!
Click the Shortcuts For up-down arrow to select Palette Menus or Tools. Then click the expand arrow next to the palette name or tool and type your shortcut. You can even save a keyboard shortcut set with a custom workspace!

CREATE AN ACTION
to increase your efficiency

Performing repeated steps is boring and time consuming. That is why Adobe created Actions. An Action is a series of commands that you can apply to an image with one click of the mouse. Unlike a keyboard shortcut, which can only open a command, an action can open a command, apply changes to an image, step through another command, apply it, and even save a file in a particular way. You can create your own actions for steps that you do repeatedly, save the actions, and add them to the Actions palette.

To create an action, you first record a sequence of steps. You then name and save your new action in the Actions palette. The next time you need to apply the same steps to an image, you play the action and Photoshop automatically applies the series of operations to the open file or even to an entire folder of files.

Actions are easy to create and they can help you automate your work for repetitive tasks leaving you more time to work on creative projects.

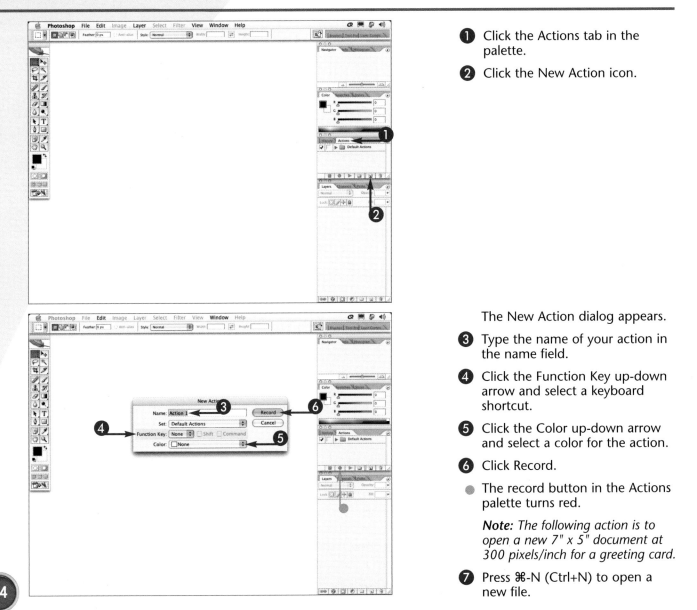

① Click the Actions tab in the palette.

② Click the New Action icon.

The New Action dialog appears.

③ Type the name of your action in the name field.

④ Click the Function Key up-down arrow and select a keyboard shortcut.

⑤ Click the Color up-down arrow and select a color for the action.

⑥ Click Record.

● The record button in the Actions palette turns red.

Note: *The following action is to open a new 7" x 5" document at 300 pixels/inch for a greeting card.*

⑦ Press ⌘-N (Ctrl+N) to open a new file.

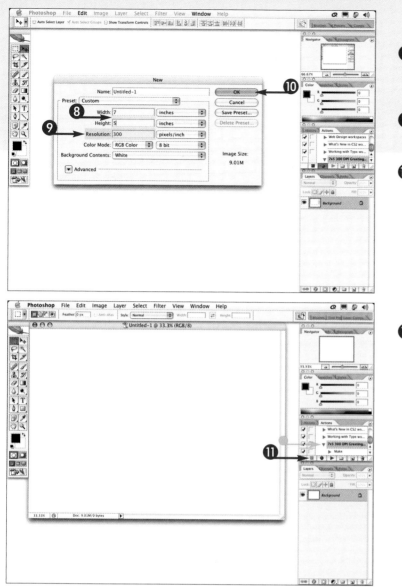

The New file dialog appears.

8 Type your specific dimensions in the Width and Height fields.

9 Type **300**, or your desired resolution, in the Resolution field.

10 Click OK.

A new untitled document appears.

11 Click the Stop Recording button in the Actions palette.

● Your custom action is now recorded and is listed in the Actions palette.

You can test it by clicking the keyboard shortcut you assigned.

An untitled, 5" x 7", 300 ppi document appears.

TIPS

More Options!

You can apply the same action to any open files or a folder of files. In the menu, click File ⇨ Automate ⇨ Batch. You can also apply an action to a group of images from the Bridge by clicking Tools ⇨ Photoshop ⇨ Batch.

Try This!

You can reduce some of the clutter in the Actions palette by setting it to Button mode. Click the Actions palette's expand arrow and select Button Mode. Your actions change to color-coded buttons, making them much easier to find.

Did You Know?

When you first open Photoshop, the Actions palette only includes the Default set for setting up workspaces. You can find other prerecorded actions by clicking the Actions palette's expand arrow. Click any sets such as Frames, Image Effects, and so on, to load these.

DESIGN A CUSTOMIZED BRUSH
with your settings

Whether you retouch photographs, design brochures, or paint from scratch, you will use the brush tools many times and in many ways. Selecting the Brush tool from the toolbar opens a variety of brushes in the pull-down menu on the Options bar.

You can modify the size, roundness, or other attributes of any of the existing brushes to suit your drawing style or your image. You can then save the modified brush as your own custom brush so it is ready to use for your next design.

A number of other tools also have modifiable brush options, including the Pencil tool, the Eraser tool, the Clone Stamp tool, the Pattern Stamp tool, the History Brush, the Art History Brush, the Blur tool, the Sharpen tool, the Smudge tool, the Dodge tool, the Burn tool, and the Sponge tool.

Customizing brush tools for your projects is a timesaving technique, and it is fun. You may find yourself experimenting with all types of brushes.

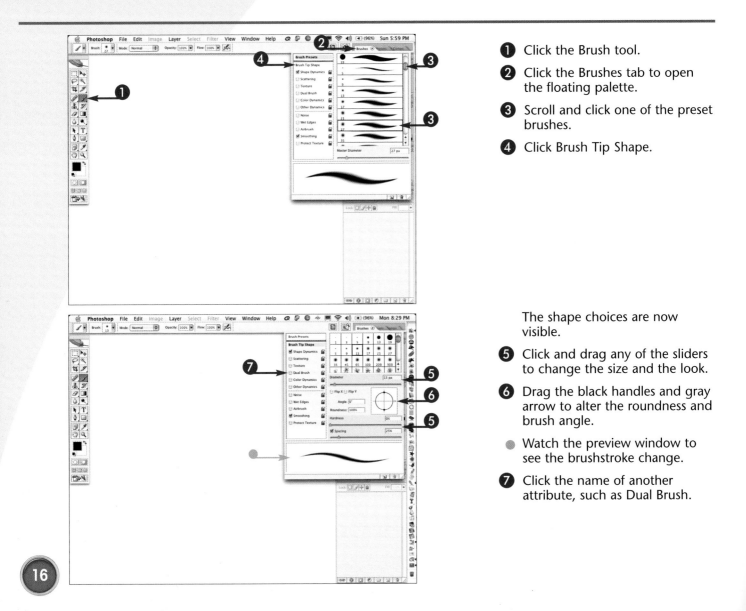

① Click the Brush tool.

② Click the Brushes tab to open the floating palette.

③ Scroll and click one of the preset brushes.

④ Click Brush Tip Shape.

The shape choices are now visible.

⑤ Click and drag any of the sliders to change the size and the look.

⑥ Drag the black handles and gray arrow to alter the roundness and brush angle.

● Watch the preview window to see the brushstroke change.

⑦ Click the name of another attribute, such as Dual Brush.

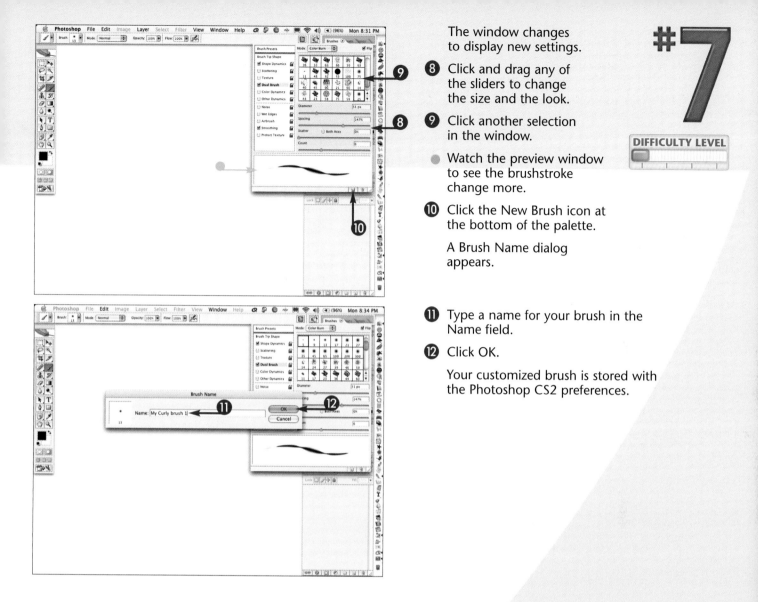

The window changes to display new settings.

⑧ Click and drag any of the sliders to change the size and the look.

⑨ Click another selection in the window.

● Watch the preview window to see the brushstroke change more.

⑩ Click the New Brush icon at the bottom of the palette.

A Brush Name dialog appears.

⑪ Type a name for your brush in the Name field.

⑫ Click OK.

Your customized brush is stored with the Photoshop CS2 preferences.

TIPS

Caution!

To avoid losing lose custom brushes if you reset Photoshop's preferences, you must save your custom brushes as part of a Brushes.abr file. Click the Brushes palette down-arrow and select Save Brushes. Name the file with the extension suffix .abr and then click Save.

Did You Know?

Photoshop CS2 includes many different brush files. You can load these brushes from the pull-down menu on the Brushes palette, or from the brush options pull-down menu in the Options bar. The brush files are listed at the bottom of these menus!

More Options!

You can choose to see the brushes listed by name rather than the stroke thumbnail. Click the expand-arrow on the Brushes tab and choose text only. You can also choose a different-sized thumbnail view as well as different-sized list views.

MAKE A SPECIAL GRADIENT
to suit your design

The Gradient tool helps you blend multiple colors as you fill an area in an image. You can use the Gradient tool in many ways, such as by itself to fill text with soft gradations of color, to fill backgrounds with a gradient, or in combination with layers and masks. Gradients are often used when making composite images. Photoshop includes default gradient color sets and has other gradient sets listed in the pull-down menu in the Options bar. You can also create your own gradient by sampling colors from areas in your image or choosing different colors altogether.

You can add intermediate colors and design a blend among multiple colors in any order you want. You can even design gradients that fade from any color to transparent.

You can also choose a style for the gradient, such as linear, radial, angled, reflected, or diamond. You customize the gradients from the Gradient Editor. Start with an existing gradient and modify the colors, the colors stops, and other variations in the dialog. The possibilities are almost endless!

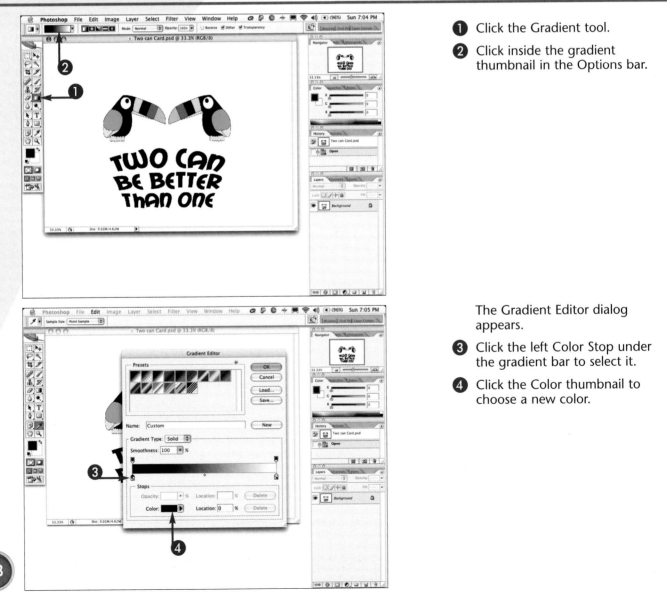

① Click the Gradient tool.

② Click inside the gradient thumbnail in the Options bar.

The Gradient Editor dialog appears.

③ Click the left Color Stop under the gradient bar to select it.

④ Click the Color thumbnail to choose a new color.

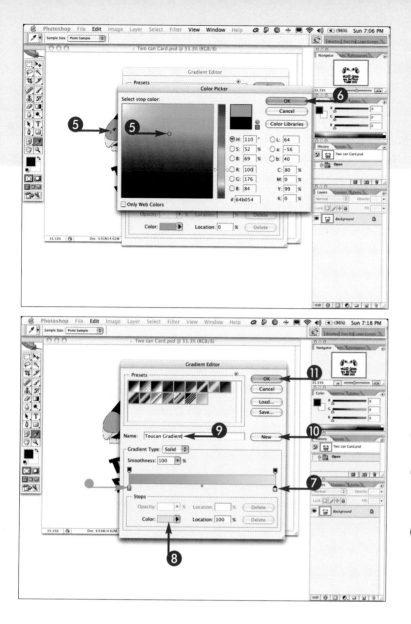

The Color Picker dialog appears.

5 Select a color from the dialog or move the cursor over the image to select a color.

6 Click OK.

● The selected color fills the left Color Stop in the Gradient Editor.

7 Click the right Color Stop under the gradient bar to select it.

8 Repeat Steps **4** to **6** to select the colors for the right Color Stop.

9 Type a name for your new gradient in the Name field.

10 Click New.

The custom gradient appears in the presets.

11 Click OK.

TIPS

Caution!

You must save your custom gradients in a presets library to avoid losing them when you reset Photoshop's preferences. Click Save in the Gradient Editor dialog or choose Save Gradients from the pull-down menu on the Gradient Picker. Type a name for your gradient library with the extension suffix .grd. Click Save and your gradients are saved in Photoshop's Presets.

More Options!

You can duplicate any of the Color Stops to vary your custom gradient. Press Option (Alt) and drag the first Color Stop to another location. You can even drag and jump a new Color Stop over other Color Stops as long as you are pressing Option (Alt). To remove a Color Stop, click on it and drag straight down.

CALIBRATE AND PROFILE
your monitor for better editing

You adjust colors in Photoshop based on what you see on the screen. Because each monitor shows color differently, you must calibrate and profile it to make sure the colors are displayed as accurately as possible.

Calibration is the process of setting your monitor to an established color standard. *Profiling* is the process of creating an International Color Consortium (ICC) profile, a description of how your monitor reproduces color.

Macintosh system preferences include a display calibration tool. On Windows, Photoshop CS2 installs a Adobe gamma utility. Both of these software-only methods are subjective, relying on the room lighting and the person viewing the screen. The best way to get your monitor to display colors within an accurate range is with a hardware calibration device called a colorimeter. A spectrophotometer offers even greater accuracy.

GretagMacbeth, X-Rite, and ColorVision all make affordable colorimeters. Using a colorimeter or spectrophotometer, such as GretagMacbeth's Eye-One Display or Eye-One Pro, is easy because the hardware and software combination do all the work.

Install the software, launch it, plug the device into a USB port, and follow the on-screen instructions.

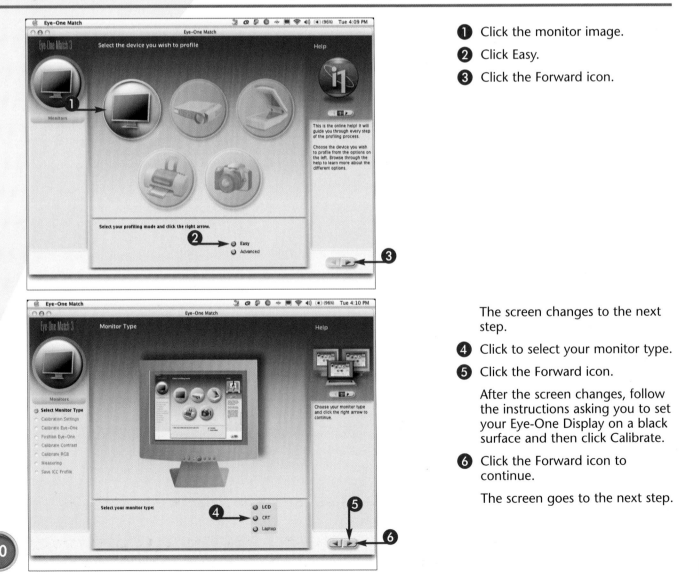

❶ Click the monitor image.

❷ Click Easy.

❸ Click the Forward icon.

The screen changes to the next step.

❹ Click to select your monitor type.

❺ Click the Forward icon.

After the screen changes, follow the instructions asking you to set your Eye-One Display on a black surface and then click Calibrate.

❻ Click the Forward icon to continue.

The screen goes to the next step.

⑦ Place the Eye-One unit on the monitor as the image shows.

⑧ Click the Forward icon.

The screen goes black and then a box appears under the colorimeter on the screen.

After the box fills with white, then black, and then colors, the device automatically measures the colors.

A new screen appears showing the name of the monitor profile created by the device.

⑨ Click the Forward icon.

● A dialog appears telling you where the profile was saved on your computer's hard drive.

⑩ Click OK.

⑪ Quit the Eye-One software application and disconnect the Eye-One Colorimeter.

 TIPS

Did You Know?

As monitors age, they lose their color accuracy more quickly. You should calibrate and profile regularly. Calibrate monthly if your monitor is new. You may need to calibrate weekly if your monitor is over two years old or for some CRTs.

Important!

Clean the monitor screen with a soft cloth before you start, but never spray any cleaning liquids on your monitor. If you have a CRT monitor, let it warm up for 30 minutes before you calibrate and create a profile.

More Options!

GretagMacbeth's software keeps a help file open in a column along the right side of the screen. You can increase your understanding of color calibration and read an explanation of each step as it is performed by clicking the arrow above the column.

TURN ON THE FULL POWER OF PHOTOSHOP
with a digitizing tablet

Using a mouse as an input device may work for placing insertion points in text or dragging a rectangular selection in Photoshop, but using a Brush tool or selecting specific areas with a mouse is similar to writing your name with a bar of soap — clunky and inaccurate. Using a pressure-sensitive digitizing tablet and stylus, such as the Wacom Intuos 3, instead of a mouse allows you to edit images with greater comfort and control. Every point on the tablet has a matching point on the screen. You do not waste time scooting the mouse around so you become more productive.

Using a tablet and stylus, you have access to many Photoshop tools that are only available when a tablet is connected to the computer. You can easily make precise selections, create blended composite images, and even paint digitally as you would with a traditional paintbrush on paper.

The key to using a tablet and stylus and turning on the full power of Photoshop is to start by setting the tablet preferences located in the System Preferences or Control Panels.

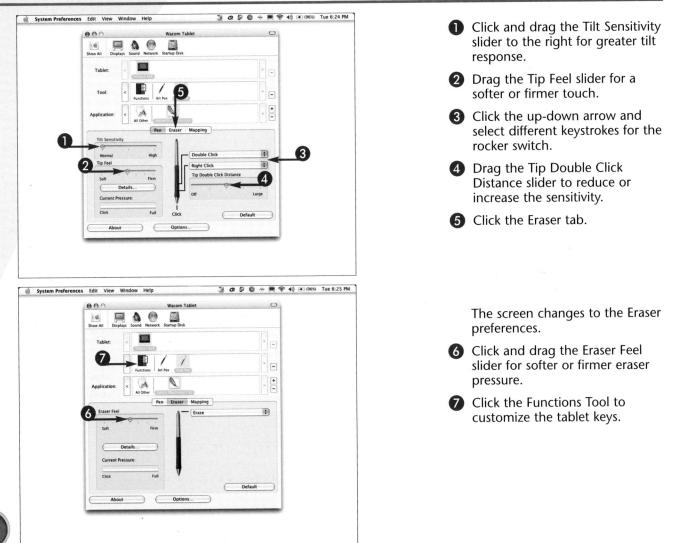

① Click and drag the Tilt Sensitivity slider to the right for greater tilt response.

② Drag the Tip Feel slider for a softer or firmer touch.

③ Click the up-down arrow and select different keystrokes for the rocker switch.

④ Drag the Tip Double Click Distance slider to reduce or increase the sensitivity.

⑤ Click the Eraser tab.

The screen changes to the Eraser preferences.

⑥ Click and drag the Eraser Feel slider for softer or firmer eraser pressure.

⑦ Click the Functions Tool to customize the tablet keys.

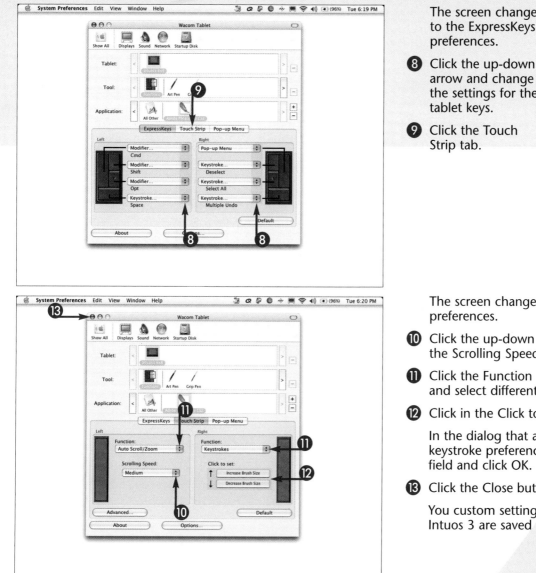

The screen changes to the ExpressKeys preferences.

8 Click the up-down arrow and change the settings for the tablet keys.

9 Click the Touch Strip tab.

The screen changes to the Touch Strip preferences.

10 Click the up-down arrow to change the Scrolling Speed.

11 Click the Function up-down arrow and select different functions.

12 Click in the Click to set boxes.

In the dialog that appears, type your keystroke preferences in the Keys data field and click OK.

13 Click the Close button.

You custom settings for the Wacom Intuos 3 are saved in the preferences.

TIPS

Try This!

You can set your tablet and stylus preferences for all applications or select specific settings for each application you use. If you have more than one stylus, you can even set different settings for each one with each application.

Did you know?

The Wacom Intuos 3 is considered the most responsive tablet and stylus on the market. Not only does working with the Wacom stylus feel like any pen or pencil, the added convenience of the ExpressKeys and Touch Strip help you become more productive.

Did you know?

Over 20 Photoshop tools are specifically designed for use with a pressure sensitive tablet and stylus. If you do not have a tablet attached to your computer, a warning sign appears for many of the settings in the Brushes palette.

Chapter 2

Working with Layers, Selections, and Masks

Unless you only use Photoshop to resize and print photographs, you will use layers, selections, and masks in some way for most projects. You may duplicate a layer as a safety step or build a complex multilayered image file with any combination of layers, selections, and masks.

Layers give real editing and designing power to Photoshop. A layer is a transparency sheet with an image on it. You can edit, transform, or add filters to a layer independently from other layers. You can make one layer alter the look of a layer above or below it. You can save a file with the layers and easily change your design later, by editing one or more of the layers. You can also drag to copy a layer from one document to another.

Selections allow you to isolate areas in your image and apply different effects or filters without affecting the rest of the image. You can even select areas on one layer and create a new layer with that selection. You can make selections with many Photoshop tools, depending on the type of area you need to isolate. You can copy, move, paste, and save selections.

You can use masks to block out one area of an image or protect it from manipulations. A mask is a selection shown as a grayscale image: the white areas are selected, the black areas are not. You can create bitmap layer masks with painting tools or resolution-independent vector masks with a shape tool.

Top 100

DUPLICATE THE BACKGROUND LAYER

#11

DIFFICULTY LEVEL

You can save yourself many hours of work if you begin most Photoshop projects by duplicating the Background layer. The Background layer is the bottommost image in the Layers palette, and the only layer when you first open a new photograph.

Duplicating the Background layer allows you to work on the image without altering the original. You can rename the copy and then experiment with various Photoshop techniques on that layer. You can easily delete the copied layer and your original image remains open and unchanged.

Working on a duplicated Background layer also makes it easy to continuously compare your modified image with the original. Click the Visibility icon, the leftmost box next to the layer thumbnail in the Layers palette, to hide the original Background layer while you work on the copy. To compare your modified image with the original, click in the box to turn on the visibility for the original Background, and click the Visibility icon for the copy layer to turn it off.

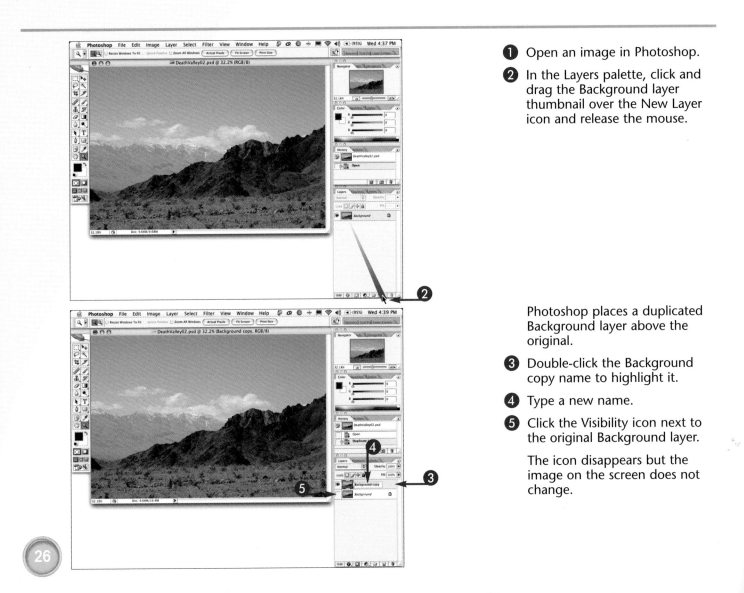

❶ Open an image in Photoshop.

❷ In the Layers palette, click and drag the Background layer thumbnail over the New Layer icon and release the mouse.

Photoshop places a duplicated Background layer above the original.

❸ Double-click the Background copy name to highlight it.

❹ Type a new name.

❺ Click the Visibility icon next to the original Background layer.

The icon disappears but the image on the screen does not change.

Quickly
FIX A FADED PHOTO

DIFFICULTY LEVEL

There are many ways to fix photos in Photoshop. In fact, there are multiple ways of doing almost any project in this powerful application. The techniques you use depend on your photos and your time.

When you scan an older photograph, the resulting image may be faded or the colors may appear washed out. You can fix the color and increase the contrast using a variety of methods and Photoshop tools, and for many photographs, you must work on the images for a while to restore them.

The quick-fix method is simply a beginning step. You can use it for photos that you do not plan to enlarge or for images that you want to reprint but are not worth multiple hours of work. This method works on some images and not others, but because it is so easy and fast, it is always worth a try. In any case, you are testing the technique on a layer above the original image, so you can always delete the new layer or use it with a different technique later.

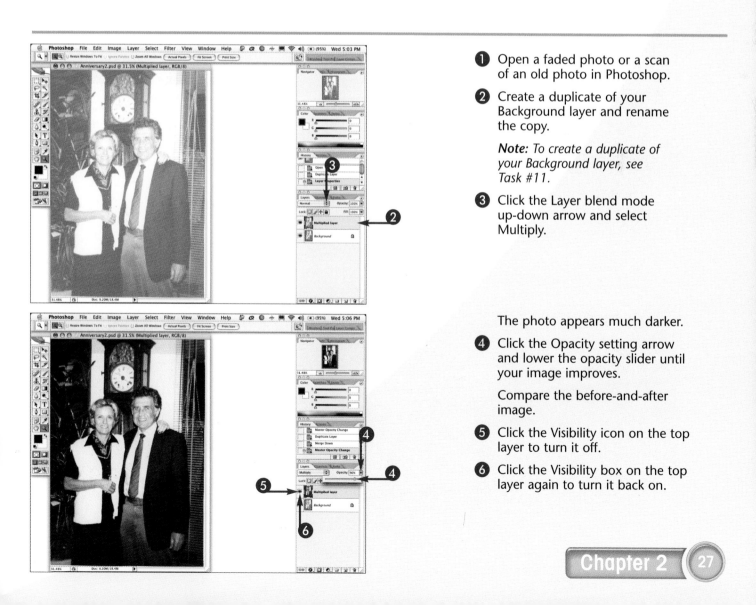

① Open a faded photo or a scan of an old photo in Photoshop.

② Create a duplicate of your Background layer and rename the copy.

Note: To create a duplicate of your Background layer, see Task #11.

③ Click the Layer blend mode up-down arrow and select Multiply.

The photo appears much darker.

④ Click the Opacity setting arrow and lower the opacity slider until your image improves.

Compare the before-and-after image.

⑤ Click the Visibility icon on the top layer to turn it off.

⑥ Click the Visibility box on the top layer again to turn it back on.

Adjust a photo with an
ADJUSTMENT LAYER

You can make a variety of adjustments on an image by clicking the Image menu and selecting Adjustments. If you made a duplicate of your Background layer, you can adjust your photo and not alter the original layer. However, each time you change the pixels in an image, you lose some data. If you combine adjustments, you lose even more pixel information.

You can use an adjustment layer instead, and apply color and tonal changes to your image without changing any pixel values.

With an adjustment layer, you can try various settings and edit the adjustment later. You can reduce the effect of the adjustment by using the opacity slider to lower the strength of the change. You can also combine various adjustment layers. An adjustment layer affects all the layers below it.

You can access the adjustment layers by clicking the Layer menu, selecting New Adjustment Layer, and then selecting the type of adjustment layer you want to apply. Photoshop includes a number of different types of adjustment layers.

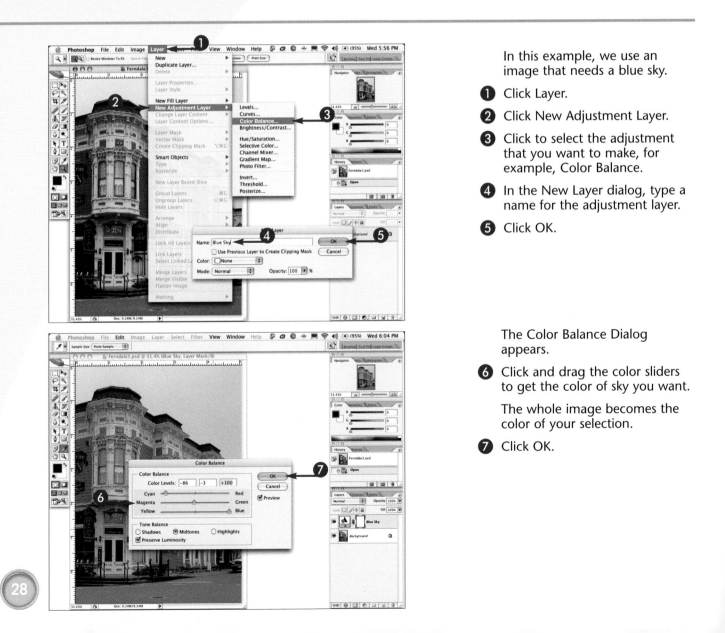

In this example, we use an image that needs a blue sky.

1 Click Layer.

2 Click New Adjustment Layer.

3 Click to select the adjustment that you want to make, for example, Color Balance.

4 In the New Layer dialog, type a name for the adjustment layer.

5 Click OK.

The Color Balance Dialog appears.

6 Click and drag the color sliders to get the color of sky you want.

The whole image becomes the color of your selection.

7 Click OK.

⑧ Click the Default Colors icon to set the default colors in the toolbar.

⑨ Click the Reverse Colors icon to change your foreground color to black.

⑩ Press Option-Delete (Alt+Backspace) to fill the adjustment layer's mask with black.

The color covering the image is now hidden by the adjustment layer's mask.

⑪ Press the Reverse colors icon to change the foreground color to white.

⑫ Click the Brush tool to select it.

⑬ Click the Brush Preset down arrow in the Options bar and select a large soft-edge brush from its menu.

⑭ Paint the area carefully.

In this example, the gray sky turns to blue as you paint.

TIPS

Did You Know?

If you accidentally paint over the building or another area that should not be changed, you can toggle the foreground and background colors by pressing X and painting with black to return the area to its original color.

Desk Top Trick!

You can quickly change the size of your brush as you paint using a keyboard shortcut. Press the right bracket key to increase the brush size, or the left bracket key to reduce the brush size.

More Options!

As you start to paint closer to the building or other areas that should not be changed, you can zoom in by pressing ⌘-Spacebar (Ctrl+Spacebar) and then lower the opacity of the brush in the Options bar.

BLEND TWO PHOTOS TOGETHER
with a layer mask

Layer masks open a world of imaging possibilities that you just cannot create with traditional tools. Using a layer mask to hide parts of one image and reveal parts of another, you can design greeting cards, posters, Web images, and more that are sure to grab a viewer's attention.

You can create very dramatic effects using a layer mask to blend one photograph into another. For example, you can blend a photograph of a wedding couple into a photo of their bouquet. You can also create comical effects with this technique if, for example, you blend a photo of a potato with a photo of a person lying on a couch.

As you paint with white on a black layer mask, the top image becomes visible. If you paint away too much, simply reverse the colors and paint with black.

This technique is especially effective if you have a digitizing tablet and stylus. By setting the painting brush to respond to pen pressure, you can easily control how much of the image you reveal with each brush stroke.

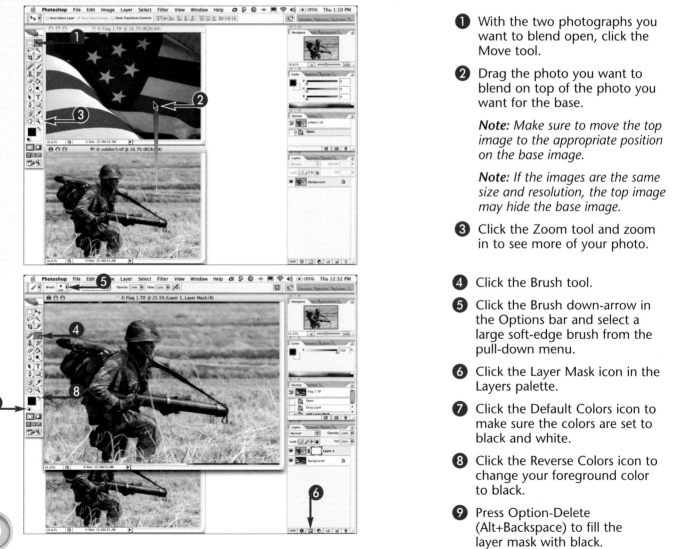

1 With the two photographs you want to blend open, click the Move tool.

2 Drag the photo you want to blend on top of the photo you want for the base.

Note: Make sure to move the top image to the appropriate position on the base image.

Note: If the images are the same size and resolution, the top image may hide the base image.

3 Click the Zoom tool and zoom in to see more of your photo.

4 Click the Brush tool.

5 Click the Brush down-arrow in the Options bar and select a large soft-edge brush from the pull-down menu.

6 Click the Layer Mask icon in the Layers palette.

7 Click the Default Colors icon to make sure the colors are set to black and white.

8 Click the Reverse Colors icon to change your foreground color to black.

9 Press Option-Delete (Alt+Backspace) to fill the layer mask with black.

A black layer mask hides the top photo, and only the base image is now visible.

⓾ Click the Reverse Foreground and Background icon to change the foreground to white.

⑪ Paint in the image using white to reveal the top photo.

⑫ Press X to reverse the foreground and background colors again.

⑬ Paint with black to fill in areas where you have painted away too much of the base image.

TIPS

Try This!
If you have a Wacom tablet and stylus, click the Brush Presets tab in the palette well. Select Pen Pressure for the Size Control under both Shape Dynamics and Other Dynamics.

Extra Help!
You can hold the Shift key as you drag the top image over the base image. Your two images will line up and be centered, one on top of the other.

More Options!
As you paint with white to reveal the top photo, try reducing the opacity of the brush in the Options bar. The images will blend even more smoothly.

JUMP A SELECTION
to its own layer

You can emphasize any area by selecting it and then jumping the selection to its own layer so you can change it. Selecting refers to specifying pixels that you want to separate and modify. When a selected area is on its own layer, you can apply layer styles and effects to transform the selected area and focus the attention. You can also change the background area it came from and create a very new look.

You can use any of Photoshop's selection tools to create a selection. A selection is indicated by a moving dashed line, commonly referred to as

marching ants. Once the selected area is on a separate layer, the dashed line is no longer visible. You can activate the selection at any time by pressing the Command (Ctrl) key and clicking the new layer in the Layers palette.

After it is on a separate layer, you can alter the look without an active selection. You can add focus by adding a border or drop shadows. You can also fade the background with an adjustment layer while preserving the selected area's color.

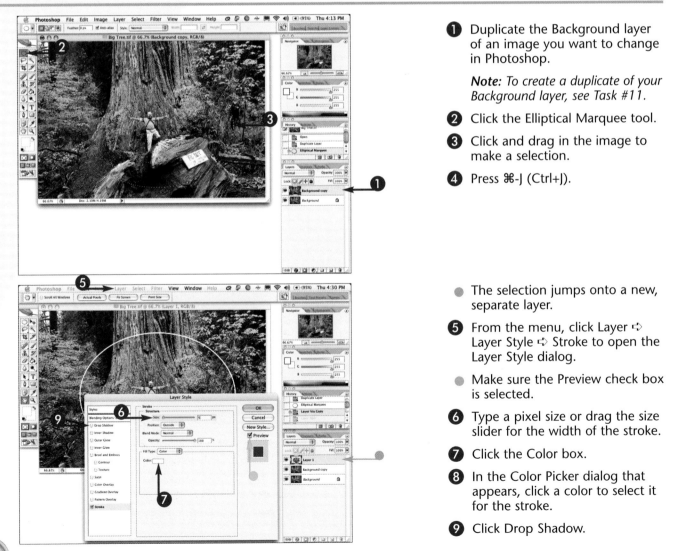

① Duplicate the Background layer of an image you want to change in Photoshop.

Note: To create a duplicate of your Background layer, see Task #11.

② Click the Elliptical Marquee tool.

③ Click and drag in the image to make a selection.

④ Press ⌘-J (Ctrl+J).

● The selection jumps onto a new, separate layer.

⑤ From the menu, click Layer ⇨ Layer Style ⇨ Stroke to open the Layer Style dialog.

● Make sure the Preview check box is selected.

⑥ Type a pixel size or drag the size slider for the width of the stroke.

⑦ Click the Color box.

⑧ In the Color Picker dialog that appears, click a color to select it for the stroke.

⑨ Click Drop Shadow.

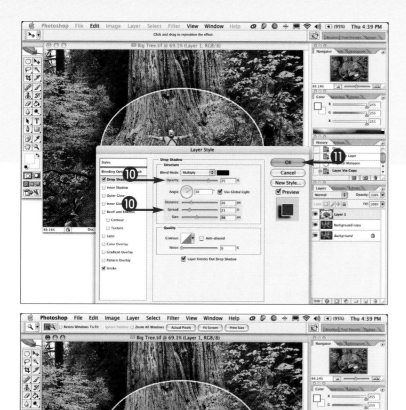

The options in the Layer style dialog change to Drop Shadow options.

⑩ Drag the sliders to set the opacity, distance, spread, and size for your image.

⑪ Click OK.

#15

DIFFICULTY LEVEL

● The stroke and drop shadow style are applied to the selection layer.

● The Layer Effect icon is visible on the layer in the Layers palette.

TIPS

Did You Know?
You can save your custom layer style. Click New Style in the Layer Style dialog. Type a name in the dialog and click OK. The next time you select Layer Style, click Styles. Your custom style appears in the last thumbnail.

More Options!
You can view the Styles by name as well as by the thumbnail. In the Layer Style dialog, click Style. Click the down-arrow next to the style thumbnails and select Large List. All the styles along with their descriptive names appear.

Try This!
You can change the attributes of the Layer Style even after it has been applied. Double-click the Layer Effects icon on the layer. The Layer Style dialog appears and you can alter the effects and styles.

USE A VECTOR SHAPE
as a decorative selection

You can add vector shapes to any image by drawing them with the Pen tools or by selecting a predesigned shape from the toolbar options. Vector shapes are resolution independent, meaning they maintain crisp edges when they are resized or saved in a PDF file.

You can access more custom shapes than the default set by clicking the custom shape options in the Options bar and clicking the down-arrow on that menu. Select one of the shapes groups at the bottom of the menu or select All to see all the installed

shapes at once. Double-click a shape thumbnail to select it.

When using shapes, you will see two boxes in the Layers palette, the fill layer, and a linked vector mask. The mask is the shape's outline. You can choose the fill layer's color in the Options bar before you draw the shape or set the fill color to a zero opacity fill.

A shape can be used as a decorative selection on a photograph. You can then alter the base image so the shaped portion stands out.

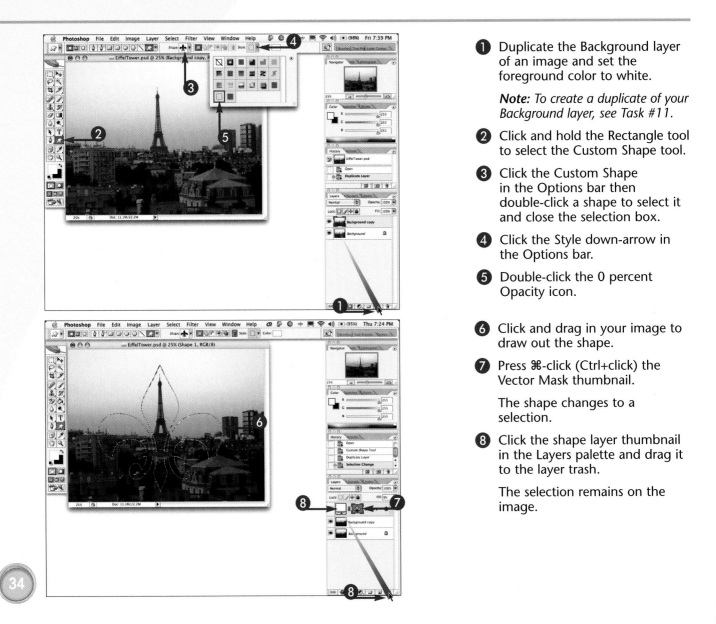

① Duplicate the Background layer of an image and set the foreground color to white.

Note: To create a duplicate of your Background layer, see Task #11.

② Click and hold the Rectangle tool to select the Custom Shape tool.

③ Click the Custom Shape in the Options bar then double-click a shape to select it and close the selection box.

④ Click the Style down-arrow in the Options bar.

⑤ Double-click the 0 percent Opacity icon.

⑥ Click and drag in your image to draw out the shape.

⑦ Press ⌘-click (Ctrl+click) the Vector Mask thumbnail.

The shape changes to a selection.

⑧ Click the shape layer thumbnail in the Layers palette and drag it to the layer trash.

The selection remains on the image.

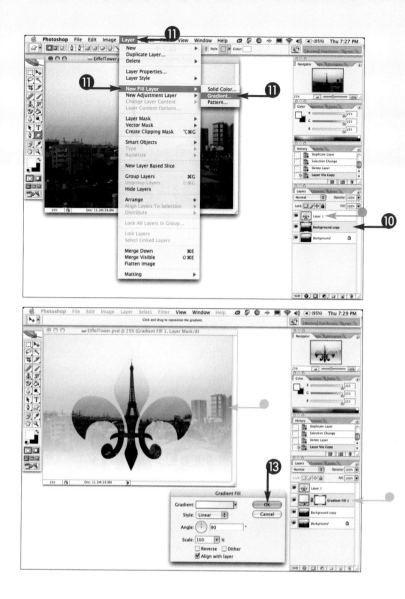

9 Press ⌘-J (Ctrl+J) to jump the selection to its own layer.

● The selection is on the new layer and not visible on the image.

10 Click the Background copy layer to select it.

11 Click Layer ⇨ New Fill Layer ⇨ Gradient.

12 When the New Layer dialog appears, click OK.

● The base image is covered with a gradient fill.

13 In the Gradient Fill dialog, click OK.

More Options!

Create a gradient fill with a color from your image for a very different look. Click the Foreground color box to open the Color Picker. Move the cursor outside of the Color Picker dialog and click a color from your image. Click OK to close the dialog. The base image blends even better with your image.

Save Two Ways!

You can save the file with all the layers so you can change it later or you can flatten the layers if you need a smaller file. To save a smaller file, Click Layer ⇨ Flatten Image from the menu before clicking File ⇨ Save As. Then save the file with a new file name.

Use a QUICK MASK TO MAKE A SELECTION

The standard selection tools in Photoshop's toolbar are useful for some images. You can select a rectangular or oval area with the Marquee tool or select a color range with the Magic Wand. The Lasso tools are great for adding to selections, but they can be difficult to use on areas with varied contours. If only you could paint directly on the areas that you want to select! You can do just that with the Brush tool and the Quick Mask mode.

The Quick Mask is an editing mode in which protected areas are covered with a translucent red mask. This is a great technique for selecting teeth that need to be whitened or a flower that you want to separate from the background.

Painting directly on the areas that you want is easier than using one of the selection tools. You can see what you are selecting. However, you are actually masking the areas you paint. Before you make any adjustments, simply inverse the selection; the areas you painted in are selected, and the rest is now masked.

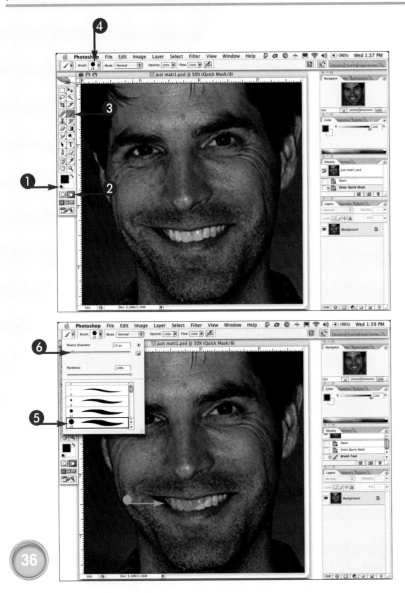

① While zoomed into the area you want to select, click the Default Colors icon in the toolbar to set the foreground color to black and the background to white.

② Click the Quick Mask Mode icon in the toolbar.

③ Click the Brush tool.

④ Click the Brush down-arrow in the Options bar.

⑤ Select a hard-edged brush.

⑥ Click and drag to adjust the Master Diameter slider.

⑦ Paint over the areas you want to select.

● The painted areas are covered with a red translucent mask.

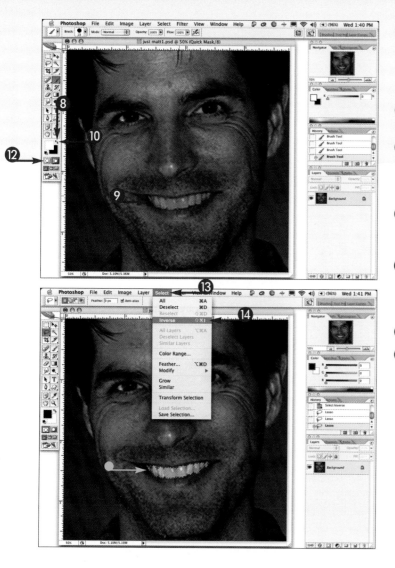

8 Click the Switch Foreground and Background Colors icon to make the foreground color white.

9 Paint over any areas that you covered accidentally.

10 Click the Switch Foreground and Background Colors icon to again make the foreground color black again.

11 Continue painting the area to select until the whole area is covered in red.

12 Click the Standard Mode icon.

● Dashed lines indicate the area that was masked by the red color.

13 Click Select.

14 Click Inverse.

The selection now includes only the area you painted in the Quick Mask mode.

#17

DIFFICULTY LEVEL

TIPS

Desktop Trick!
To change the brush size quickly, press the right bracket (]) to increase the paintbrush diameter, and the left bracket ([) to reduce it. To toggle the foreground and background colors, press X.

Important!
Painting with a hard-edge brush is easier to see; however, you need to feather the selection before you make adjustments. Click Select and click Feather. For the selection of the teeth, use a 1- or 2-pixel feather.

More Options!
If the image you are painting on is very red, change the masking color. Double-click the Quick Mask Mode icon and click the color box in the Quick Mask Options dialog to pick a new color.

REMOVE AN OBJECT
from the background

You will often want to separate a person or an object from the background so you can use the person or object on a separate layer or in another image. You could painstakingly paint over the person or object with a brush in the Quick Mask mode or select the area with the Lasso tool; however, the Extract filter often makes a better selection and does so more easily than any other Photoshop tool, especially for delicate or detailed areas, such as lace or hair.

When you use the Extract filter, Photoshop erases the background of the selected area and makes it

transparent. The filter looks for contrasting edges under the area you highlight. For pixels on the edges, it removes any color derived from the background to avoid having an edge halo when the item is placed on another background.

Although it is a sophisticated tool, the Extract filter may leave some areas that need to be touched up before your selection is complete. You can easily refine and fix the extraction with another layer and other Photoshop tools.

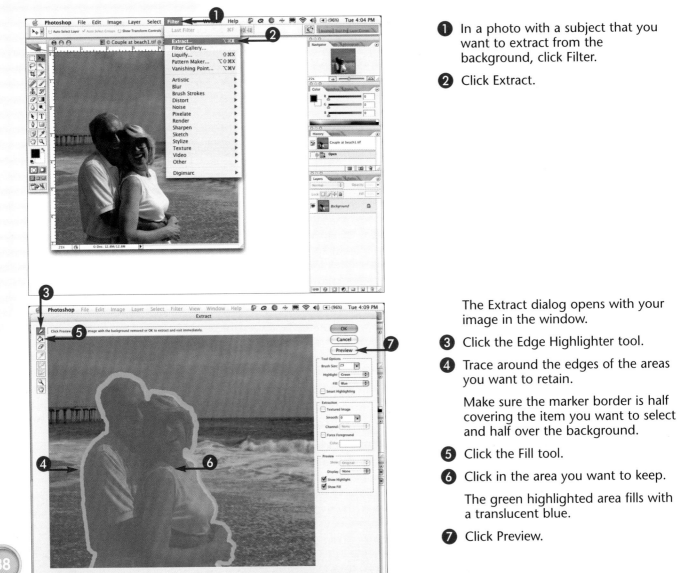

① In a photo with a subject that you want to extract from the background, click Filter.

② Click Extract.

The Extract dialog opens with your image in the window.

③ Click the Edge Highlighter tool.

④ Trace around the edges of the areas you want to retain.

Make sure the marker border is half covering the item you want to select and half over the background.

⑤ Click the Fill tool.

⑥ Click in the area you want to keep.

The green highlighted area fills with a translucent blue.

⑦ Click Preview.

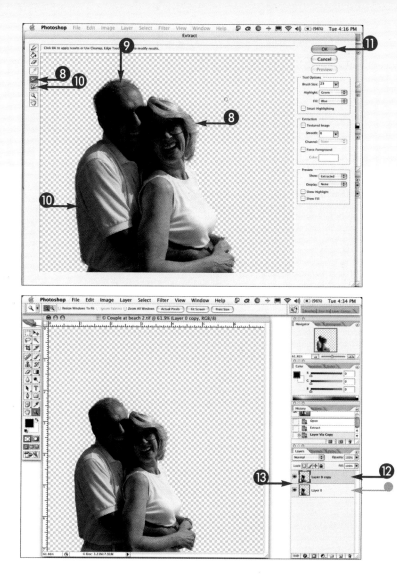

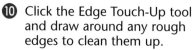

The extracted area appears on a transparent background.

8 Click the Clean Up tool and draw around any ragged edges to remove excess background.

9 Hold the Option (Alt) key down and fill in any areas that dropped out.

10 Click the Edge Touch-Up tool and draw around any rough edges to clean them up.

11 Click OK.

● The selected area is extracted and placed on an editable layer named Layer 0.

12 Press ⌘-J (Ctrl+J) to duplicate the layer.

Duplicating the layer often fixes other dropped-out areas.

13 Press ⌘-E (Ctrl+E) to merge the two layers.

TIPS

Caution!
If the blue fill color spills into the rest of the image, your subject was not completely enclosed by the highlight border. Press ⌘-Z (Ctrl+Z) to undo and outline the edge completely before filling.

More Options!
Press the left ([) or right (]) bracket keys to change the brush size as you highlight the object. Use a small brush to highlight well-defined areas and a larger brush to highlight wispy areas, such as hair.

Try This!
To preview the extraction against a plain background, click the Display expand arrow in the Preview palette on the right. Select Gray Matte or any other color that makes it easy to see your selection.

ACCENTUATE A SKY
easily with a gradient fill layer

You may have a scenic photo in which the sky is a bit dull. The lighting may have called for a different exposure setting or require a neutral density filter or polarizing filter on the camera. Still you may want to use the photo in an album or a graphic design project. Adding a little blue to darken the sky or adding some black to make a gray sky more foreboding can greatly improve an otherwise boring tourist photo.

Adding a gradient fill layer allows you to easily improve a washed-out blue sky or make a gray sky look stormy. You can visually adjust the amount of color you add, and because you are using a fill layer, you can go back and increase or decrease the amount of color after you apply it. You can even change the color that you apply to get a different effect or to create a dramatic look. This technique is most effective on a photo with a large sky area and an open horizon.

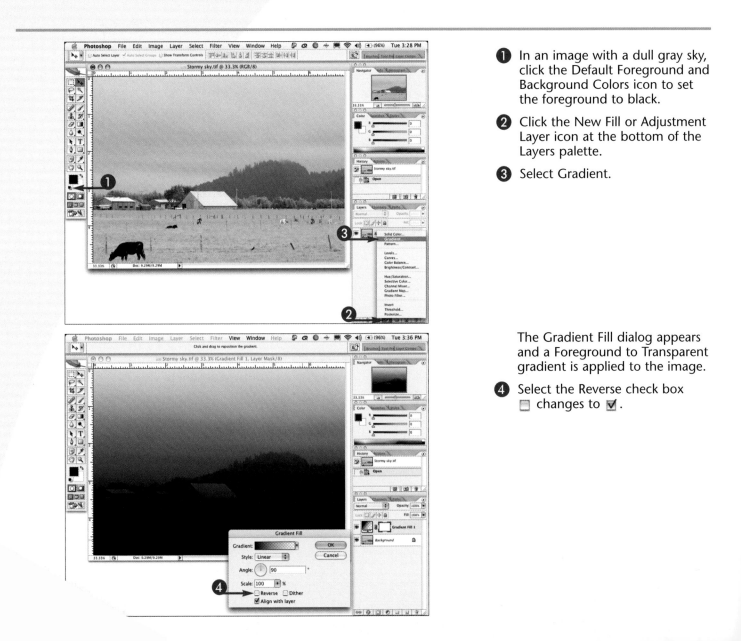

① In an image with a dull gray sky, click the Default Foreground and Background Colors icon to set the foreground to black.

② Click the New Fill or Adjustment Layer icon at the bottom of the Layers palette.

③ Select Gradient.

The Gradient Fill dialog appears and a Foreground to Transparent gradient is applied to the image.

④ Select the Reverse check box ☐ changes to ☑.

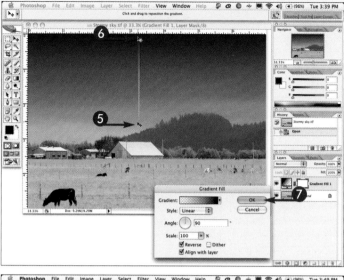

The gradient reverses to black at the top, changing to transparent at the bottom of the image.

⑤ Position the cursor over the image.

⑥ Drag upward in the image until the gradient covers only the sky and the clouds look menacing.

⑦ Click OK to apply the gradient.

● The ominous sky is applied as a layer above the Background layer.

⑧ Click the Blending mode menu up-down arrow in the Layers palette and select Overlay.

⑨ Double-click the layer thumbnail in the Layers palette for the gradient fill.

⑩ Repeat Steps **5** to **7** to increase or reduce the effect.

TIPS

More Options!

If your image has a gray sky that requires more drama, set the Foreground color in the toolbar to black. If the sky in your photo is blue, set the Foreground color in the toolbar to a dark blue before you apply the gradient fill layer. You can even accentuate a sunset by using a reddish-orange as the Foreground color.

Did you know?

Multiple layers increase the file size of your image. Because Photoshop requires more memory to work on larger files, you should merge layers that will not be adjusted later. Pressing ⌘-E (Ctrl+E) merges the highlighted layer with the layer below. Pressing ⌘-Shift-E (Ctrl+Shift+E) merges all the visible layers.

CREATE SMART OBJECTS LAYERS
to preserve quality

Creating a multilayer document in Photoshop has always been easy. However, each layer adopts the characteristics of the new base image. If you resize or alter a layer, the image may lose some quality. A Smart Objects layer is a new type of layer in Photoshop CS2. You can now place any Photoshop image or layer, or an Illustrator file as a Smart Objects layer, into a Photoshop file and the embedded layer remains fully editable while keeping all the characteristics from the original file.

You can then scale, rotate, and warp a Smart Objects layer without losing any of the original image data.

You can also place multiple copies of a layer by duplicating a Smart Objects layer in a document. When you edit one layer, all the instances of the same Smart Objects are automatically updated. You can replace the contents of a Smart Objects layer and automatically update one or multiple instances in a document at the same time. Using Smart Objects layers is a simple step, yet it gives you complete creative flexibility when designing any multilayer documents.

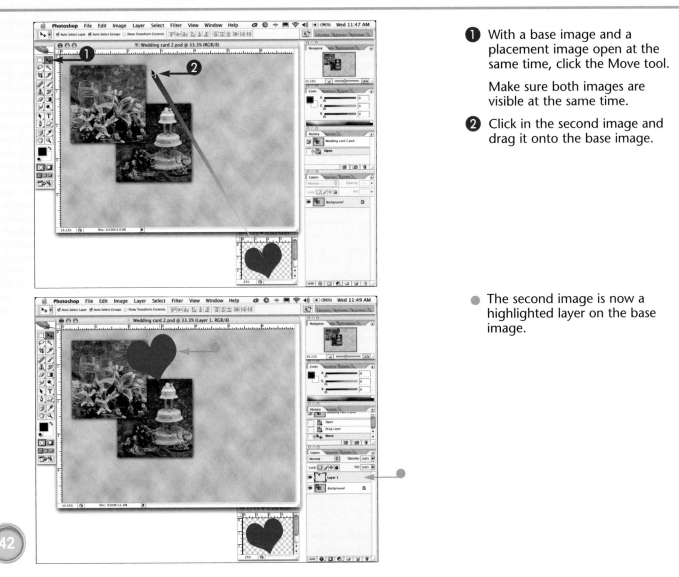

① With a base image and a placement image open at the same time, click the Move tool.

Make sure both images are visible at the same time.

② Click in the second image and drag it onto the base image.

● The second image is now a highlighted layer on the base image.

③ Click Layer.

④ Select Smart Objects.

⑤ Select Group into New Smart Object.

● The layer is converted into a Smart Objects layer.

⑥ Click and drag the Smart Objects layer's thumbnail over the New Layer icon in the Layers palette to duplicate it.

TIPS

More Options!

Click Layer ➪ Smart Objects ➪ Edit Contents. Click OK in the warning dialog that appears. The original file is displayed. You can make any color or size changes to the original file and press ⌘-S (Ctrl+S). When you close the file, the multilayered image is updated to reflect the changes, also.

Try This!

You can double-click on a Smart Objects layer thumbnail in the Layers palette instead of clicking Layer ➪ Smart Objects ➪ Edit Contents, to alter the original image. Make sure you double-click directly on the Smart Objects icon and not on the empty space in the Layers palette.

CREATE SMART OBJECTS LAYERS
to preserve quality

A Smart Objects layer acts as a pointer to the original image file. When you transform the Smart Objects layer, Photoshop uses the original pixels from the original file to make the changes. For example, if you place a photograph as a regular layer, and then use the Transformation command to make the image smaller, the actual dimensions of the image on the layer are reduced. If you then want to increase the size of the photo, your image will lose quality, because your previous transformation destroyed

pixels to reduce the size. If you place the same photograph as a Smart Objects layer, you can transform the layer and change your mind as many times as you like. Photoshop always uses the information in the original file as it transforms a Smart Objects layer. Using Smart Objects when placing RAW photos into a document is particularly convenient because you can readjust the colors and size of photo as you import the RAW file.

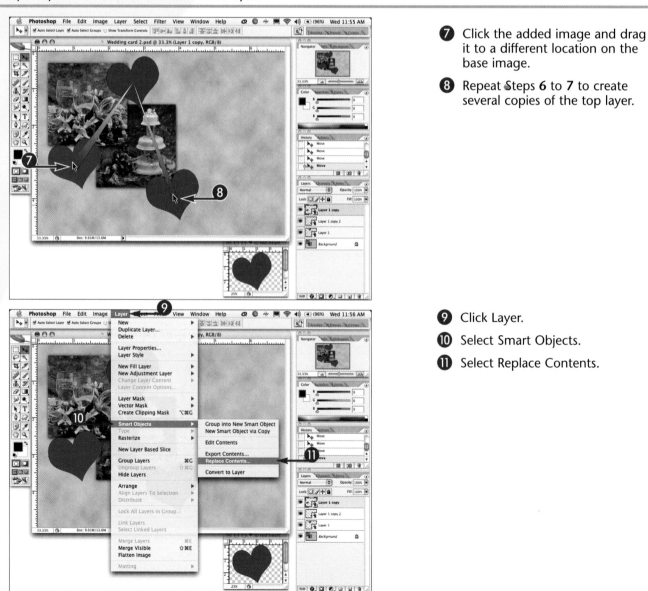

7 Click the added image and drag it to a different location on the base image.

8 Repeat Steps **6** to **7** to create several copies of the top layer.

9 Click Layer.

10 Select Smart Objects.

11 Select Replace Contents.

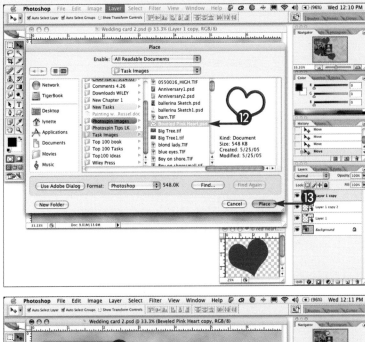

A Place dialog appears.

⑫ Navigate to the file you want to use.

⑬ Click Place.

● The new content is placed in the Smart Objects layer.

● Duplicated Smart Objects are also updated.

Did you know?

You can place a camera RAW image from the Bridge as a Smart Objects layer into a Photoshop file. The Smart Objects layer remains completely editable as a camera RAW file without any data loss.

Try This!

You can add layer styles such as bevels or drop shadows to the original image in a Smart Objects layer, and the style changes are reflected in the multilayered image.

More Options!

You can create a duplicate Smart Object that is not linked to the original. Click Layer ➪ Smart Objects ➪ New Smart Object Via Copy. Any changes you now make to the original Smart Object will not affect this copy.

Straightening, Cropping, and Resizing Magic

A well-balanced image, free from odd-looking distortions, can mean the difference between a snapshot and a good photograph. The overall layout of the image, how it is cropped, and where the main subject is placed in relation to the background are important in both design and photography. A crooked horizon or unbalanced subject matter can make even a great image look like the work of a beginner. You may have buildings that appear top heavy or out of perspective and your photos will not always be the size you need for your projects. Even the best photographers have images that require some cropping or resizing.

With Photoshop CS2, you can crop images for better composition with a variety of tools and

easily straighten the horizon in any photo. You can also straighten and crop several crookedly scanned photos in one step. You can even make multiple photos from one original image or create a panorama from several separate images. You can fix various types of camera lens distortions and correct the perspective on buildings, and Photoshop does most of the work for you. You can even enlarge an image easily without a major loss in quality.

Photoshop CS2 makes all such previously time-consuming or difficult tasks quick and easy. New tools and new resampling algorithms help you straighten, crop, adjust, and resize images, saving hours of tedious work to make all your images look better.

Top 100

CROP YOUR IMAGES
to improve composition

Designers and photographers use various techniques to balance an image and catch the viewer's attention. They may change the placement of the horizon to the upper or lower third of the image. They may divide the entire image into thirds horizontally and vertically and place the main subject at the intersection of the thirds. They may just offset the main subject to guide the viewer into the image. Perfectly composing a photograph in the camera's viewfinder is not always possible; however, you can recompose and improve that photo by cropping it in Photoshop.

You can use Photoshop's Rulers and drag guides to divide the image or just to mark the center of focus as a visual reference. Then use the Crop tool to recompose your image, placing the main subject where it is most effective.

The Crop tool dims the areas to be cut away giving you a preview of the cropped image. You can crop visually, specify dimensions in the Options bar, use one of the preset sizes, or create a crop size and save it as a preset.

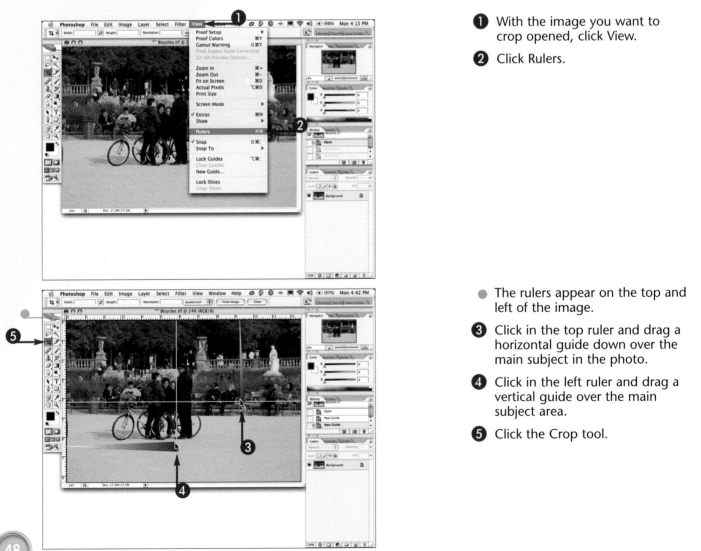

① With the image you want to crop opened, click View.

② Click Rulers.

● The rulers appear on the top and left of the image.

③ Click in the top ruler and drag a horizontal guide down over the main subject in the photo.

④ Click in the left ruler and drag a vertical guide over the main subject area.

⑤ Click the Crop tool.

6 Click and drag in the image to select the area you want to crop.

The cropped area is highlighted and the surrounding area is darkened.

7 Click and drag the corner or side anchors to reposition the cropped area.

8 Click the Commit button in the Options bar to commit the crop.

● The Crop tool crops away the unselected portions leaving a more balanced composition.

You can click View ➪ Clear Guides to remove the guides.

TIPS

Try This!

You can use the Crop tool to rotate the area and get a different composition. Drag out a marquee with the Crop tool. Then move the cursor just outside the area. It changes to a double-headed arrow. The crop rotates as you move the cursor. Click the Commit button to commit the crop.

Customize It!

Create your own Crop tool preset. Click the Crop tool and type your values in the Options bar. Click the Tool Preset Picker, the left-most thumbnail in the Options bar. Click the New Tool Preset icon on the right in the pull-down menu. Name your tool in the dialog and click OK. Your custom cropping tool is added to the menu.

Create a
LEVEL HORIZON

You may have a photograph that is perfect for your design but the photo was shot at a crooked angle. You can easily fix that photograph in Photoshop without doing any math to adjust the angle of the horizon line.

Photoshop includes a Measure tool, found in the toolbar under the Eyedropper tool. This tool is intended to help you position elements precisely in a design layout and can calculate distances between two points in the unit of measure that you have set

in the preferences. When you click and drag the tool across your image, a nonprinting line is drawn and the Options bar displays all the numeric information relating to the line and angle.

You can also use this tool to let Photoshop calculate how many degrees your image should be rotated to level the horizon and then let Photoshop straighten the photo for you. You can then use the Crop tool to cut off the angled edges of the image, and give your photograph a straight horizon line.

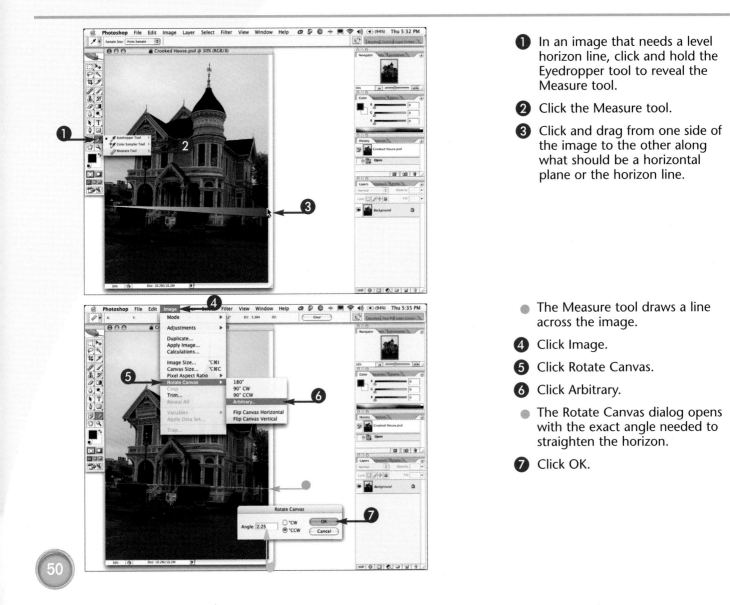

① In an image that needs a level horizon line, click and hold the Eyedropper tool to reveal the Measure tool.

② Click the Measure tool.

③ Click and drag from one side of the image to the other along what should be a horizontal plane or the horizon line.

● The Measure tool draws a line across the image.

④ Click Image.

⑤ Click Rotate Canvas.

⑥ Click Arbitrary.

● The Rotate Canvas dialog opens with the exact angle needed to straighten the horizon.

⑦ Click OK.

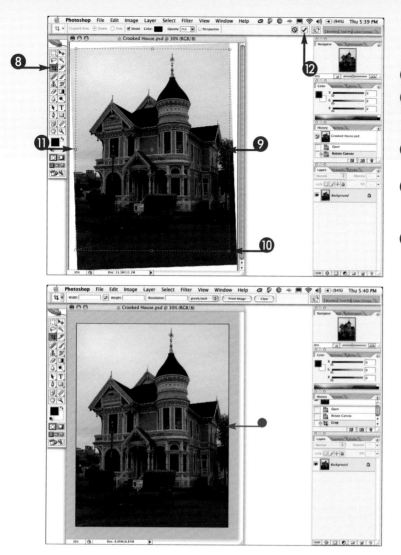

The image is rotated and the horizon is now more level.

⑧ Click the Crop tool.

⑨ Click and drag in the image to select the area you want to crop.

⑩ Drag the corner anchors to the edges.

⑪ Drag the Center anchors up or down to fit the image.

⑫ Click the Commit button in the Options bar to commit the crop.

● The image is cropped and the horizon is now straight.

TIPS

Did You Know?
You can easily check the dimensions of an open photo without opening the Image Size dialog. Select the Crop tool and click Front Image in the Options bar. The current width, height, and resolution are shown in the data fields.

Attention!
The Crop tool retains the dimensions of the previous crop. Be sure to click Clear in the Options bar to reset the tool and remove any old settings before you click and drag the Crop marquee in a new image.

Try This!
Although you have less control over the area to be cropped, you can crop a photo using the Rectangular Marquee tool. Click and drag a selection in the image with the Marquee tool. Click Image ➪ Crop.

TRY A REVERSE CROP
to expand the canvas

When you think of cropping, you generally think of reducing the physical size of an image by cutting away areas around the borders. In Photoshop, you can also use the Crop tool to expand your canvas, give your photo or image a wider border, or quickly create a new colored background for a photo.

Although using the Image Size menu and dialog is more precise, expanding the canvas with the Crop tool is quick and you can see exactly how your enlarged canvas appears. In addition, using the reverse crop method, you can create a border that is

uneven, larger on one side than the other for a page layout, or larger on the bottom than on the top as in a gallery print.

You can use this technique to enlarge your canvas visually or with precise dimensions for your final image. If you are working on a series of images with specific sizes, you can create a custom Crop tool preset and then use that tool to quickly reverse crop the photos. All your images then have the same-sized canvas, making your design and layout tasks much easier.

① In an opened image, click the Default Color icon in the toolbar to set the foreground to black and the background to white.

② Click the Zoom tool

③ Click the Zoom Out box in the Options bar.

④ Click in the image several times to zoom out.

The image becomes smaller on a gray background area.

⑤ Click the Crop tool.

⑥ Click and drag across the entire image.

● The crop marquee surrounds the image.

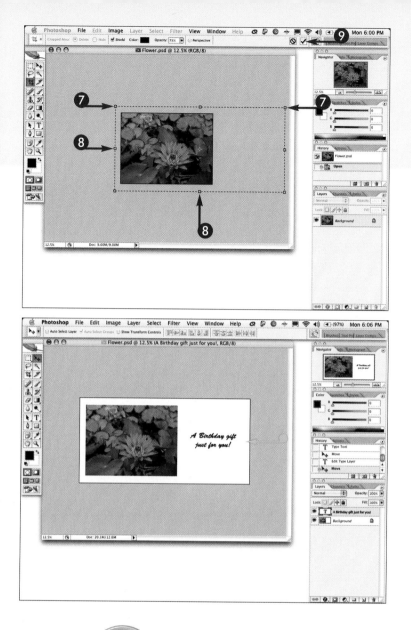

7 Click and drag on the corner anchor points of the crop marquee to extend the crop area.

8 Click and drag on the center anchor points until the borders fit your design.

9 Click the Commit button in the Options bar to commit the crop.

● The canvas is enlarged and filled with the default background color.

DIFFICULTY LEVEL

TIPS

More Options!
You can use this technique to quickly create a gift tag or a note card. Enlarge the canvas as in the task, click the Type tool and type some text in the white canvas area.

Try This!
Click the Background Color box in the Toolbar and select another color. When you enlarge the canvas using the reverse crop method, the area will fill with your selected color instead of white.

Change It!
Click the Crop tool and type the width and height for your finished design in the boxes in the Options bar. When you click and drag out the crop marquee in the image, it maintains the exact proportions you typed.

CROP AND STRAIGHTEN
in Camera Raw

Many digital cameras can save image files in the Camera Raw format. Camera Raw image files are the digital negatives and contain the actual picture data from the digital camera's image sensor without any in-camera processing applied. Photographers often prefer editing in Camera Raw to maintain more control because they can interpret the image data rather than let the camera make the adjustments and conversions automatically.

Photoshop CS2 not only allows you to set the white balance, tonal range, contrast, color saturation, and

sharpening in Camera Raw, you can now crop and straighten images in Camera Raw before opening them in Photoshop.

Once you crop and straighten the image files in the Camera Raw dialog, you can save them in Camera Raw and reprocess the file at any time with maximum control. You can also continue to edit and refine them in Photoshop and save them in a standard file format.

Using Camera Raw to crop and straighten gives you more options for editing and saving images.

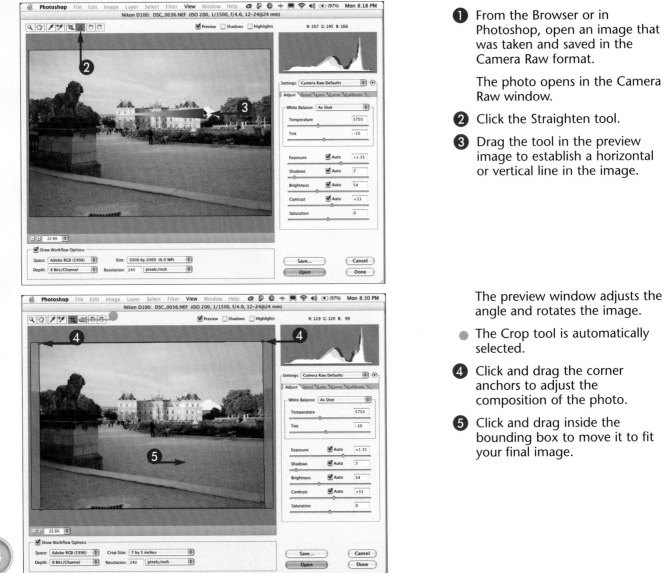

① From the Browser or in Photoshop, open an image that was taken and saved in the Camera Raw format.

The photo opens in the Camera Raw window.

② Click the Straighten tool.

③ Drag the tool in the preview image to establish a horizontal or vertical line in the image.

The preview window adjusts the angle and rotates the image.

● The Crop tool is automatically selected.

④ Click and drag the corner anchors to adjust the composition of the photo.

⑤ Click and drag inside the bounding box to move it to fit your final image.

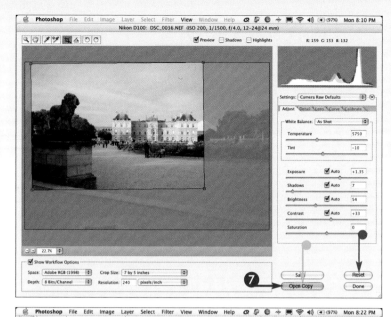

The bounding box moves to the desired area of the photograph.

⑥ Press and hold Option (Alt).

● The Open button changes to Open Copy.

⑦ Click Open Copy to open the image in Photoshop without altering your original.

● Holding the Option (Alt) key down also changes the Cancel button to Reset so you can start over.

DIFFICULTY LEVEL

The cropped and straightened image opens in Photoshop.

TIPS

Did You Know?

You can apply the same cropping dimensions to multiple images. Open the images in Camera Raw. Click Select All on the left of the dialog. Click Synchronize and then select the check box (☐) for Crop in the Synchronize dialog. Click OK to close the dialog. Select the Crop tool and crop the top-most image. All selected images are cropped in the same way.

More Options!

You can make a crop with specific proportions in Camera Raw. Click and hold the Crop tool to reveal the pop-up menu. Click one of the presets or click Custom. In the Custom Crop dialog, type the exact proportions or dimensions you need and click OK. The Crop tool is set for your specific size.

STRAIGHTEN CROOKED SCANS
quickly

When you are not bogged down with repetitive tasks, you can be more productive and creative. Photoshop has many features, such as automated image processing, to help both your productivity and your creativity.

Scanning images one by one is one of those redundant projects and can be very time consuming. You have to scan one image, crop it, and save it, then lift the scanner top, reposition another image on the scanner bed, and start over.

Using Photoshop CS2, you can scan multiple images on a flat bed scanner at one time and let Photoshop

separate these into multiple files. This automation tool can also save time when scanning just one photo. You no longer need to line it up perfectly on the scanner bed, because Photoshop's Crop and Straighten Photos command can also crop and straighten just one scanned photo.

The Crop and Straighten Photos command works best when the images have clearly defined edges and there is at least 1/8 inch between each image. The command may also work more quickly if all the images have similar tones.

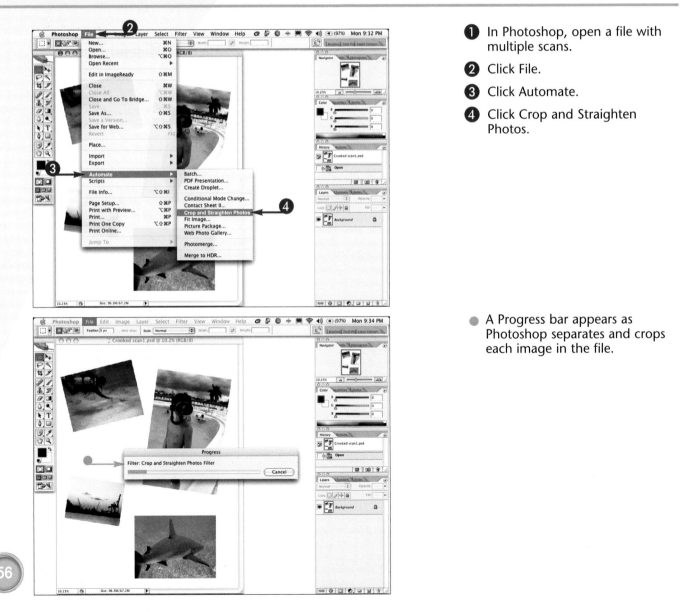

① In Photoshop, open a file with multiple scans.

② Click File.

③ Click Automate.

④ Click Crop and Straighten Photos.

● A Progress bar appears as Photoshop separates and crops each image in the file.

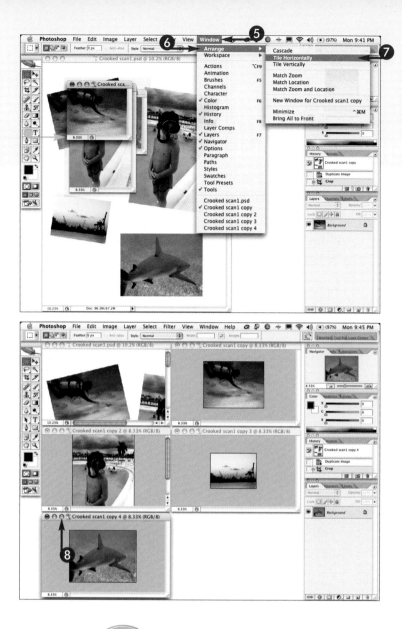

- Each image is opened in its own window.

5 Click Window.

6 Click Arrange.

7 Click Tile Horizontally (or Tile Vertically).

Photoshop arranges the original scan and all the separate images on the screen.

8 Click the Maximize button to view each image at full size.

TIPS

Important!

Photoshop does not replace the original scan with the separated photos and it does not automatically save the separate images. Instead, it renames each separated file using the same name as the original scan and labeling it copy, copy 2, and so on. You can Click File ➪ Save As and rename each file before you save it.

More Options!

You might scan multiple images at once and decide you only want to keep one of them. Make a selection border around one image, including some background. Press and hold Option (Alt) as you select File ➪ Automate ➪ Crop and Straighten Photos. Photoshop crops and straightens that one photo and puts it in a separate file.

CROP MULTIPLE IMAGES
from one original

Although tools such as the Crop and Straighten Photos command are meant as productivity aids to crop and straighten multiple images at one time, you can use the same tool in various creative ways.

You can create multiple images from one file by using the command to divide one photograph into multiple sections. You can make individual photographs from each section of the original or apply a diptych or triptych look to an image, making two or three panels for the image, which you can print and frame separately.

Select a plain, rectangular frame shape as a custom shape to designate the areas you want to crop into new images. Photoshop turns those separate shapes into separate images that you can save as new files. The trick to this technique is to leave a small margin around each of the shape selections and to create a separate layer for each shape when you use the Custom Shape tool. You can use the shape as part of your final print, or because it is on a separate layer, you can delete it for a different look.

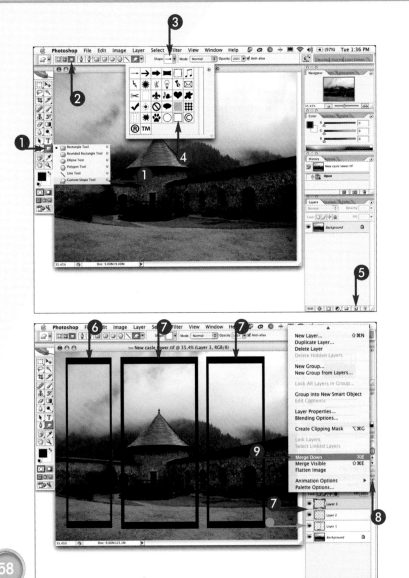

1. In a large file, click and hold the Rectangle tool and select the Custom Shape Tool.

2. Click the Fill Pixels icon in the Options bar.

3. Click the Shape down-arrow.

4. Select the square thin frame shape.

5. Click the New Layer icon in the Layers palette.

- A new blank layer is placed above the background.

6. Click and drag a frame shape in the image.

7. Repeat Steps **5** to **6** twice to add two more layers and two more frame shapes.

8. Click the Layers palette expand arrow.

9. Select Merge Down from the pop-up menu.

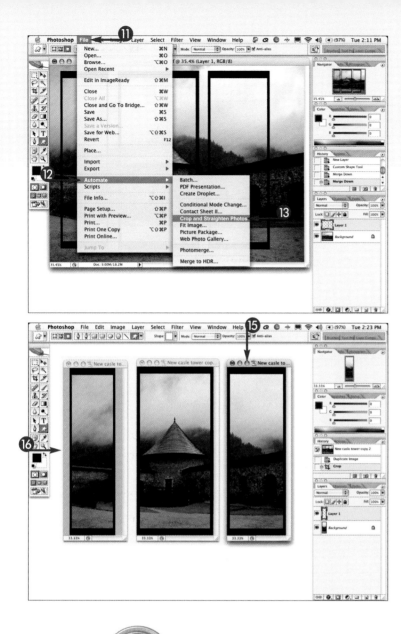

⑩ Repeat Steps **8** to **9** until there is only one layer above the background layer.

⑪ Click File.

⑫ Click Automate.

⑬ Click Crop and Straighten Photos.

Photoshop separates the segments and creates three new files with the name of the original and copy, copy 2, and copy 3.

⑭ Click the Close button of the original file.

⑮ Click the Maximize button on each of the three new files to enlarge them.

⑯ Align the three new files to make a triptych.

TIPS

Caution!

Be sure to create a new layer for each frame you draw. You can then resize and rotate the shapes by clicking Edit ⇨ Free Transform and transforming the frame shape with the Transformation anchors. Before you apply the Crop and Straighten Photos command, merge all the custom shape layers into one layer above the original image.

More Options!

You can delete the shape layer for each file by dragging it to the Layers palette trash, or use the shape to give your finished images a framed look. Use the Magic Wand tool to select the shape. Change its color by clicking Edit ⇨ Fill and selecting a new color. Then Click Layer ⇨ Layer Style and apply a bevel and drop shadow to the layer.

CHANGE YOUR PERSPECTIVE
with the crop tool

When you photograph an object from an angle rather than from a straight-on view, the object appears out of perspective, displaying keystone distortion. The top edges of a tall building photographed from ground level appear closer to each other at the top than they do at the bottom. If you photograph a window and cannot get directly in front of it to take the shot, the window appears more like a trapezoid. Depending on the photograph, you can correct this type of distortion with a number of Photoshop's tools.

The Crop tool in Photoshop CS2 has a special option that allows you to transform the perspective in an image and quickly adjust the keystone distortion. Your image must have an object that was rectangular in the original scene for the Crop tool's perspective function to work properly. You first adjust the cropping marquee to match the rectangular object's edges, and then extend the marquee to fit your image. When you click the Commit button, Photoshop crops the image as large as possible while maintaining the angles of the rectangular object.

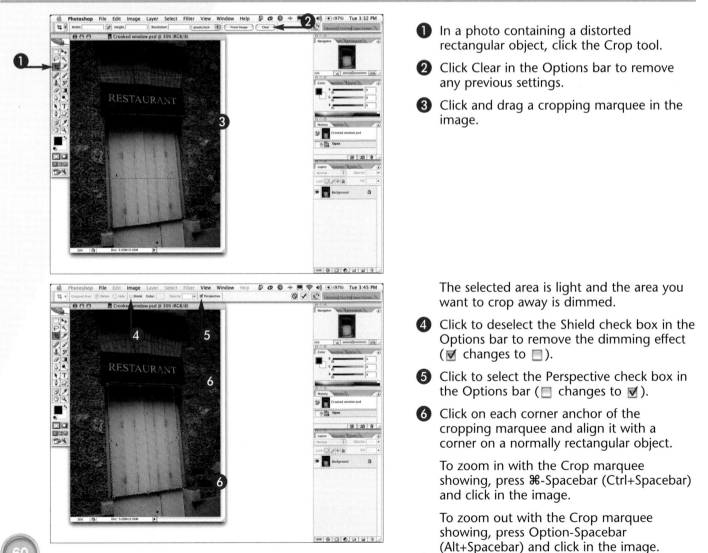

① In a photo containing a distorted rectangular object, click the Crop tool.

② Click Clear in the Options bar to remove any previous settings.

③ Click and drag a cropping marquee in the image.

The selected area is light and the area you want to crop away is dimmed.

④ Click to deselect the Shield check box in the Options bar to remove the dimming effect (☑ changes to ☐).

⑤ Click to select the Perspective check box in the Options bar (☐ changes to ☑).

⑥ Click on each corner anchor of the cropping marquee and align it with a corner on a normally rectangular object.

To zoom in with the Crop marquee showing, press ⌘-Spacebar (Ctrl+Spacebar) and click in the image.

To zoom out with the Crop marquee showing, press Option-Spacebar (Alt+Spacebar) and click in the image.

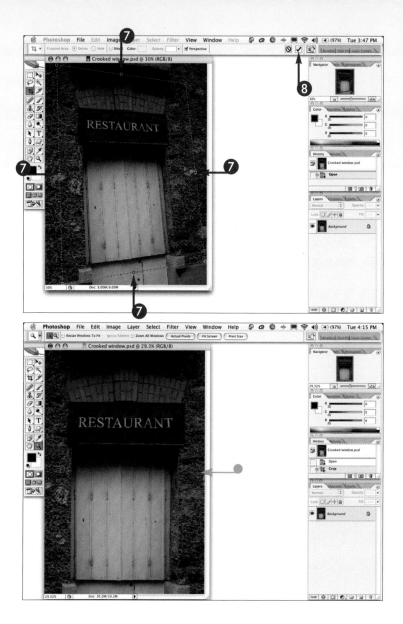

7 Click and drag out each of the center anchor points to fit the edges of the entire image.

8 Click the Commit button in the Options bar to commit the crop.

● Photoshop realigns the image and changes the perspective.

TIPS

Caution!
Photoshop's Crop tool will not work to correct keystoning on all images. The Crop tool may not fix the perspective distortion if it is applied to an image that has already been cropped for size.

Important!
By default, the area set off for cropping is darkened as you draw out the cropping marquee in the preview. To see the whole image as you line up the marquee and set the perspective with the Crop tool, deselect the check box (☑) for Shield in the Options bar before you start lining up the rectangle.

Attention!
If Photoshop shows an error, you may not have placed the corner handles correctly. Click the Cancel icon in the Options bar and adjust the cropping marquee before clicking the Commit button and committing the crop.

STRAIGHTEN BUILDINGS
with one filter

Depending on the focal length of a camera lens or the f-stop used, a photograph may show common lens flaws such as barrel and pincushion distortion. Barrel distortion causes straight lines to bow out toward the edges of the image. Pincushion distortion is the opposite effect, where straight lines bend inward. If the camera tilts up or down or at any angle, the perspective also appears distorted. The new Lens Correction filter in Photoshop CS2 can help you fix these and other lens defects easily.

When you photograph tall buildings, the tops of the buildings may appear to be larger at the top than the bottom. The Lens Correction filter allows you to easily line up perspective of the buildings with a vertical plane. You can use the filter's image grid to make your adjustments more accurately, or you can turn the grid off if you choose. The filter even has an option to let you select how to correct the missing areas along the edges that occurred when the perspective was repaired.

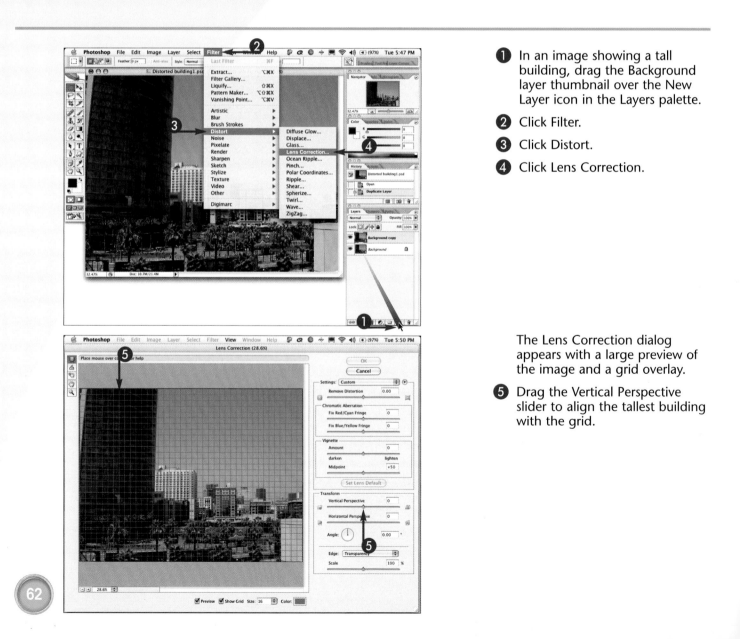

1. In an image showing a tall building, drag the Background layer thumbnail over the New Layer icon in the Layers palette.

2. Click Filter.

3. Click Distort.

4. Click Lens Correction.

The Lens Correction dialog appears with a large preview of the image and a grid overlay.

5. Drag the Vertical Perspective slider to align the tallest building with the grid.

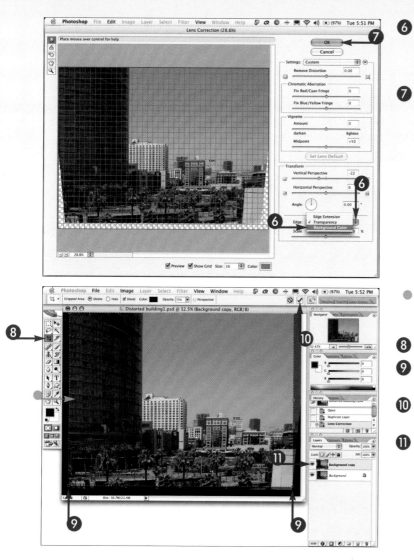

6 Click the Edge up-down arrow and select Background Color from the menu.

7 Click OK to commit the changes.

● The adjusted image reopens in Photoshop with a black border over the moved edges.

8 Click the Crop tool.

9 Click and drag in the image using the black border as a guide.

10 Click the Commit button in the Options bar to apply the crop.

11 Click the Visibility (eye) icon to turn off the background copy layer to compare the original image and the corrected one.

TIPS

Try This!
You can reset the adjustments in the dialog by pressing Option (Alt). The Cancel button changes to Reset. Click Reset to remove the changes and start over. You can change Cancel buttons in most dialogs to Reset by pressing Option (Alt).

More Options!
You can save the Lens Correction settings and reapply them to other images. Set the options in the dialog box. Click the Manage Settings down-arrow and choose Save Settings. The saved settings appear in the Settings pull-down menu.

Did You Know?
The Lens Correction filter can adjust both Barrel distortion and Pincushion distortion. In addition, it can fix Chromatic Aberration, a colored fringe along the edges of objects, and Vignetting, the appearance of darker corners or edges in the image.

CREATE A PANORAMA
from multiple photos

You can combine multiple photographs into one continuous image to create a panorama. For example, you can take three or more overlapping photographs of a scenic horizon, and then assemble them in Photoshop. You can also scan all four corners of a large document on a letter- or legal-size scanner and combine these to re-create the document as an image file. The Photomerge command can assemble photos that are tiled horizontally as well as vertically.

Photos or scans intended for merging should have an overlap of 25 percent to 40 percent. Using a tripod to keep the camera level when taking photos for a photomerge can help Photoshop assemble the images more accurately. To make the merge as successful as possible, try to maintain the same exposure for each photograph or keep the same scanning settings for each scan. After Photoshop has created a merged file, you can fine-tune the image using various tools to better blend the edges of the individual photos.

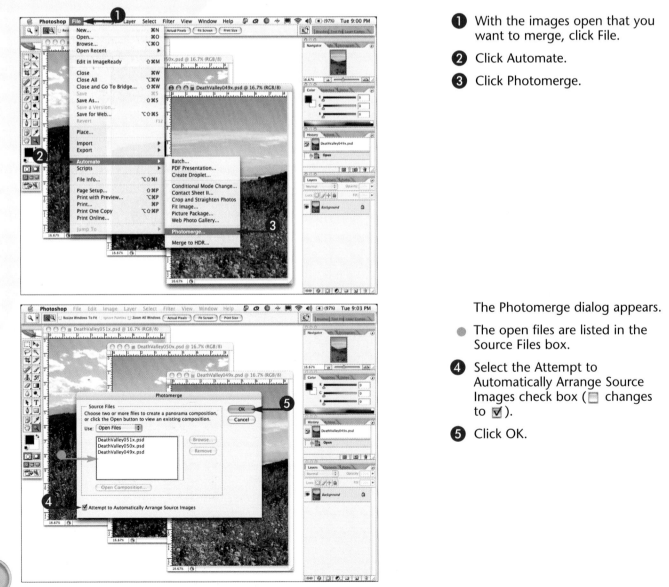

① With the images open that you want to merge, click File.

② Click Automate.

③ Click Photomerge.

The Photomerge dialog appears.

● The open files are listed in the Source Files box.

④ Select the Attempt to Automatically Arrange Source Images check box (☐ changes to ☑).

⑤ Click OK.

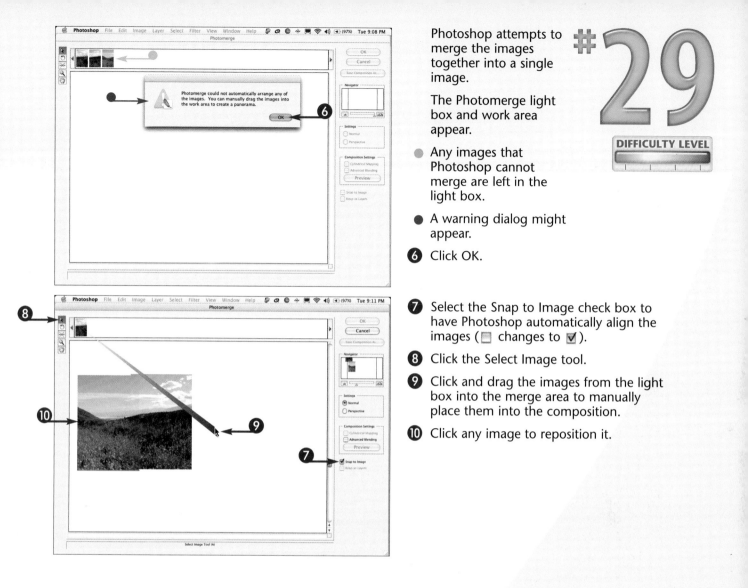

Photoshop attempts to merge the images together into a single image.

The Photomerge light box and work area appear.

● Any images that Photoshop cannot merge are left in the light box.

● A warning dialog might appear.

⑥ Click OK.

⑦ Select the Snap to Image check box to have Photoshop automatically align the images (□ changes to ☑).

⑧ Click the Select Image tool.

⑨ Click and drag the images from the light box into the merge area to manually place them into the composition.

⑩ Click any image to reposition it.

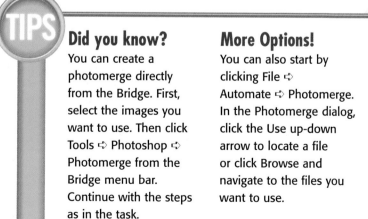

TIPS

Did you know?

You can create a photomerge directly from the Bridge. First, select the images you want to use. Then click Tools ➪ Photoshop ➪ Photomerge from the Bridge menu bar. Continue with the steps as in the task.

More Options!

You can also start by clicking File ➪ Automate ➪ Photomerge. In the Photomerge dialog, click the Use up-down arrow to locate a file or click Browse and navigate to the files you want to use.

Change It!

You can add more files by clicking the Browse button again and navigating to add source files. You can always remove a file from the Source Files list by selecting the file and clicking Remove.

CREATE A PANORAMA
from multiple photos

The most difficult part of a successful Photomerge is controlling or correcting exposure problems. Even a slight deviation in exposure can make the merge look odd. If your panorama displays color shifts even after using Advanced Blending, as in the example, you can click Cancel instead of clicking OK. Click on one of the photos that did blend correctly. Then click on the open photo segment that had a different exposure compared to the others. Click Image, click Adjustments, and click Match Color. In the Match Color dialog, select the first photo, the one with the

correct exposure, as the Source image. Move the dialog so you can see both images and use the preview to compare the colors. You can adjust the amount of change by using the Color Intensity slider until the two images match as closely as possible. Click OK to apply the color changes to the photo. When you use the Photomerge command after editing the colors of the image that originally did not blend well, Photoshop can usually blend the images into a successful panorama.

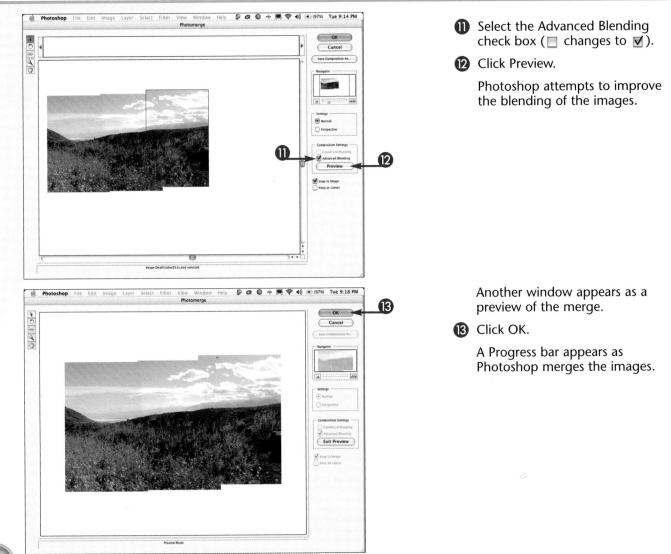

⑪ Select the Advanced Blending check box (☐ changes to ☑).

⑫ Click Preview.

Photoshop attempts to improve the blending of the images.

Another window appears as a preview of the merge.

⑬ Click OK.

A Progress bar appears as Photoshop merges the images.

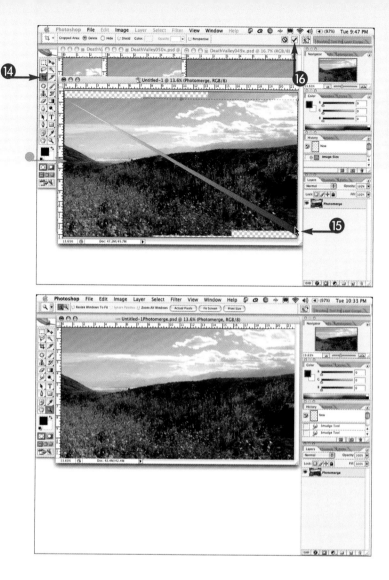

● The resulting photomerge appears in an untitled window.

⑭ Click the Crop tool.

⑮ Drag across the image to crop away any uneven edges.

⑯ Click the Commit button to apply the crop.

The final merged file appears in a new window.

Note: The image may need some blending or color adjustment in the merged areas.

TIPS

Attention!

If the composition cannot be automatically assembled, a message appears on-screen. You can try to assemble the composition manually in the Photomerge dialog using the light box. You may need to adjust some of the images first.

More Options!

When the new panorama appears in the Photomerge dialog, you can add or remove individual source files. You can rearrange the order of the images, drag an image in the work area to reposition it, or rearrange the images in the light box.

Important!

You can save each image in the composition in individual layers. Select the Keep as Layers check box (☑). This is useful if you need to correct the color of each image separately before finishing the file.

MAXIMIZE YOUR IMAGES
with minimal visible loss

Whether you print on an inkjet printer or a printing press, or use the image for the Web or e-mail, you often need a different size than the original. You can resize images using the Image Size dialog.

You can adjust the width, height, or resolution without affecting pixel dimensions or image quality by deselecting the Resample Image check box in the dialog. To change the overall size of an image, you must check the box and Photoshop resamples by adding or removing pixels to adjust for the changes.

Photoshop CS2 has dramatically improved its interpolation methods — the way it assigns values to

added pixels and smoothes transitions between juxtaposing pixels. You can now preserve most of the quality and detail when you enlarge or reduce images.

When you change the overall size of the image, the recommended resampling method is Bicubic Sharper for reducing image size and Bicubic Smoother for enlarging the image. However, many photographers are finding that the Bicubic Sharper resampling method, along with a resolution of 360 ppi, actually works best for both enlarging and reducing photos.

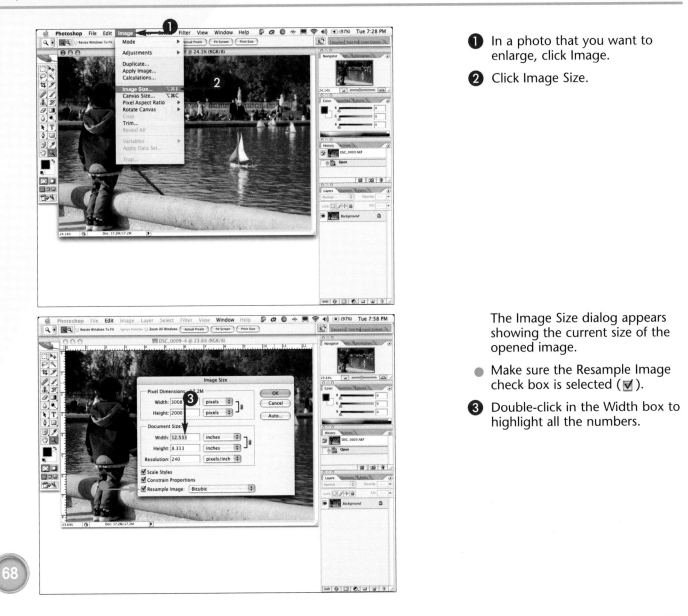

① In a photo that you want to enlarge, click Image.

② Click Image Size.

The Image Size dialog appears showing the current size of the opened image.

● Make sure the Resample Image check box is selected (☑).

③ Double-click in the Width box to highlight all the numbers.

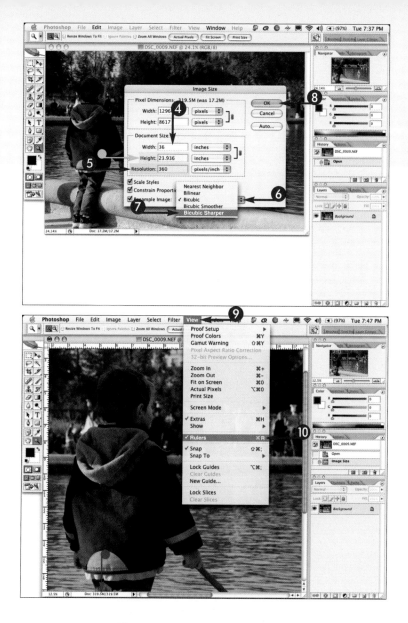

4 Type the desired width for the final printed image.

● The height automatically adjusts proportionally.

5 Type **360** in the Resolution box.

6 Click the Resample Image up-down arrow.

7 Select Bicubic Sharper from the pop-up menu.

8 Click OK.

A Progress bar appears as Photoshop processes the enlargement.

The enlarged photo appears.

● Check the file size in the window frame.

9 Click View.

10 Click Rulers to turn the rulers on and see the new dimensions.

TIPS

Test It!
Enlarge an image twice, once using Bicubic Smoother and once using Bicubic Sharper. Crop the same 4-x-6-inch section on both enlargements and paste these into two new documents. Because resampling may reduce detail and sharpness, apply the Smart Sharpen filter with the same settings to each new document and print them for comparison.

Did You Know?
A resolution of 150 to 360 ppi is generally recommended for inkjet printing. Images for on-screen viewing only need a resolution of 72 ppi. Images intended for a printing press require a resolution of twice the line screen of the press. If the line screen is 133 dpi, the resolution should be 266 ppi. Rounding up to 300 ppi is generally recommended.

Chapter

4

Retouching Portraits

You can use Photoshop to give your subjects a digital makeover and make them look more beautiful, younger, and healthier. However, it is so easy to alter images in Photoshop that new users often overdo it and make people look like plastic versions of themselves. You are trying to enhance a person's best features and minimize other areas, not turn him or her into someone else. If your subject looks at his photo and thinks he looks good, you have done your job well.

Use different layers to make all these changes so your image is not permanently changed until you save a flattened version. Using layers also allows you to blend or reduce the effects you apply making them appear more natural. In addition, you should always work on a duplicate of the original file even when you

make minor enhancements. Just do not show the original untouched photo to the subject!

You can use Photoshop CS2 for removing blemishes and red eye, enhancing the eyes, reducing wrinkles, whitening teeth, softening the face, and more. You can also change someone's hair color or eye color to fit a client's request. You can add richness to an image with a soft diffused digital glow. You can even reduce certain undesirable sags without plastic surgery or a bulge here and there to get your subject into better shape.

Because these enhancements should be subtle, using a digitizing tablet and stylus, such as the Wacom Intuos 3, is particularly useful when retouching portraits.

REMOVE BLEMISHES
to improve the skin

You can greatly improve a portrait by removing skin imperfections. Blemishes may be natural but they are rarely a desirable feature in a photograph. With Photoshop, you can easily remove or reduce the number of blemishes. You can even leave some while making them less obvious.

With previous versions of Photoshop, you could use the Clone Stamp tool or the Patch tool for this task. Photoshop CS introduced the Healing Brush, which is even better for repairing certain skin imperfections.

The new Spot Healing Brush in Photoshop CS2 is the simplest tool to use for removing blemishes. This tool automatically samples the areas around the spot to be removed and blends the pixels. The key to using the Spot Healing Brush is to choose a brush size that is just slightly larger than the blemish.

Create a new blank layer above the photo layer. You can then change the opacity of this layer and make the changes less obvious. If you do not like the changes, you can simply discard the layer.

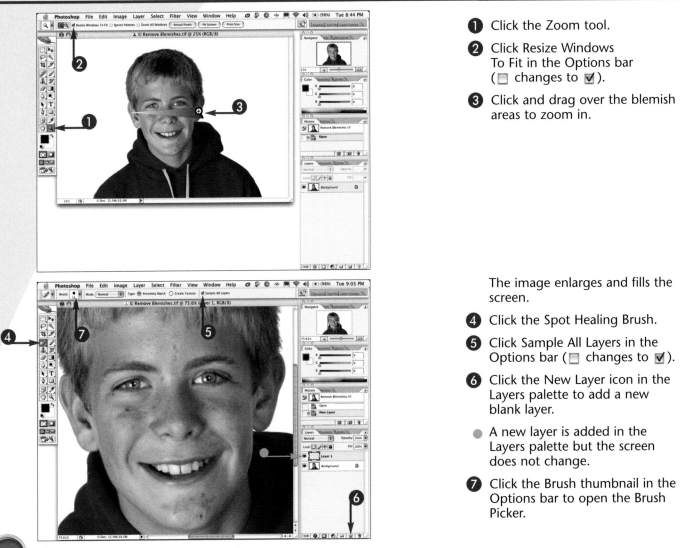

① Click the Zoom tool.

② Click Resize Windows To Fit in the Options bar (☐ changes to ☑).

③ Click and drag over the blemish areas to zoom in.

The image enlarges and fills the screen.

④ Click the Spot Healing Brush.

⑤ Click Sample All Layers in the Options bar (☐ changes to ☑).

⑥ Click the New Layer icon in the Layers palette to add a new blank layer.

● A new layer is added in the Layers palette but the screen does not change.

⑦ Click the Brush thumbnail in the Options bar to open the Brush Picker.

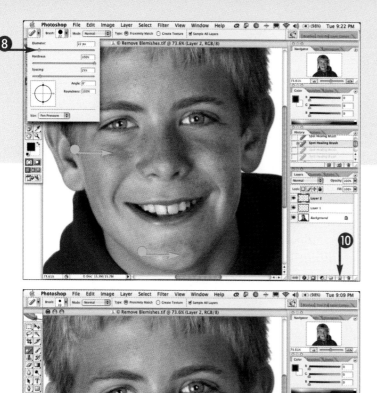

8 Click and drag the Diameter slider to adjust the size of the brush.

The brush size should be just larger than the blemish you want to remove.

9 Click each of the worst blemishes of a similar size first.

● Photoshop removes the blemishes blending the surrounding skin area.

10 Click the New Layer icon in the Layers palette to add another blank layer.

11 Repeat Steps **7** to **9**, clicking the other blemishes.

● Layer 2 should be highlighted in the Layers palette.

12 Click the Opacity expand arrow in the Layers palette.

13 Drag the Opacity slider for Layer 2 to the left until the skin looks natural.

TIPS

Attention!
Moles, freckles, or other distinguishing marks are a distinct feature. Unlike most blemishes, theses permanent marks may be considered essential to the person's character. Be sure to check with the subject or the art director first before removing these.

Did You Know?
You should always adjust images using a copy of the original file; however, you should also work on a different layer than the original Background layer. That way, you can easily discard the layer if you dislike your changes.

More Options!
With a digitizing tablet, you can set the Size in the Brush Picker to Pen Pressure and set the Brush size to be larger than the largest blemish. Press harder to remove large blemishes, and press lightly to remove smaller blemishes.

REMOVE RED EYE
to quickly improve any photo

You can remove the red eye effect from all photographs whether they are scanned from film or prints or start out as digital files. Photoshop CS2 introduces a new Red Eye tool making the process very easy.

Red eye is caused by the reflection of a camera flash in a person's retina. When you shoot in a darkened room, the subject's irises are wide open and their pupils enlarged, increasing the chances for red eye photos. Using a camera with the flash mounted

directly above the lens also causes more red eyes than using a bounce flash or a flash unit that is positioned away from the camera lens.

By default, Photoshop's Red Eye tool uses a large brush and makes the areas around the pupil black. You can change the default settings in the Options bar to fit the size of your subject's eyes. Changing the red areas to a gray color rather than black makes your subject look more natural and allows you to change the eye color later if needed.

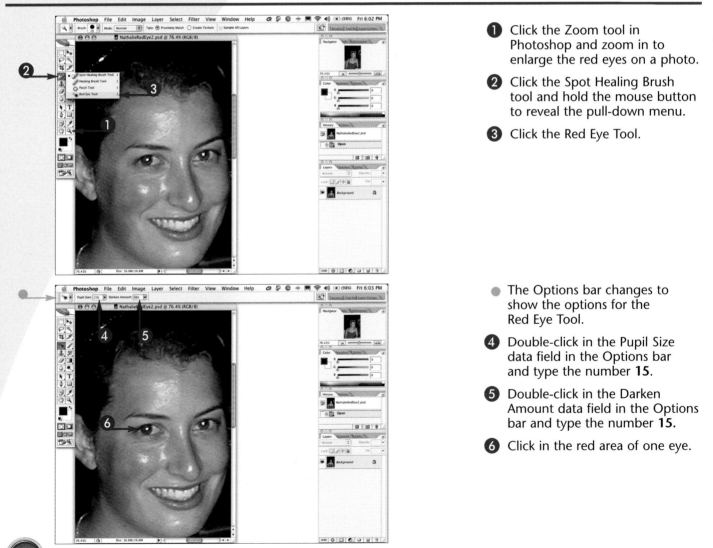

① Click the Zoom tool in Photoshop and zoom in to enlarge the red eyes on a photo.

② Click the Spot Healing Brush tool and hold the mouse button to reveal the pull-down menu.

③ Click the Red Eye Tool.

● The Options bar changes to show the options for the Red Eye Tool.

④ Double-click in the Pupil Size data field in the Options bar and type the number **15**.

⑤ Double-click in the Darken Amount data field in the Options bar and type the number **15**.

⑥ Click in the red area of one eye.

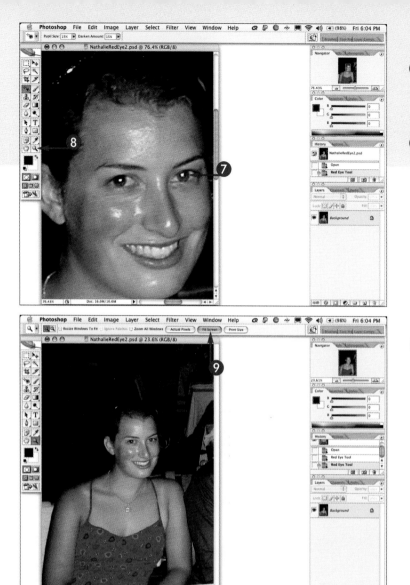

Photoshop replaces the red with a neutral gray.

⑦ Click in the red area of the other eye.

Photoshop replaces the red with a neutral gray.

⑧ Click the Zoom tool.

The Options bar changes.

⑨ Click Fit Screen to zoom out and see the entire image and a more natural looking eye color.

TIPS

Desktop Trick!

Pressing J selects the Spot Healing Brush tool. Press Shift as you press J again three times to select the Red Eye tool. With the tool selected, press Return (Enter) and the first data field in the Options bar is highlighted. Type your settings and press Tab to highlight the next data field.

Try This!

You can select all tools even faster using a one-letter keyboard shortcut. Click Photoshop (Edit), Preferences, and then General. Deselect the Use Shift Key for Tool Switch check box (☐) in the Options section of the dialog. Click OK. When you press the letter corresponding to a tool, you cycle through all the tools hidden below the first one.

CHANGE EYE COLOR
digitally

Using the Red Eye tool works well to eliminate the red eye effect. However, it leaves the eyes a gray color. You can improve many photos by simply adding back a little color or colorizing the iris of the eyes.

When you colorize the eyes, you are looking for a natural eye color. If you have another photo of the same person, you can sample the eye color from the first photo and paint it into the one with gray eyes. You can also select any color as the foreground color and paint in the irises. Colorizing the eyes naturally

depends on specific brush options you set in the Options bar.

You can also use the same technique to apply one person's eye color to another subject's eyes. Agencies often request a specific eye color for a model to better blend into the color scheme of an advertising piece. You can save time by using Photoshop to change the eye color in the original photo and avoid finding and photographing a different model.

① Click and drag the Background layer thumbnail in the Layers palette over the New Layer icon to duplicate the layer.

② Click the Zoom tool and zoom in to enlarge the eyes.

③ Click the Eyedropper tool.

④ Click the Sample Size up-down arrow in the Options bar and select 3 by 3 Average.

⑤ Click in the iris to set the foreground color.

⑥ Click the Brush tool.

The Options bar changes.

⑦ Click in the Brush thumbnail in the Options bar to open the Brush Picker.

⑧ Drag the Master Diameter slider to set a brush size just smaller than one-half the iris.

⑨ Click and drag the Hardness slider to 50 percent.

⑩ Click the Mode up-down arrow and click Color.

⑪ Click the Airbrush icon to enable it.

⑫ Click the foreground color box in the toolbar.

The Color Picker dialog appears.

⑬ Click and drag the Hue slider to another color.

⑭ Click OK to close the Color Picker.

#33

DIFFICULTY LEVEL

⑮ Click and drag to paint the new color in both irises.

⑯ Click the Eraser tool and erase if you paint over other areas.

⑰ Click the Opacity expand arrow in the Layers palette and drag the slider to the left until the eyes are the color you want.

TIPS

More Options!
If you have another photo with an appropriate eye color, you can also use the Color Replacement tool instead of the standard Brush tool. Select that tool. Option-click in the first photo to sample the color of the eyes you want to use, and apply it with soft brush strokes to the image you are correcting.

Did You Know?
You can avoid red eye in many photos if you use the red eye reduction feature included with some newer cameras. This feature minimizes the red eye effect in flash photos by firing several flashes an instant before the photo is taken, forcing the pupils to close slightly just as the final flash and shutter are released.

REDUCE WRINKLES
with a soft touch

You can remove wrinkles with Photoshop in a variety of ways. You can clone them away with the Clone Stamp tool or patch them using the Patch tool sampling the skin from other areas in the face. However, if you remove all the wrinkles and give a person perfectly smooth skin, the effect is not believable. Using the Healing Brush tool, you can maintain more control over the corrections and give your subject a rejuvenated yet natural appearance.

You can modify the Healing Brush and change its shape and angle so your brush strokes are not as visible when you literally paint away the wrinkles. You can create your wrinkle-removing brush by changing attributes in the Brush Picker in the Options bar. The effect appears even more realistic if you use a pressure-sensitive stylus and digitizing tablet and set the Healing Brush to respond to pressure.

Once you brush away the years, you can change the opacity of the altered layer to reintroduce just enough wrinkles to appear natural.

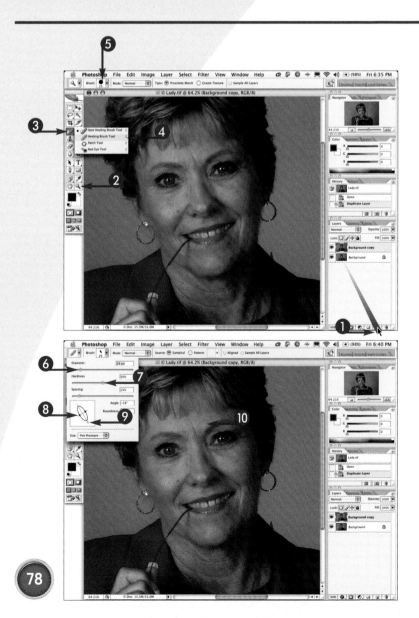

❶ Click and drag the Background layer thumbnail in the Layers palette over the New Layer icon to duplicate the layer.

❷ Click the Zoom tool and zoom in to enlarge the areas with wrinkles.

❸ Click the Spot Healing Brush tool and hold the mouse button to reveal the pull-down menu.

❹ Click the Healing Brush Tool.

❺ Click the Brush thumbnail in the Options bar to open the Brush Picker.

❻ Set the Master Diameter slider to a brush size wide enough to cover the deepest wrinkles.

❼ Drag the Hardness slider to about 50 percent.

❽ Click one dot on the circle in the thumbnail and drag toward the center to change the Roundness of the brush.

❾ Drag the arrowhead to change the angle of the stroke in the direction of the deepest wrinkles.

❿ Option-click (Alt+click) an area of clear skin near one wrinkle to sample.

⓫ Click and drag directly on the first wrinkles to paint them away.

⓬ Repeat Steps **8** to **11** changing the brush angle and roundness for the other wrinkles.

⓭ Click the Zoom tool.

⓮ Press Option (Alt) and click in the image to zoom out.

⓯ Click the Opacity expand arrow in the Layers palette and drag the slider until the wrinkles look natural.

TIPS

Try This!
Use many small strokes rather than one larger one when you paint over wrinkles with the Healing Brush and sample nearby areas of clear skin often. The skin tones match more closely and the results appear more natural.

Desktop Trick!
You need to zoom in and out often when removing wrinkles. Instead of changing tools when the Healing Brush is selected, press ⌘-Spacebar (Ctrl+Spacebar) and click to zoom in. Press Option-Spacebar (Alt+Spacebar) to zoom out.

Customize It!
With a Wacom Intuos3 stylus, you can set the rocker switch on the pen to the Option (Alt) key. You can then press the rocker switch instead of reaching for your keyboard to sample areas with the Healing Brush tool.

WHITEN TEETH
to add a youthful look

You can greatly improve every portrait in which the subject is smiling by applying a little digital tooth whitening. Yellow teeth always dull a smile as well as the overall look of the photo.

Whitening the teeth is easier using Photoshop than using tooth-whitening gels. You first select the teeth and feather, or soften the selection, to avoid a visible line between the areas that are lightened and the rest of the image. Although there are many ways to make a selection in Photoshop, using the Quick Mask mode and the Brush tool, as described in Chapter 2,

works well when making a detailed selection such as selecting a person's teeth.

Once the teeth are selected, whitening is a two-step process. You have to remove the yellow and then brighten the teeth by adjusting the saturation. Zoom in to make the detailed selection, but be sure to zoom out to see the whole image before adjusting the color. Digital tooth whitening should be a subtle adjustment to keep the smile and the person looking natural.

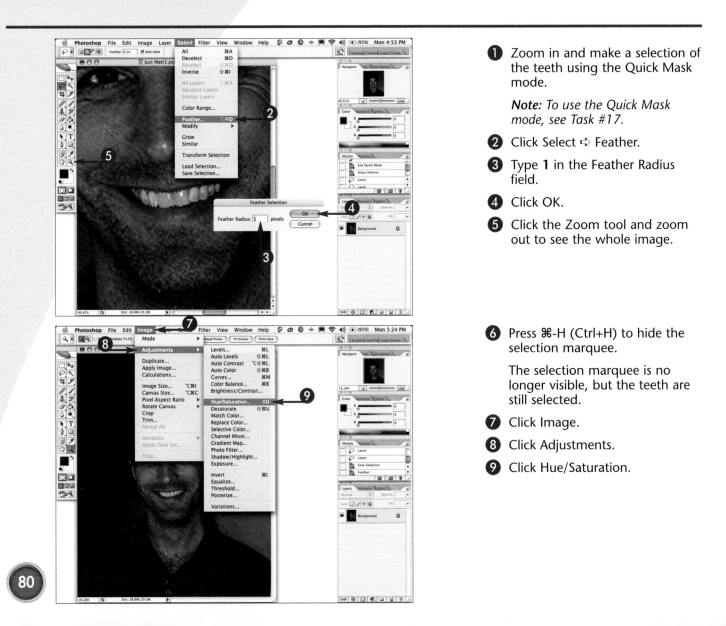

① Zoom in and make a selection of the teeth using the Quick Mask mode.

Note: *To use the Quick Mask mode, see Task #17.*

② Click Select ➪ Feather.

③ Type **1** in the Feather Radius field.

④ Click OK.

⑤ Click the Zoom tool and zoom out to see the whole image.

⑥ Press ⌘-H (Ctrl+H) to hide the selection marquee.

The selection marquee is no longer visible, but the teeth are still selected.

⑦ Click Image.

⑧ Click Adjustments.

⑨ Click Hue/Saturation.

The Hue/Saturation dialog appears.

Move it to one side so you can see the teeth.

⑩ Click the Edit up-down arrow and select Yellows.

⑪ Click and drag the Saturation slider to the left to remove the yellow.

⑫ Click the Edit up-down arrow again and select Master.

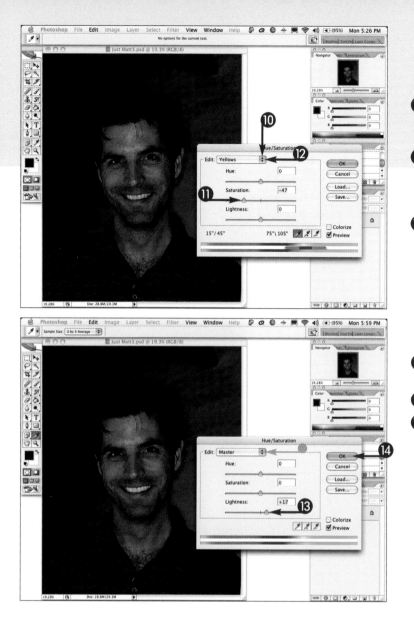

● The Hue/Saturation dialog remains with Master in the Edit field.

⑬ Click and drag the Lightness slider slowly to the right to brighten the teeth.

⑭ Click OK to apply the changes.

⑮ Press ⌘-D (Ctrl+D) to deselect the teeth.

TIPS

Desktop Trick!

When zooming in on an image, hold the Spacebar and the pointer temporarily changes to the Hand tool. You can click and drag around your image with the Hand tool and easily move to the area that needs to be adjusted. When you release the Spacebar, you change back to the tool you previously selected.

Did You Know?

Feathering softens the edge of a selection and smooths the transition between two distinct areas. You type a number of pixels for the Feather Radius in the Feather Selection dialog. The higher the number, the softer the edge. You cannot see the result of the feathering until you move the selected area or adjust it.

BRIGHTEN THE EYES
by lightening the whites

One way to quickly enhance a portrait is to draw attention to the eyes. The eyes are the most important feature of the face and the key to a person's individuality. Whether the whites of the eyes are bloodshot or just appear dull, lightening them can enhance the whole face. Brightening and desaturating the white area draws the viewer right into the subject's personality.

Lightening the whites of the eyes is a multi-step and multi-layer process. You first select the whites and remove the redness using a Hue/Saturation

adjustment layer. Then you brighten the eyes with a Curves adjustment layer and change the blending mode of the layers.

People do not have perfectly white eyes, so this adjustment requires not only a precise selection, it is also important to view the entire photo as you apply the changes. Because the adjustments are on separate layers, you can easily go back and modify the adjustments to enhance the overall image and keep the subject looking natural.

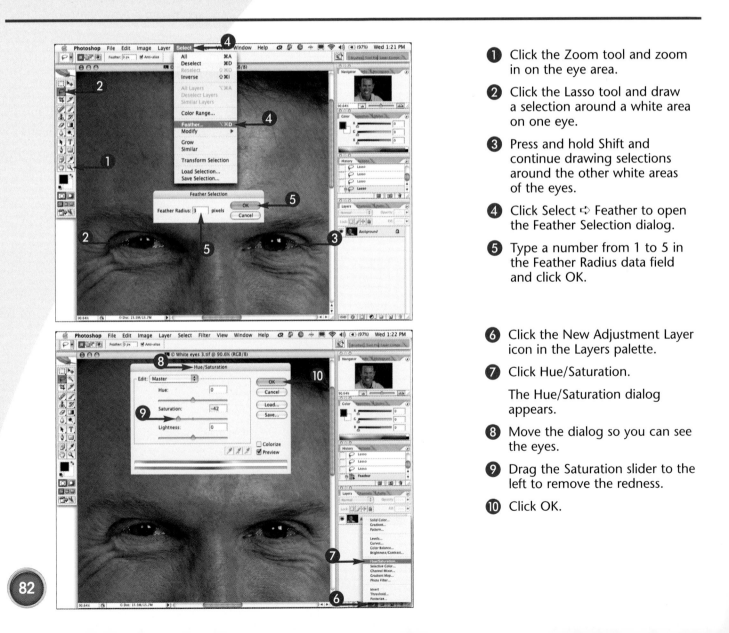

① Click the Zoom tool and zoom in on the eye area.

② Click the Lasso tool and draw a selection around a white area on one eye.

③ Press and hold Shift and continue drawing selections around the other white areas of the eyes.

④ Click Select ➪ Feather to open the Feather Selection dialog.

⑤ Type a number from 1 to 5 in the Feather Radius data field and click OK.

⑥ Click the New Adjustment Layer icon in the Layers palette.

⑦ Click Hue/Saturation.

The Hue/Saturation dialog appears.

⑧ Move the dialog so you can see the eyes.

⑨ Drag the Saturation slider to the left to remove the redness.

⑩ Click OK.

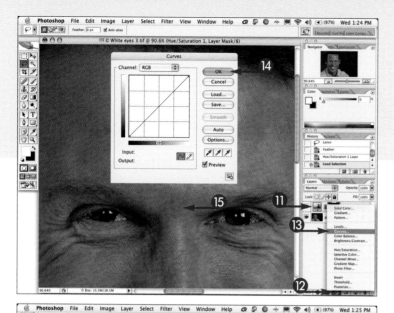

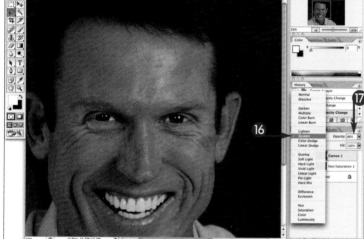

11 ⌘-click the layer mask thumbnail in the Layers palette to load the selection of the eye whites.

12 Click the New Adjustment Layer icon in the Layers palette.

13 Click Curves.

The Curves dialog appears.

14 Click OK in the dialog without making any changes.

15 Press Option-Spacebar (Alt+Spacebar) and click in the image to zoom out and see the whole face.

16 Click the Layer Blending mode up-down arrow on the Layers palette and select Screen.

17 Click and drag across the word Opacity to activate the Scrubby Slider and reduce the opacity of the layer until the eyes look good.

36

DIFFICULTY LEVEL

TIPS

More Options!
In some palettes, dialogs, and options bars, clicking and dragging on the word associated with a slider activates the Scrubby Sliders. The cursor changes to a pointing finger. Click and drag across the word changing the amount in the data field.

Did You Know?
Pressing Shift as you select with a selection tool allows you to add to a selected area or add a separate selection. Pressing Option (Alt) as you drag over a selected area allows you to remove areas from that selection.

Try This!
You can quickly access the Feather dialog, or other options, for any selection by pressing the Control key (right-click) in the selection area. A pop-up contextual menu appears listing options such as feather, save, fill, and stroke.

ADD DEPTH TO THE EYES
to emphasize them

Removing red eye and lightening the whites of the eyes improves any photograph. You can also make your subject more interesting by adding other adjustments that emphasize the eyes. You can add more contrast to the iris, the colored portion surrounding the pupil, by lightening some areas and darkening others. You can add depth to the eyes by darkening the eyelashes and the natural outline of the eyes. This digital technique is similar to dodging and burning in the darkroom.

Instead of using Photoshop's Dodge and Burn tools on the image, you can use the Brush tool on separate blank layers and vary the opacity of each layer to control the adjustments. Painting with white lightens areas. Painting with black darkens areas, lengthens the eyelashes, and adds definition to the eyes. Using the opacity setting in the Layers palette, you can fine-tune the adjustments before you finalize the image.

Making the eyes sparkle by using a variation of digital dodging and burning in Photoshop helps draw the viewer's attention to the eyes and engages them in the photo.

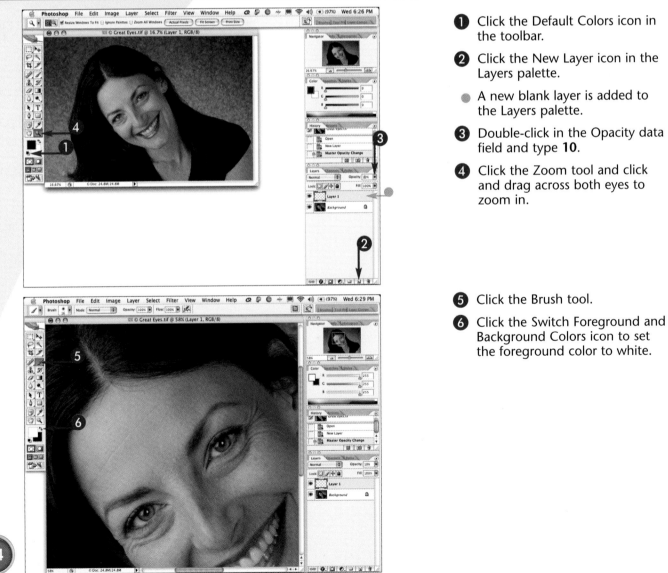

① Click the Default Colors icon in the toolbar.

② Click the New Layer icon in the Layers palette.

● A new blank layer is added to the Layers palette.

③ Double-click in the Opacity data field and type **10**.

④ Click the Zoom tool and click and drag across both eyes to zoom in.

⑤ Click the Brush tool.

⑥ Click the Switch Foreground and Background Colors icon to set the foreground color to white.

⑦ Click the Brush thumbnail in the Options bar to open the Brush Picker.

⑧ Click and drag the Master Diameter slider to select a small brush that fits inside the iris.

⑨ Click and drag the Hardness slider to 0 percent.

⑩ Paint with white in the center of both irises.

⑪ Click the Switch Foreground and Background colors icon to set the foreground color to black.

⑫ Paint with black around the edges of the irises and in the pupils.

⑬ Click the New Layer icon in the Layers palette to add a second blank layer.

⑭ Double-click in the Opacity data field and type **9**.

⑮ Click the Brushes tab to open the Brushes Palette and presets.

⑯ Press ⌘-Spacebar (Ctrl+Spacebar) and then click in the image to zoom in to see the eyelashes.

TIPS

Did You Know?
You can save and reuse an eyelash brush. Use the settings in the Brush Tip Shape in the Brushes palette to create the brush. Click the down-arrow on the Brushes palette. Click New Brush Preset. Type a name in the dialog and click OK.

Try This!
Press D to set the foreground and background colors to the default black and white. Press X to quickly switch the foreground and background colors as you digitally dodge and burn.

Try This!
To lighten dark brown eyes, try setting the foreground color to a dark red or burgundy color instead of white. Paint in the irises on a separate layer and adjust the opacity. Adding red to dark brown eyes softens the look.

ADD DEPTH TO THE EYES
to emphasize them

Retouching portraits is always tricky. You want to improve the image and still preserve the person's character. Because the eyes can define personality, enhancing the eyes usually helps the overall portrait and helps the viewer focus on the subject.

When you work on any portrait and especially when you work on the eyes, you need to make small changes. Large changes are too often obvious and your subjects want to see themselves and be seen at their best, not different. Use light brush strokes instead of heavy ones. Make small changes and repeat these on several layers. You can easily adjust the opacity of each layer independently, creating more variations in brush strokes and colors. With adjustments on multiple layers, it is also easier to change or delete enhancements that do not seem natural.

Using a pressure-sensitive digitizing tablet and stylus also gives more variety to brush strokes. Many of the brush options can be set to respond to pressure or tilt, allowing you to alter brush styles with fewer trips to the Brushes palette.

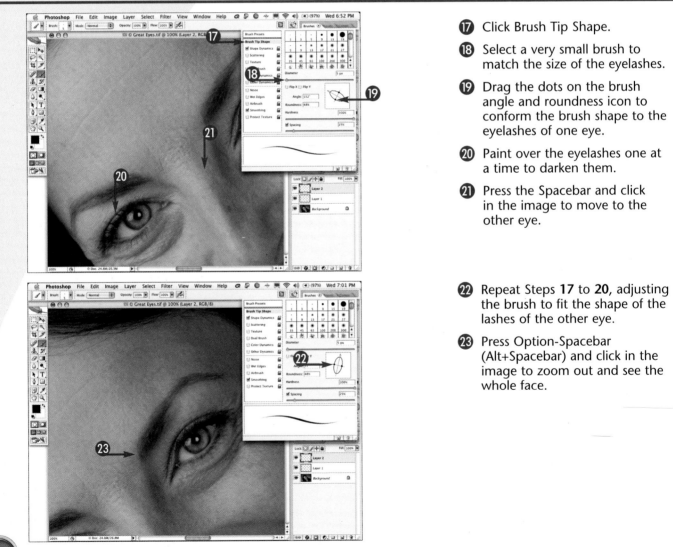

⑰ Click Brush Tip Shape.

⑱ Select a very small brush to match the size of the eyelashes.

⑲ Drag the dots on the brush angle and roundness icon to conform the brush shape to the eyelashes of one eye.

⑳ Paint over the eyelashes one at a time to darken them.

㉑ Press the Spacebar and click in the image to move to the other eye.

㉒ Repeat Steps **17** to **20**, adjusting the brush to fit the shape of the lashes of the other eye.

㉓ Press Option-Spacebar (Alt+Spacebar) and click in the image to zoom out and see the whole face.

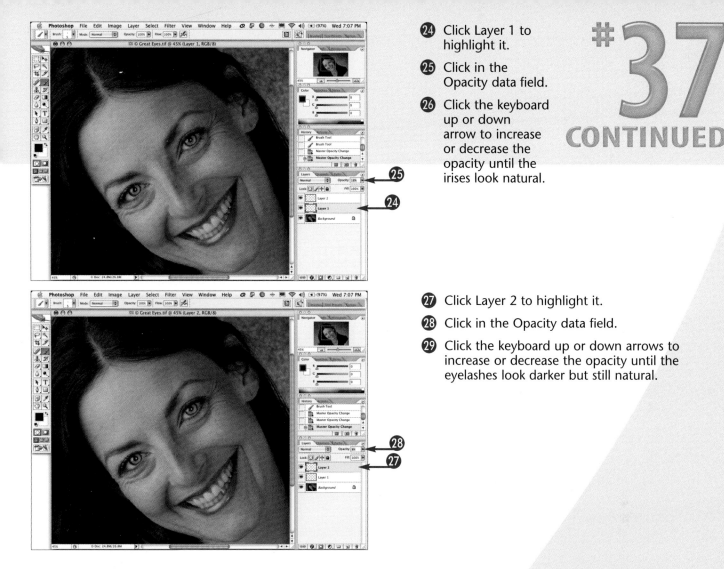

24 Click Layer 1 to highlight it.

25 Click in the Opacity data field.

26 Click the keyboard up or down arrow to increase or decrease the opacity until the irises look natural.

#37 CONTINUED

27 Click Layer 2 to highlight it.

28 Click in the Opacity data field.

29 Click the keyboard up or down arrows to increase or decrease the opacity until the eyelashes look darker but still natural.

More Options!

You can add eyeliner to the eyes in a photograph. Add another layer. Lower the opacity to about 18 percent. Paint with black at the edge of the eyelashes on each eye. Click in the Opacity data field and use the keyboard up and down arrows to increase or reduce the opacity of the layer until the eyeliner looks natural.

Did You Know?

You can use the same technique to enhance light eyebrows. Add a layer and reduce the opacity to 8 percent. Open the Brushes palette and click Brush Tip Shape. Set the hardness to 0 percent and change the Size, Angle, and Roundness to match the shape of the eyebrows. Paint a few smooth strokes over both eyebrows using black. Change the layer's opacity as needed.

SHARPEN JUST THE EYES
to add focus

The final step to enhancing the eyes in a photograph is to sharpen the eye area. You want to add focus and draw the viewer into the photo, but you do not necessarily want to sharpen the rest of the face or the skin. You can selectively sharpen the eyes by using a Sharpen filter and then applying the filter with the History palette and History Brush.

The techniques for sharpening in Photoshop had not changed in about ten years or more. Until now the standard Sharpening filter has been the Unsharp

Mask. With Photoshop CS2, you can now sharpen using the new Smart Sharpen filter. This new filter is not only easier to use, it has added features including a much larger preview.

Once you sharpen the entire portrait, you can hide the effect using the History palette to go back to a version of the photo before the sharpening was applied. Then, using the History Brush, you can paint the sharpening effect on the eye area where you want the focus.

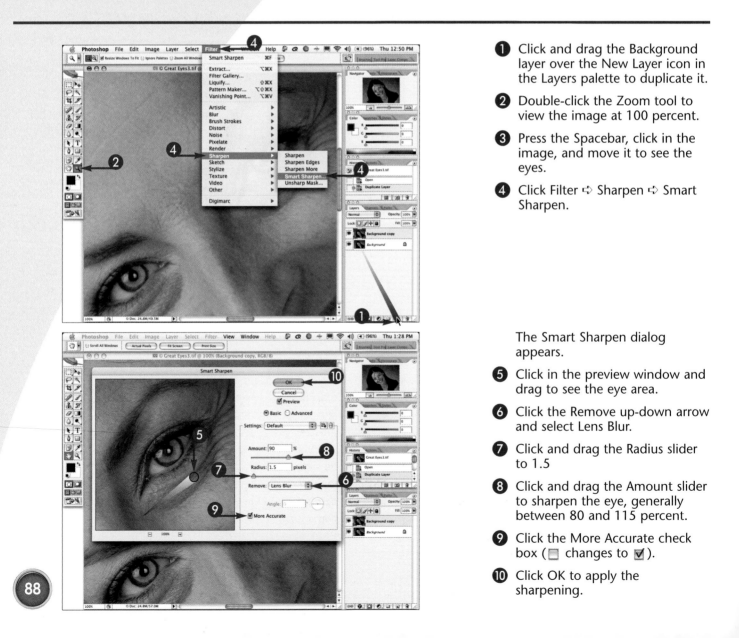

① Click and drag the Background layer over the New Layer icon in the Layers palette to duplicate it.

② Double-click the Zoom tool to view the image at 100 percent.

③ Press the Spacebar, click in the image, and move it to see the eyes.

④ Click Filter ⇨ Sharpen ⇨ Smart Sharpen.

The Smart Sharpen dialog appears.

⑤ Click in the preview window and drag to see the eye area.

⑥ Click the Remove up-down arrow and select Lens Blur.

⑦ Click and drag the Radius slider to 1.5

⑧ Click and drag the Amount slider to sharpen the eye, generally between 80 and 115 percent.

⑨ Click the More Accurate check box (☐ changes to ☑).

⑩ Click OK to apply the sharpening.

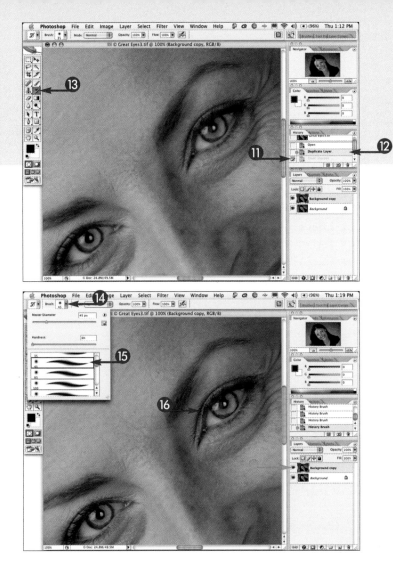

The Smart Sharpen filter Progress bar appears, and sharpening is applied to the Background copy layer.

⑪ Click the box to the left of the Smart Sharpen step in the History palette to set the source for the History Brush.

⑫ Click the previous state in the History palette.

⑬ Click the History Brush on the toolbar.

⑭ Click the Brush thumbnail in the Options bar to open the Brush Picker.

⑮ Select a soft-edge brush at 0 percent Hardness that is large enough to cover the edge of the eyes.

⑯ Paint over the eyes, eyelashes, and eyebrows with the History Brush to apply the sharpening.

● Click the Visibility icon (👁) for the Background copy on and off to compare before and after sharpening.

38

DIFFICULTY LEVEL

TIPS

Attention!

The Smart Sharpen filter only applies to one layer. You must merge any layers before sharpening. Click the New Layer icon in the Layers palette to place a new blank layer above the other layers. Press ⌘-Option-Shift-E (Ctrl+Alt+Shift+E). The adjustment layers and the Background copy merge in the new layer. All the adjustment layers, Background copy, and original Background layers remain unchanged.

Did You Know?

Always view the image at 100 percent magnification when you use a Sharpening filter to get the most accurate view on-screen of your changes. Still, the amount of detail visible in a print may be slightly different than what you see on the screen. The amount of detail can vary depending on the type of printer and paper used.

APPLY DIGITAL PLASTIC SURGERY
for a younger look

You can use Photoshop to perform digital plastic surgery and easily improve a nose or other facial features. Sometimes even the simplest touch of the digital brush can take years off a person's face. You can use the Liquify command for body sculpting to lessen a bulging waistline or improve any figure. You can also use the Liquify tool on other animate and inanimate objects to improve or add variety to your images.

The Liquify command is more powerful than the various Distort filters under the Filters menu. Liquify modifies and moves pixels around instead of applying a uniform effect across a layer as the distortion filters do. You can create many different effects such as warp, twirl, expand, contract, and more in this one dialog. Because the Liquify command allows you to reset the dialog instead of applying or canceling the effect, you can experiment with different looks before you actually move any pixels in the image.

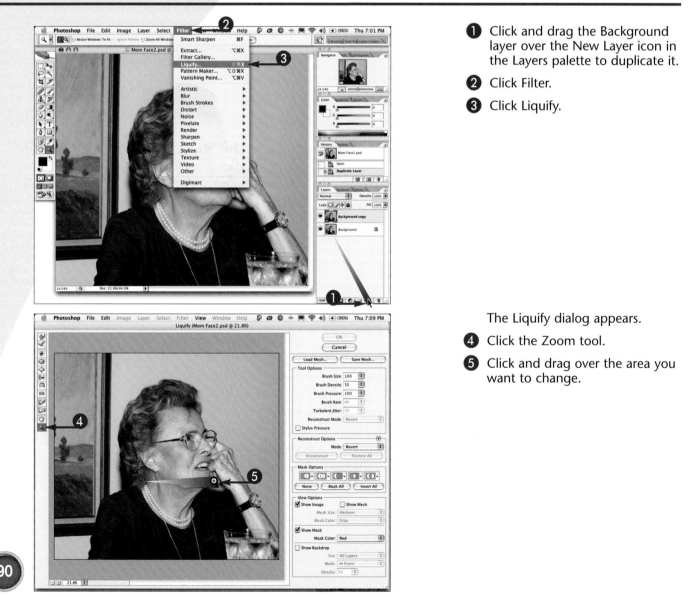

① Click and drag the Background layer over the New Layer icon in the Layers palette to duplicate it.

② Click Filter.

③ Click Liquify.

The Liquify dialog appears.

④ Click the Zoom tool.

⑤ Click and drag over the area you want to change.

6 Click the Forward Warp tool.

7 Click the Brush Size up-down arrow and drag the slider to adjust the brush size.

8 Click the Brush Pressure up-down arrow and drag the slider to lower the brush pressure.

● If you are using a pressure-sensitive tablet and stylus, click the Stylus Pressure box instead.

9 Drag over the area to move the pixels around, placing the brush cross hair at the edge of the area you want to move.

10 Repeat Steps 7 to 9 to get the desired look.

11 Click OK to apply the changes.

A Progress bar appears and the filter is applied to the image.

12 Click the Visibility icon (👁) for the Background copy on and off to compare before and after the use of the Liquify command.

TIPS

Did You Know?
You can use the Freeze Mask tool in the Liquify toolbar to mask areas that you do not want to affect. To remove areas from the mask, paint with the Thaw Mask tool, also in the Liquify toolbar.

More Options!
If you do not like your changes, press Option (Alt) and the Cancel button changes to a Reset button. Click Reset and your image remains unchanged without canceling out of the dialog allowing you to try other modifications.

Attention!
When you paint with a Liquify Brush, select a brush size larger than the area you want to alter to avoid making any abrupt and unnatural changes. Lowering the brush pressure also helps soften the effect of any changes.

ADD A SOFT FOCUS EFFECT
to make a portrait glow

You can apply Photoshop's filters to mimic the photographic filters used in traditional film photography. However, by using a combination of Photoshop filters, layers, and blending modes you can add special effects and create unique images with a painterly quality that go beyond the possibilities of film photography. You can add a soft focus effect to a portrait that not only minimizes skin imperfections but also adds a romantic glow to the subject's skin and still keep the subject's main features in focus.

You first apply a filter and change the blending mode to modify the effect. Make other changes using the layer's opacity setting. When the overall effect is pleasing, you can refocus the eyes and other areas to help draw the viewer into the portrait.

Whenever you use various filters, you can control the effects by working on a duplicate of the original Background layer and then adjust the effects with layer modes and opacity changes. Duplicated layers are also great for experimenting with different creative techniques. If you do not like the changes, simply delete the layer.

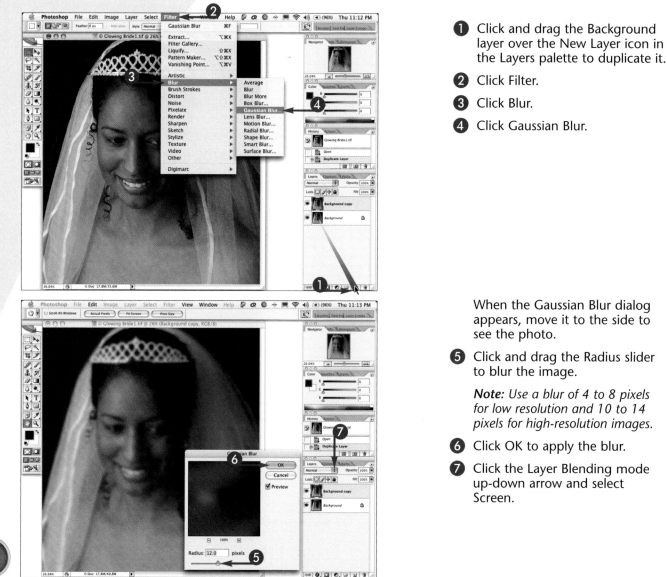

① Click and drag the Background layer over the New Layer icon in the Layers palette to duplicate it.

② Click Filter.

③ Click Blur.

④ Click Gaussian Blur.

When the Gaussian Blur dialog appears, move it to the side to see the photo.

⑤ Click and drag the Radius slider to blur the image.

Note: Use a blur of 4 to 8 pixels for low resolution and 10 to 14 pixels for high-resolution images.

⑥ Click OK to apply the blur.

⑦ Click the Layer Blending mode up-down arrow and select Screen.

The image becomes very light.

⑧ Click the Layer Mask icon in the Layers palette to add a layer mask.

⑨ Click the Foreground Color icon in the toolbar and set it to black.

⑩ Press B to select the Brush tool.

⑪ Click the Brush thumbnail in the Options bar to open the Brush Picker.

⑫ Click an Airbrush just large enough to outline the eye area.

● The Airbrush thumbnail in the Options bar is automatically selected.

⑬ Click the Opacity expand arrow in the Options bar and drag the stroke opacity slider to 40 percent.

⑭ Paint with black over the eyes and other important features to bring them out.

⑮ Click the Opacity expand arrow in the Layers palette and drag the Layer Opacity slider to get the right amount of glow.

#40

DIFFICULTY LEVEL

TIPS

Did You Know?
Dragging the original Background layer over the New Layer icon automatically names the duplicated layer Background copy. You can also duplicate the Background layer by pressing ⌘-J (Ctrl+J). In this case, the duplicated Background layer is named Layer 1.

Try This!
To experiment with a layer mask on which you previously worked, duplicate the layer. Click the Visibility icon (👁) to hide the original layer with the layer mask. Make changes to the duplicate. You can always discard it and return to the original.

More Options!
You can select and modify your brushes from either the Brush Picker in the Options bar or from the floating Brushes palette. When you edit or save a brush in one place, the brush is automatically updated in the other.

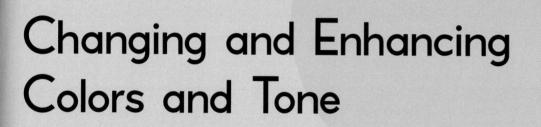

Chapter 5

Changing and Enhancing Colors and Tone

Color is the heart of Photoshop. Whether you work on a design or a photograph, you often want to adjust the hue, saturation, brightness, or tone of an image. Using Photoshop you can change, remove, and add colors with many different techniques and using a variety of tools. You can fine-tune the shadows and highlights or completely alter the overall tone of a photograph. You can transform a color photograph into a grayscale or black-and-white image, and you can add color to a grayscale image by colorizing it. Photoshop even helps you reduce image noise, those random extraneous pixels that are not really a part of the image.

Because some pixel information is discarded whenever you make color and tonal adjustments to an image, you should be judicious with any corrections. You can also save yourself a lot of work and preserve more of your image quality by using layers and especially adjustment layers. Adjustment layers make changes without permanently altering pixel values. By making small adjustments on multiple layers, you can minimize the image data loss because Photoshop combines all the adjustments before it applies them. In addition, you can edit adjustment layers any time before you flatten the image.

Whenever you make color or tonal adjustments, start by calibrating and profiling your monitor. Otherwise, you may be changing colors that are not really in the image and what you see on your monitor can look very different when it is printed.

Top 100

Try a better than
AUTOMATIC QUICK COLOR FIX

Photoshop includes Auto buttons in the dialogs for Levels and Curves, as well as several Auto color-correction tools, Auto Levels, Auto Contrast, and Auto Color, under the Adjustments submenu of the Image menu. Generally, the Auto Color adjustment is the best of the three; however, applying any auto correction may or may not work depending on the image.

The Auto Color command tries to neutralize the midtones and clips the shadows and highlights to adjust the contrast and color. You can improve the

Auto Color correction tool and actually make it quite useful by changing the default settings before you apply it.

These adjustments are related. The options for the Auto Color Correction control the tone and color adjustments for all three Auto corrections, as well as the auto choices in both the levels and curves. You can change and save the options for Auto Color and all the auto corrections have these settings applied. When you need to make a quick color fix, you can apply the modified Auto Color adjustment to improve the photo.

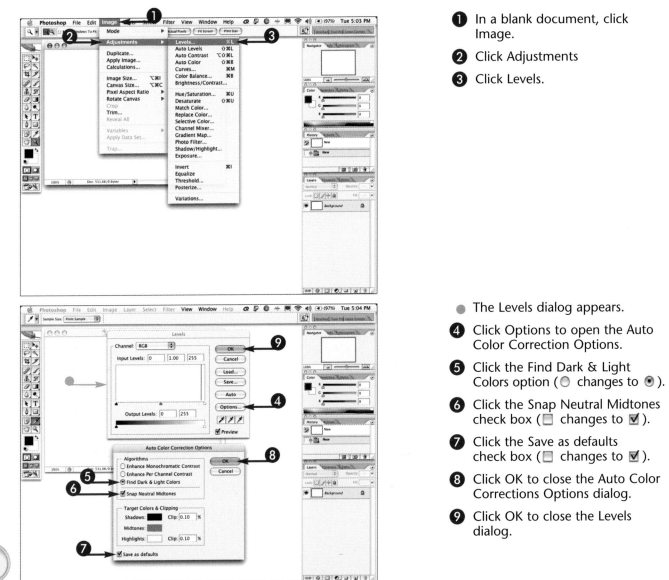

① In a blank document, click Image.

② Click Adjustments

③ Click Levels.

● The Levels dialog appears.

④ Click Options to open the Auto Color Correction Options.

⑤ Click the Find Dark & Light Colors option (○ changes to ⦿).

⑥ Click the Snap Neutral Midtones check box (☐ changes to ☑).

⑦ Click the Save as defaults check box (☐ changes to ☑).

⑧ Click OK to close the Auto Color Corrections Options dialog.

⑨ Click OK to close the Levels dialog.

10 Click File ⇨ Open and navigate to open a photograph.

11 Click and drag the Background layer over the New Layer icon in the layers palette to duplicate it.

12 Click Image.

13 Click Adjustments.

14 Click Auto Color.

Photoshop applies the Auto Color Correction to the duplicate layer.

15 Click the Visibility icon on the top layer on and off to compare the before-and-after image.

TIPS

Try This!

You can change the effect a command such as Auto Color has on an image by clicking Edit and then Fade Auto Color or Fade plus the name of the command. Move the slider to fade the effect. The Fade command is only available immediately after the original command was applied. From the same Fade menu, you can also change the blending mode.

Customize It!

You can improve Auto Color more by also changing the Target Colors and Clipping settings in the dialog. Click the Shadows color box and type **5** in each of the RGB fields in the Color Picker dialog. Click OK. Click the Highlights color box and type **245** in each of the RGB fields. Click OK. Save those settings as the defaults before applying Auto Color.

IMPROVE AN UNDEREXPOSED PHOTO
in two steps

You may find a photograph that is perfect for your project or has the subject just the way you want, but it is underexposed. Fixing an underexposed photograph with traditional photography tools was difficult. Fixing such a photo with Photoshop is much easier and there are many ways you can accomplish the correction. You can use a variety of Photoshop filters and adjustments to correct the exposure. However, you can easily make a quick correction using a duplicated layer and altering the layer blend mode. This two-step technique is worth a try before you work with any of the other methods.

Depending on the photo, the exposure may appear corrected the first time you apply the technique. For other images, you may need to repeat the steps once or even twice. You can even apply a half step by duplicating the layer with the changed blend mode and then reducing the effect the top layer has on the overall image by changing the opacity of the layer.

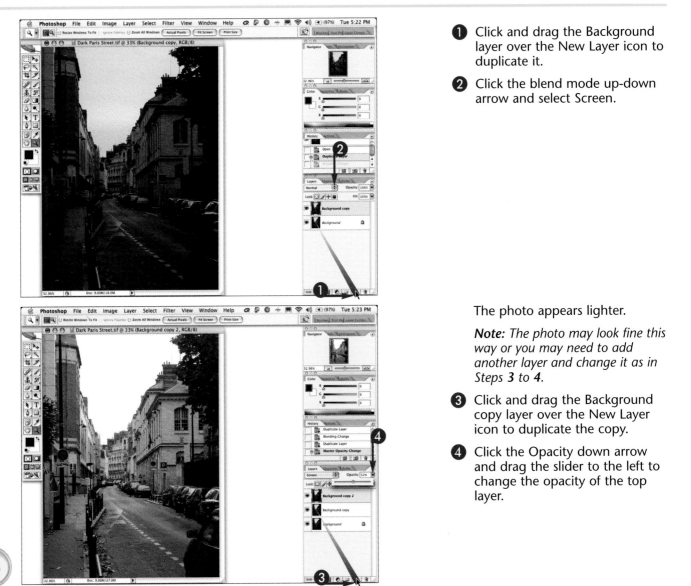

① Click and drag the Background layer over the New Layer icon to duplicate it.

② Click the blend mode up-down arrow and select Screen.

The photo appears lighter.

Note: The photo may look fine this way or you may need to add another layer and change it as in Steps 3 to 4.

③ Click and drag the Background copy layer over the New Layer icon to duplicate the copy.

④ Click the Opacity down arrow and drag the slider to the left to change the opacity of the top layer.

IMPROVE AN OVEREXPOSED PHOTO

in three steps

An overexposed photograph is impossible to salvage with traditional darkroom techniques. Too much light means there is nothing in the film to print. Digital photography and Photoshop can change and improve photos in new and almost magical ways. Although it may be easier to lighten a dark photo, you can easily reduce some of the highlights in an overly bright photograph and often improve the image enough to make it worth printing. You can use the Shadow/Highlight command in the basic mode to effectively reduce the highlights.

With most dialogs in Photoshop, when you move the slider to the right you increase the amount. When you use the Shadow/Highlight adjustment to reduce the highlights, it works in the opposite fashion.

As with every project in Photoshop, you can accomplish the task in a variety of ways. This three-step technique for reducing the highlights and improving an overexposed photo is so easy it is always worth testing before spending time with other methods or discarding the photo.

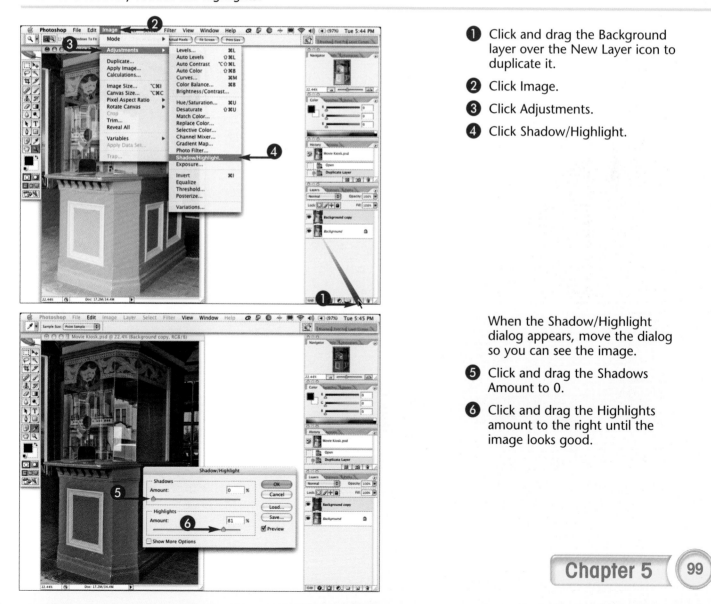

① Click and drag the Background layer over the New Layer icon to duplicate it.

② Click Image.

③ Click Adjustments.

④ Click Shadow/Highlight.

When the Shadow/Highlight dialog appears, move the dialog so you can see the image.

⑤ Click and drag the Shadows Amount to 0.

⑥ Click and drag the Highlights amount to the right until the image looks good.

REMOVE A COLORCAST
to improve the overall color

Whether you have a scanned image or one from a digital camera, your image may show a colorcast due to improper lighting, white balance settings, or other factors. A colorcast appears as a reddish, bluish, or greenish tint over the whole image. Photoshop has many tools that you can use to remove colorcasts, and sometimes you may need to try different ones. Although intended for matching the colors between two images, the Match Color command can also be applied to one image to remove a colorcast.

The Match Color command uses advanced algorithms to adjust the brightness, color saturation, and color balance in an image. Because you can adjust the controls in different combinations, using this command on just one image allows you to better control the color and luminance of the image than many other tools.

By using the Match Color command on a duplicated layer, you can use the layer's Opacity slider to fade the effect to achieve the best color for your image, as well as compare the before and after images.

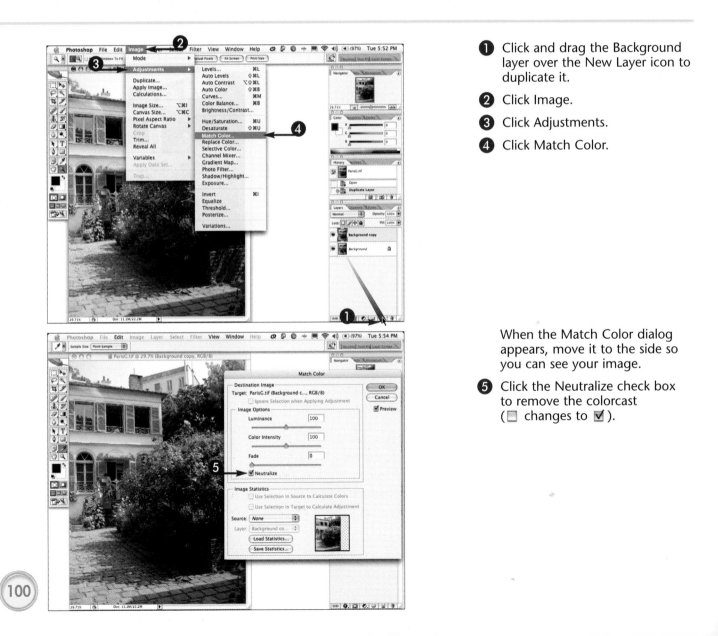

① Click and drag the Background layer over the New Layer icon to duplicate it.

② Click Image.

③ Click Adjustments.

④ Click Match Color.

When the Match Color dialog appears, move it to the side so you can see your image.

⑤ Click the Neutralize check box to remove the colorcast (☐ changes to ☑).

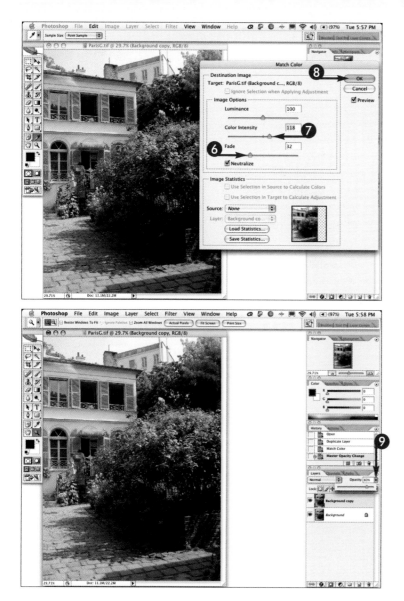

6 Click and drag the Fade slider slowly to the right to reduce the effect.

7 Click and drag the Color Intensity to the right to increase the color range if necessary.

8 Click OK to apply the change.

44

DIFFICULTY LEVEL

9 Click the Opacity expand arrow on the Layers palette and drag the slider to adjust the overall effect.

TIPS

Did You Know?

You can view the floating Histogram palette and see the color changes as they are made. Click the pull-down menu on the Histogram tab and click All Channels View. Click the pull-down menu again and click Show Channels in Color. Click and drag the Histogram palette so you keep it open and still see the image and your other palettes.

More Options!

If there is an area in the image that is normally neutral gray, you can also correct a colorcast using levels. Click Layer ➪ New Adjustment Layer ➪ Levels. Click OK in the New Layer dialog. Click the Set Gray Point Eyedropper, the middle eyedropper in the Levels dialog. Click in the part of the image that should be neutral gray.

REDUCE DIGITAL NOISE
to enhance the image

Image noise appears in many photos because of underexposure, shooting with a high ISO setting on a digital camera, or when photographing dark areas with a slow shutter speed. You may get more image noise with lower-end cameras. When you scan a photograph, the original film grain can also appear as noise in the scanned images. You can remove digital noise in the image while preserving edge details using Photoshop's new advanced Noise Reduction filter.

The Reduce Noise filter can also help reduce JPEG artifacts, which appear as halos around edges in the image. The lower the JPEG quality setting used to save the image, the more artifacts you see. Click the Remove JPEG Artifact check box in the dialog and the filter removes many of these halos.

In most cases, you should make other color adjustments first because the Shadow/Highlight command and other color modifications may bring out more image noise. Also, be sure to zoom in to exaggerate the details and view the corrections in the large preview in the dialog.

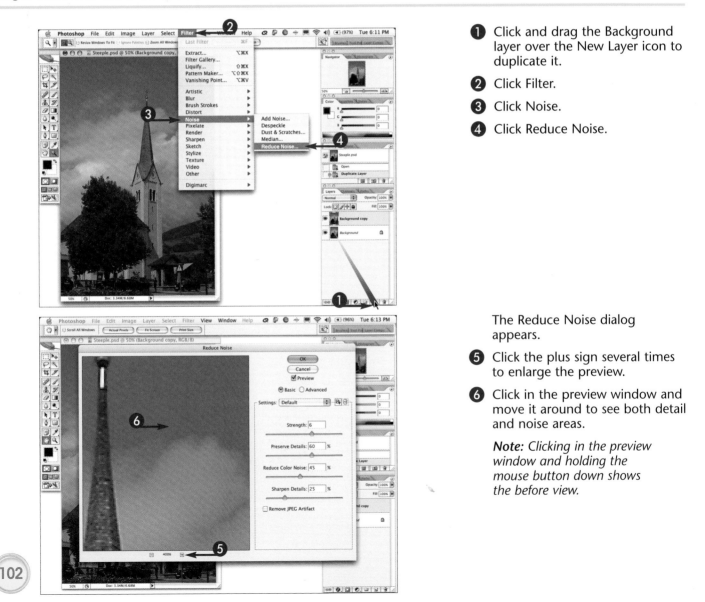

1 Click and drag the Background layer over the New Layer icon to duplicate it.

2 Click Filter.

3 Click Noise.

4 Click Reduce Noise.

The Reduce Noise dialog appears.

5 Click the plus sign several times to enlarge the preview.

6 Click in the preview window and move it around to see both detail and noise areas.

Note: Clicking in the preview window and holding the mouse button down shows the before view.

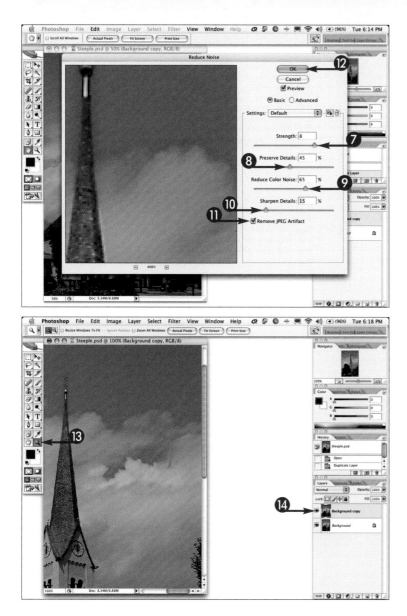

7 Click and drag the Strength slider to about 8.

8 Click and drag the Preserve Details slider to about 45 percent.

9 Click and drag the Reduce Color Noise slider to about 65 percent.

10 Click and drag the Sharpen Details slider to no more than 20 percent.

11 Click the Remove JPEG Artifact check box (☐ changes to ☑).

12 Click OK.

The filter is applied to the layer.

13 Double-click the Zoom tool to view at 100 percent.

14 Click the Visibility icon next to the Background copy layer to compare before and after the noise reduction.

TIPS

Did You Know?
Keep the Sharpen Details amount in the Reduce Noise dialog below 20 percent. You get better results if you apply the Smart Sharpen filter after using the Reduce Noise filter instead of trying to fix everything with one filter.

More Options!
You can try different settings and start over easily by resetting the dialog box. Press and hold Option (Alt) and the Cancel button becomes a Reset button. Click Reset and try different settings to reduce the digital noise.

Did You Know?
Digital noise includes color noise or miscellaneous colored artifacts, and luminance or grayscale noise, which is often more obvious in one channel. You can apply the Reduce Noise filter in Advanced mode to correct the individual channels and preserve more image detail.

Find the
DETAILS IN THE SHADOWS

You can automatically bring out the details in the shadow areas of a photograph using Photoshop's Shadow/Highlight command. In Photoshop CS, this command could only be used on RGB images. In Photoshop CS2, you can use Shadow/Highlight to correct 8- or 16-bit RGB, CMYK, or lab images.

Images with good tonal range have some very light areas, some very dark areas, and include a complete range of tones between the lightest and darkest areas. A photograph may be well lit in most areas and have dark areas of shadow with no details.

Photographs that are backlit, with the light source coming from behind the subject, often display overly dark shadow areas. Sometimes the photographer forgot to use a fill flash to lighten shadows when taking the photo. All these photos can be improved with the Shadow/Highlight command.

You can bring out more detail and enhance the overall image by simply moving the sliders in the collapsed dialog or you can use all the additional options available in the command to fix your photo.

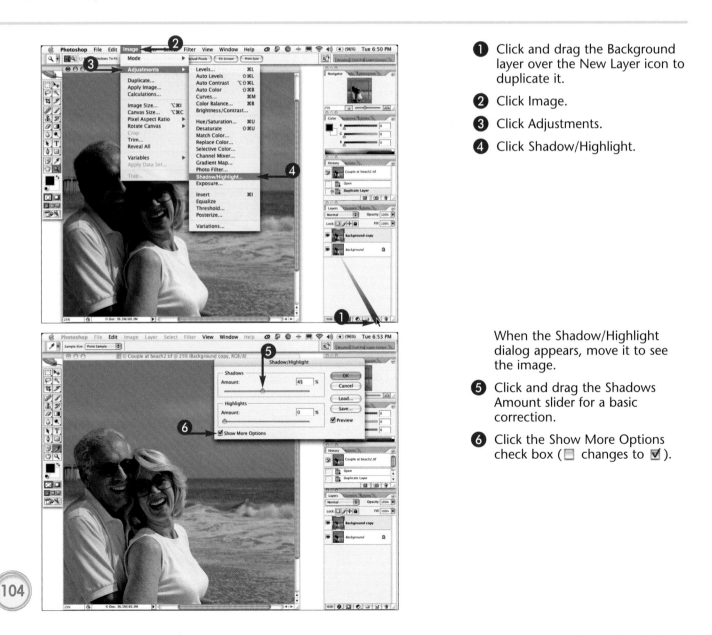

① Click and drag the Background layer over the New Layer icon to duplicate it.

② Click Image.

③ Click Adjustments.

④ Click Shadow/Highlight.

When the Shadow/Highlight dialog appears, move it to see the image.

⑤ Click and drag the Shadows Amount slider for a basic correction.

⑥ Click the Show More Options check box (☐ changes to ☑).

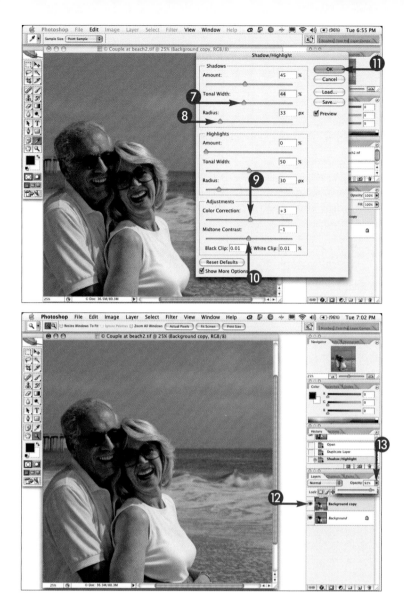

The full dialog appears with many more sliders.

7 Click and drag the Shadows Tonal Width slider lower to affect only the darkest shadows.

8 Click and drag the Radius amount to change the range of pixels affected.

9 Click and drag the Color Correction slider to reduce overly saturated colors.

10 Click and drag the Midtone Contrast if necessary.

11 Click OK to close the dialog and apply the changes.

12 Click the Visibility icon next to the Background copy layer to compare the before and after images.

13 Click the Opacity expand arrow on the Layers palette and drag the slider to adjust the overall effect.

TIPS

Attention!

Before you make tonal adjustments with the Shadow/Highlight command, be sure to remove any blemishes and scratches from the image first using Photoshop's Healing, Patching, or Cloning tools. Even dust spots become more visible after a tonal adjustment.

More Options!

You can also apply a selective adjustment. Make a selection of the area that needs adjustment and click ⌘-H (Ctrl+H) to hide the selection marquee. When you use the Shadow/Highlight command, the tonal adjustment is confined to the selected areas.

Did You Know?

You can save your Shadow/Highlight settings by clicking Save in the dialog, then naming and saving them on your hard drive. You can then apply the settings to other photos shot under the same lighting conditions and displaying the same blocked shadows.

ADD A SEPIA TONE
for a special effect

You can make a new photograph look antique or change the mood of any image by giving it a sepia tone. Old photographs often appear to have a brown tone, sometimes due to aging and sometimes because the photo was actually printed with a sepia tint. You can use Photoshop to easily turn a color photo into a simulated sepia-toned image.

Most techniques involve starting with a grayscale image or changing a color image to a grayscale image and then adding a brown color to tone the

image. Photoshop CS2 even includes a sepia photo filter, which you can apply to a grayscale image. This quick sepia change is much simpler and involves fewer steps.

You can use this technique without first changing the image to grayscale and then back to RGB to create the tone. The image remains in RGB mode so you do not lose any color data in the underlying image. You can also use the same method to give a photo a tint of a different color.

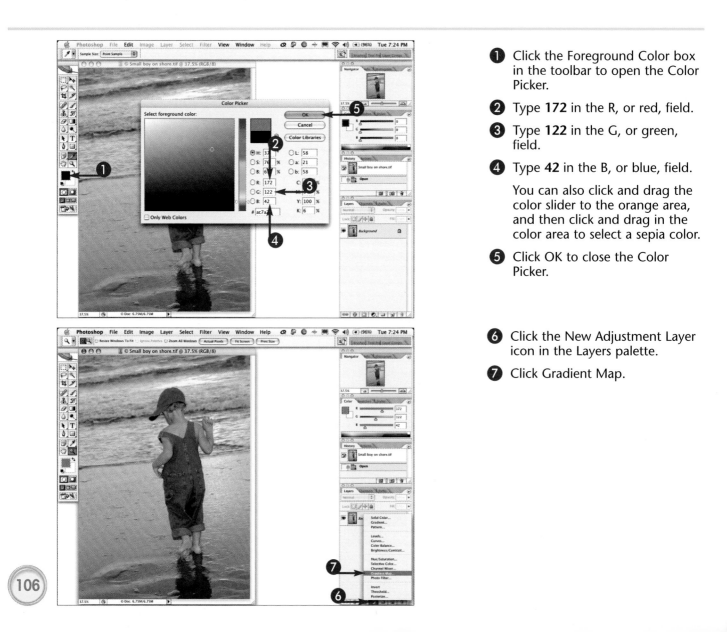

① Click the Foreground Color box in the toolbar to open the Color Picker.

② Type **172** in the R, or red, field.

③ Type **122** in the G, or green, field.

④ Type **42** in the B, or blue, field.

You can also click and drag the color slider to the orange area, and then click and drag in the color area to select a sepia color.

⑤ Click OK to close the Color Picker.

⑥ Click the New Adjustment Layer icon in the Layers palette.

⑦ Click Gradient Map.

The Gradient Map dialog appears and applies a very light sepia tone to the image.

⑧ Click OK to close the dialog.

⑨ Click the Layer Blend mode up-down arrow and click Color.

TIPS

Did You Know?

If you like the sepia tone you create, you can use it on another open image without going through the steps in the task. Click and drag on the Gradient Map thumbnail in the Layers palette of the first image and drag it over the other open image. The sepia tone is automatically applied to the image.

More Options!

You can change the sepia color to a different brown or to any other color by double-clicking in the Gradient Map thumbnail in the Layers palette. Then click the gradient in the dialog that appears to open the Gradient Editor. Double-click the brown color stop to open the Color Picker and choose another color. Click OK.

COLORIZE AN OLD GRAYSCALE
photo

Hand coloring a photograph can be a difficult process using traditional paints and traditional film photos. With Photoshop, hand coloring an old black-and-white image is much easier. You can use any black-and-white photo, called a grayscale image, and paint areas using any colors you choose.

You can start with larger areas and then focus in on specific parts to colorizing these individually and on additional layers. By making selections of detailed areas and then applying the colors, you can be as

precise as necessary to achieve the effect. Zoom in to select and paint detailed areas and then zoom out to see the overall effect. Continue making different selections and choosing other colors until the whole image is colorized.

You can vary the size of the Brush tool as you paint or use a pressure-sensitive stylus and set the brush size to pressure. Once the entire image is painted, you can lower the opacity of each colored layer as a final touch.

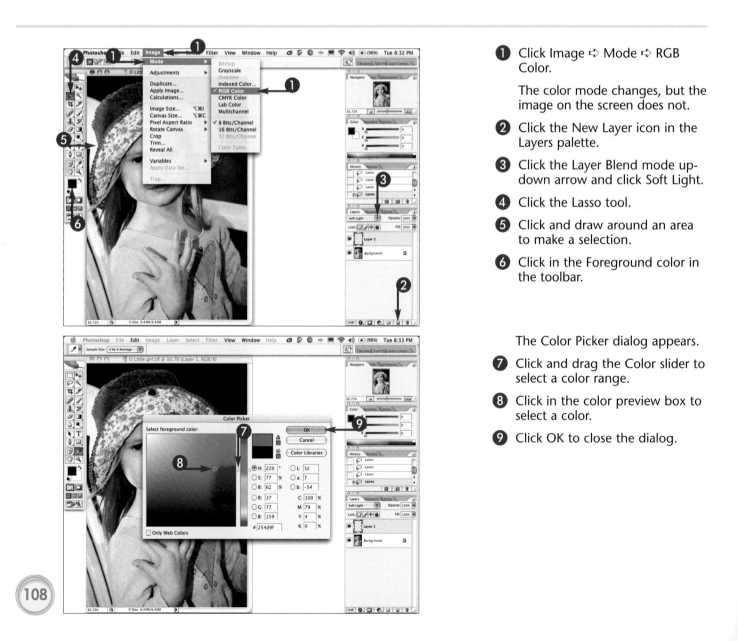

① Click Image ➪ Mode ➪ RGB Color.

The color mode changes, but the image on the screen does not.

② Click the New Layer icon in the Layers palette.

③ Click the Layer Blend mode up-down arrow and click Soft Light.

④ Click the Lasso tool.

⑤ Click and draw around an area to make a selection.

⑥ Click in the Foreground color in the toolbar.

The Color Picker dialog appears.

⑦ Click and drag the Color slider to select a color range.

⑧ Click in the color preview box to select a color.

⑨ Click OK to close the dialog.

⑩ Press B to select the Brush tool.

⑪ Click in the Brush thumbnail in the Options bar to open the Brush Picker.

⑫ Click a soft-edged brush.

⑬ Paint over the selected areas to apply the color.

DIFFICULTY LEVEL

⑭ Click the Opacity arrow.

⑮ Drag the Opacity slider for the layer to adjust the color.

⑯ Repeat Steps **2** to **15** until the entire image is painted.

TIPS

Try This!

Instead of clicking the foreground color, simply click in the Set foreground color box in the Color palette to open the Color Picker without changing tools. You can also move the cursor over the Color palette and click in the multicolored bar to select a color all without changing tools. Click and drag the RGB sliders to adjust the colors.

More Options!

You can select more realistic colors for skin or hair by selecting the colors from another color image. Keep the other image open on the screen while you are colorizing the grayscale photo. With the Color Picker open, move the cursor outside the dialog to sample real colors from the color image. Then paint in the grayscale image with those colors.

Turn a
COLOR PHOTO INTO A
GRAYSCALE PHOTO

You can convert a color image to grayscale in many ways using Photoshop. You always want to preserve as much of the image data as possible to be able to vary the range of tones depending on your image. Simply changing the mode of the file to grayscale discards pixel data and gives you an image that appears flat and has a small tonal range. Selecting Desaturate from the Adjustments menu also tends to flatten the contrast of the image. You can use two separate adjustment layers instead to retain much

more control over the tone of the image and even continue to adjust the light and dark areas after the adjustment.

Even if you want the result to be a black-and-white photograph, always shoot the photo in color and scan black-and-white photos in the RGB mode. There is more pixel data in an RGB image than in a grayscale image — three times as much. You can always remove the color from a photograph but you cannot put real colors back in.

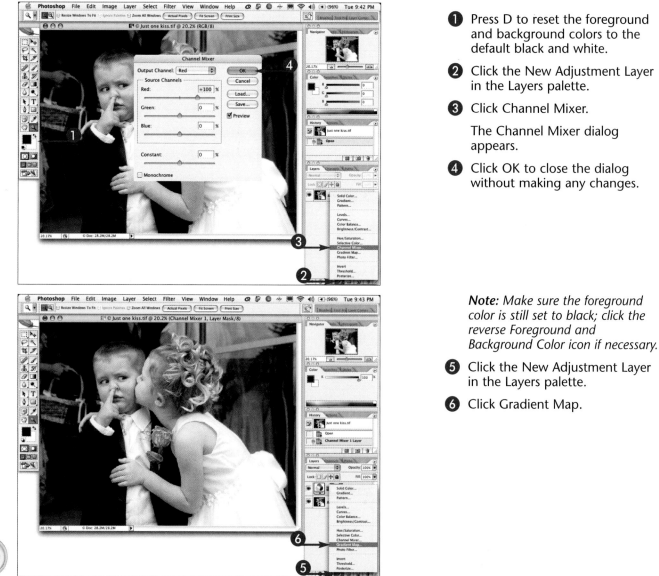

① Press D to reset the foreground and background colors to the default black and white.

② Click the New Adjustment Layer in the Layers palette.

③ Click Channel Mixer.

   The Channel Mixer dialog appears.

④ Click OK to close the dialog without making any changes.

Note: Make sure the foreground color is still set to black; click the reverse Foreground and Background Color icon if necessary.

⑤ Click the New Adjustment Layer in the Layers palette.

⑥ Click Gradient Map.

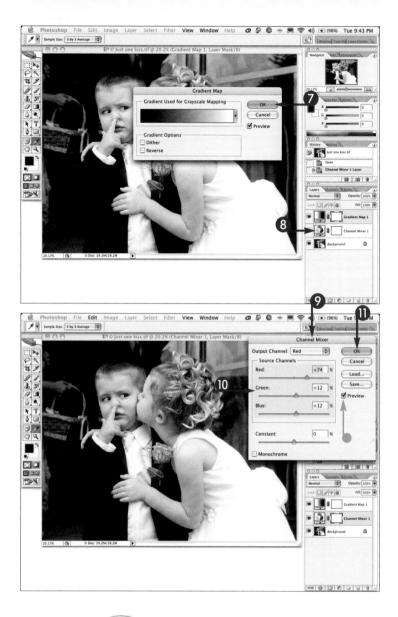

The Gradient Map dialog appears and the image behind it changes to grayscale.

7 Click OK to close the dialog.

8 Double-click the Channel Mixer Adjustment thumbnail in the Layers palette.

The Channel Mixer dialog appears.

● Make sure the Preview check box is selected in the dialog.

9 Click and drag the dialog to one side so you can see the image.

10 Click and drag the sliders for each Source Channel to get the contrast you want.

11 Click OK.

TIPS

Did You Know?

The Output Channel color sets the Source sliders for that specific color channel to 100 percent and the other color source channels to 0 percent. The Constant slider adjusts the grayscale values for each color's output channel. Move the Constant slider to the left to darken the grays that correspond to that color and to the right to lighten them.

More Options!

Another way to convert to grayscale quickly but without adjustment possibilities is to look at each individual channel on the Channels tab in the Layers palette. Press ⌘-1, then ⌘-2, then ⌘-3 (Ctrl+1, Ctrl+2, Ctrl+3) to cycle through the individual channels. Select the one that looks best and drag the other two color channels to the Layers palette trash.

Chapter 5: Changing and Enhancing Colors and Tone

Give a color photo an
OLD COLORIZED LOOK

When you colorize an old grayscale photo, you create an antique look. You get a very different look by starting with a color photo, converting it into a grayscale image, and then colorizing one area. You can use the colorizing methods described in Task 48 and use any colors you choose. However, if you keep a copy of the original color photo on a layer beneath the grayscale layer, you can use the Eraser tool with a low Opacity setting and bring the original color back in specific areas. You can even create a more or less muted colorized effect by changing the Opacity of the tool as you erase.

If you have already saved the grayscale photo without the original layers, you can still use this method. Start by opening the original color image and the converted grayscale photo. Using the Move tool, hold the Shift key as you click and drag the grayscale version onto the original color photo. Follow Steps 7 to 14 in this task to paint a very creative image.

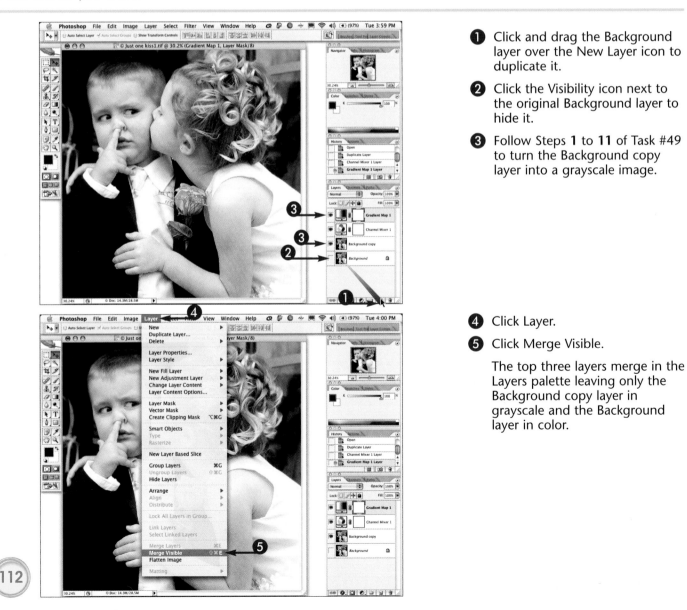

❶ Click and drag the Background layer over the New Layer icon to duplicate it.

❷ Click the Visibility icon next to the original Background layer to hide it.

❸ Follow Steps **1** to **11** of Task #49 to turn the Background copy layer into a grayscale image.

❹ Click Layer.

❺ Click Merge Visible.

The top three layers merge in the Layers palette leaving only the Background copy layer in grayscale and the Background layer in color.

6 Click in the Visibility box by the original Background layer to make it visible.

7 Click the Eraser tool.

8 Click the Brush options to select a brush size.

9 Click the Airbrush thumbnail in the Options menu.

10 Double-click in the Opacity data field in the Options menu and type **20**.

11 Erase over the area to be colorized.

12 Double-click in the Opacity data field in the Options menu and type **40**.

13 Click the Brush options and drag the slider to reduce the brush size.

14 Erase over parts of the colored area to increase the color.

The viewer's attention is drawn to the perfect spot.

#50

DIFFICULTY LEVEL

TIPS

Desktop Trick!

You can change the size of the Eraser tool by pressing the Right Bracket key to increase the size and the Left Bracket key to reduce the size. You can also change the Opacity of the Eraser tool by clicking once in the data field and pressing the up or down arrow on the keyboard to increase and reduce the Opacity.

Did You Know?

You can vary the hardness or softness of the Eraser or Brush tools using the keyboard instead of the Brush Picker. Click the Eraser or Brush tool to select it. Hold the Shift key down as you repeatedly press the Right Bracket key to increase the hardness, or the Left Bracket key to increase the softness of the tool.

Making Magic with Digital Special Effects

Since its inception, photographers and graphic designers alike have been using Photoshop for digital imaging and photo manipulation. Photoshop can transform an average shot into a good photograph, a good photograph into a great one, and a great image into creative fine art. Photoshop CS2 adds even more power and control to digital image editing. Just as with the previous versions, there are many different ways to create a design or enhance a photograph. You can use the old tools in new ways and in combination with the new techniques to create, improve, or completely alter any image.

You can simulate the effect of using traditional photographic filters to enhance the colors or change the areas in focus in an image. You can draw attention to one part of the image using a vignette or give an ordinary photo a painterly glow. Using the new Merge to HDR feature, you can combine multiple exposures to realize a photo with a wider range of tones than the camera can capture in one shot. You can also use one photo and the flexibility of the Smart Objects feature to vary the luminosity of the scene. You can even use parts of a photo and multiple layers to create an original design. The new Vanishing Point filter allows you to remove unwanted items from photographs or place different elements into an image while maintaining the basic perspective. You can even try a remodeling project using a keyboard and mouse.

Top 100

Apply a
DIGITAL PHOTO FILTER
for emphasis

DIFFICULTY LEVEL

Different lighting conditions produce different color temperatures, creating colorcasts especially on film that is not prebalanced for the specific type of light source. Photographers often use colored lens filters to correct the lighting differences, change the color balance in their photos, or to create a more dramatic image. Digital images also display different color temperatures depending on the white balance settings used. You can use the Photo Filter in Photoshop to apply a traditional lens filter effect to

an image whether it is digital or scanned from film. Because Photoshop considers the Photo Filter an adjustment rather than a filter, you find the Photo Filter under both the Adjustments and Adjustments Layer menus. Using a Photo Filter adjustment can visually change the time of day in the photo, turning midday into sunset. You can also repurpose or revive an image, turning a bland photo into a dramatic one by applying a blue or violet filter across the entire image, or warming a cool photo by applying a warming filter.

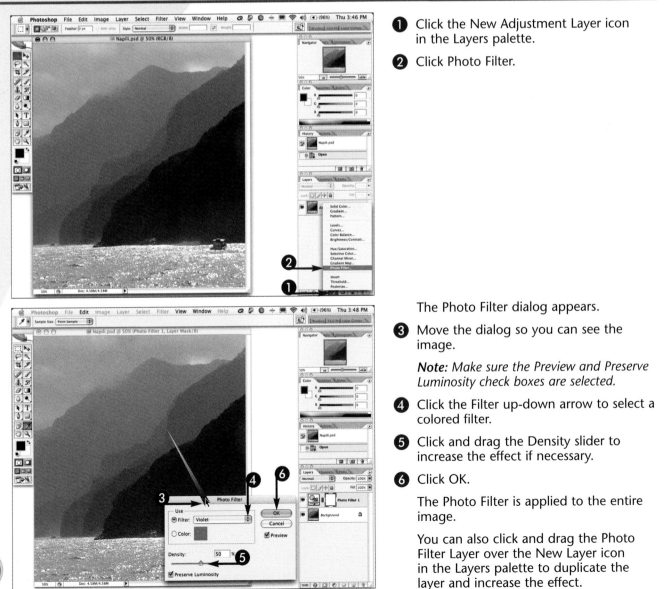

① Click the New Adjustment Layer icon in the Layers palette.

② Click Photo Filter.

The Photo Filter dialog appears.

③ Move the dialog so you can see the image.

Note: Make sure the Preview and Preserve Luminosity check boxes are selected.

④ Click the Filter up-down arrow to select a colored filter.

⑤ Click and drag the Density slider to increase the effect if necessary.

⑥ Click OK.

The Photo Filter is applied to the entire image.

You can also click and drag the Photo Filter Layer over the New Layer icon in the Layers palette to duplicate the layer and increase the effect.

Create a dreamlike image with a
SOFT FOCUS EFFECT

Photographers sometimes purposely blur a photograph to create a very different type of image. They may shoot through a piece of material or use a soft focus filter to change the look of a photo. Using Photoshop and the Gaussian Blur filter, you can apply a similar effect to any scanned or digital photo and even give a dreamlike glow to the image.

Digital photographs are often praised for their sharpness and a sharp photograph can be very effective, especially in architectural scenes. However,

adding a soft focus effect to a nature photo or even some portraits can create a romantic or nostalgic look. Using the Gaussian Blur filter in Photoshop with a very high radius setting blurs the image beyond recognition. However, when you apply the blur to a duplicated layer, and then change the opacity of the blurred layer, the two layers blend together creating a glow that makes your photo appear as though it is painted onto a canvas.

DIFFICULTY LEVEL

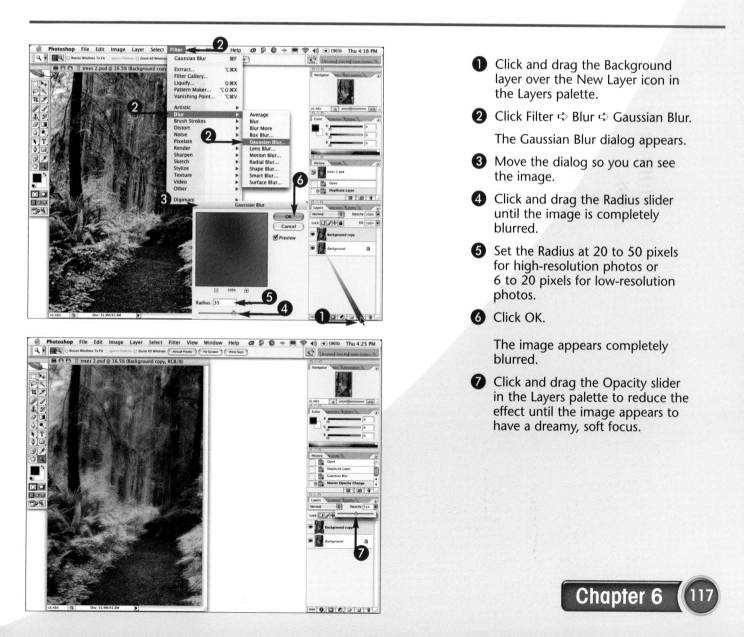

① Click and drag the Background layer over the New Layer icon in the Layers palette.

② Click Filter ➪ Blur ➪ Gaussian Blur.

The Gaussian Blur dialog appears.

③ Move the dialog so you can see the image.

④ Click and drag the Radius slider until the image is completely blurred.

⑤ Set the Radius at 20 to 50 pixels for high-resolution photos or 6 to 20 pixels for low-resolution photos.

⑥ Click OK.

The image appears completely blurred.

⑦ Click and drag the Opacity slider in the Layers palette to reduce the effect until the image appears to have a dreamy, soft focus.

Add action with a simulated
MOTION BLUR

You can add a greater sense of movement to action shots by using a filter to simulate the motion of the subjects. Photoshop includes a number of blur filters, including one for motion blur. Unlike the Gaussian Blur filter, which blurs pixels in clusters, the Motion Blur filter blurs pixels in both directions along straight lines. You can choose the angle of movement and the distance in pixels that are affected by the blur in the filter dialog to simulate both the direction and speed of motion of the subject of the photo.

The Motion Blur filter blurs the entire image, removing all details. The subject matter as well as the background are blurred, making the photo look as though the camera and not the subject was moving when the shot was taken. By adding a layer mask filled with black to hide the motion blur, you can then selectively paint in white over certain areas to create the illusion of movement while keeping the main subject and the background in focus.

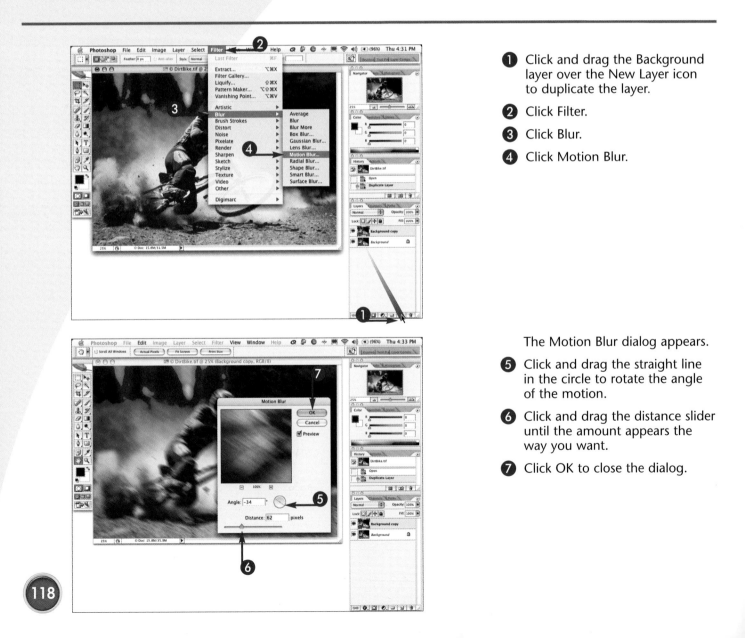

① Click and drag the Background layer over the New Layer icon to duplicate the layer.

② Click Filter.

③ Click Blur.

④ Click Motion Blur.

The Motion Blur dialog appears.

⑤ Click and drag the straight line in the circle to rotate the angle of the motion.

⑥ Click and drag the distance slider until the amount appears the way you want.

⑦ Click OK to close the dialog.

The filter is applied to the Background Copy layer.

⑧ Press Option (Alt) and click the Layer Mask icon in the Layers palette.

A black layer mask is added to the layer and hides the motion blur.

⑨ Press D to set the foreground and background colors so that white is now the foreground color.

⑩ Click the Brush tool.

⑪ Click the Brush thumbnail in the Options bar and click a soft-edge brush from the Brush Picker.

⑫ Paint over the edges to make the motion blur appear only where you want it.

TIPS

Did You Know?

You can also use the Wind filter for linear motion effect. After duplicating the layer, click Filter ➪ Stylize ➪ Wind. Click From the Right or From the Left to select the direction of the movement. Click OK to close the dialog. Then follow Steps 8 to 12 to add a layer mask and selectively paint in the appropriate motion.

More Options!

You can add movement to the entire image leaving only the subject in focus by following Steps 1 to 7. Instead of applying a layer mask, click the Eraser tool. Select a soft-edged eraser from the Brush Picker and erase over the subject of the photo. This technique works well to focus on one person in a moving crowd.

Focus on the subject with a
DARK-EDGED VIGNETTE EFFECT

You can create a vignette effect in an image by either lightening or darkening the area around the main subject. Portraits often show the subject in a soft-edged oval surrounded by a lighter area. In other images, the corners and edges may be darker than the center. A dark vignette effect is often due to the light falloff in the camera lens, but darkening the edges of an image can simulate the look of an old photograph. Used on a portrait, it can create a dramatic look by appearing to focus a soft light on the subject. With a landscape, you can simulate

a burned-in edge, essentially enhancing the center of the image. Either way, vignetting helps draw the attention of the viewer to the subject and away from the edges of the photo.

You can create a dark-edged vignette effect in many ways with Photoshop. However, using a Photo Filter Adjustment layer allows you to change not only the color for the outside edges but also the size and shape of the vignette effect, even after it is applied.

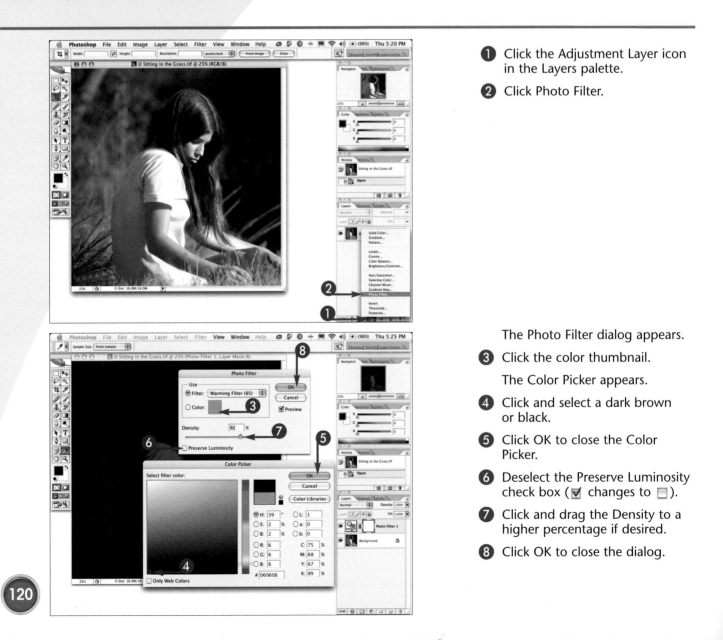

1 Click the Adjustment Layer icon in the Layers palette.

2 Click Photo Filter.

The Photo Filter dialog appears.

3 Click the color thumbnail.

The Color Picker appears.

4 Click and select a dark brown or black.

5 Click OK to close the Color Picker.

6 Deselect the Preserve Luminosity check box (☑ changes to ☐).

7 Click and drag the Density to a higher percentage if desired.

8 Click OK to close the dialog.

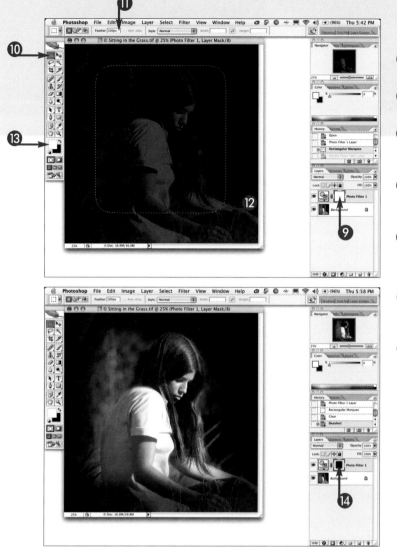

A dark filter covers the image.

⑨ Click the layer mask thumbnail.

⑩ Click the Rectangular Marquee tool.

⑪ Click the Feather data field and type **100** for a hi-resolution photo.

⑫ Click and drag a selection over the center of the image.

⑬ Press D to set the foreground color to white.

⑭ Press Delete (Backspace) to fill the selection with black.

⑮ Click ⌘-D (Ctrl+D) to deselect the marquee.

TIPS

More Options!
You can change the darkness of the vignette anytime. Double-click the Adjustment layer thumbnail in the Layers palette to reopen the Photo Filter dialog. Drag the Density slider to the right to darken and to the left to lighten the effect.

Did You Know?
When you click the Adjustment Layer icon in the Layers palette and select from one of the choices, such as Photo Filter, a Layer mask is automatically applied and the default colors are reversed with black becoming the background color.

Desktop Trick!
Pressing D resets the default colors. Pressing X reverses the foreground and background colors. Pressing ⌘-Delete (Ctrl+Backspace) fills a selection with the background color. Pressing Option-Delete (Alt+Backspace) fills a selection with the foreground color.

MERGE MULTIPLE RAW PHOTOS
to 32-Bit HDR

The human eye can adapt to different brightness levels in the real world but the camera cannot. Using Photoshop CS2, you can merge multiple photos of the same scene but with different exposures into a High Dynamic Range (HDR) image, which can show luminosity levels even beyond what the human eye can see. The dynamic range in a photo refers to the ratio between the dark and bright areas. By blending multiple exposures into an HDR photo, the image can represent the complete dynamic range in the visible world. HDR images are mostly used for motion

pictures and special lighting effects in some high-end photography. Using this new tool, you can combine images for more dynamic photographs.

Because you can only use some of Photoshop's tools on 32-bit HDR images, you need to convert the resulting photo to a 16-bit image before editing and printing the image. Photoshop also includes a preview adjustment in the dialog because a standard monitor is not capable of displaying all the brightness of an HDR photo.

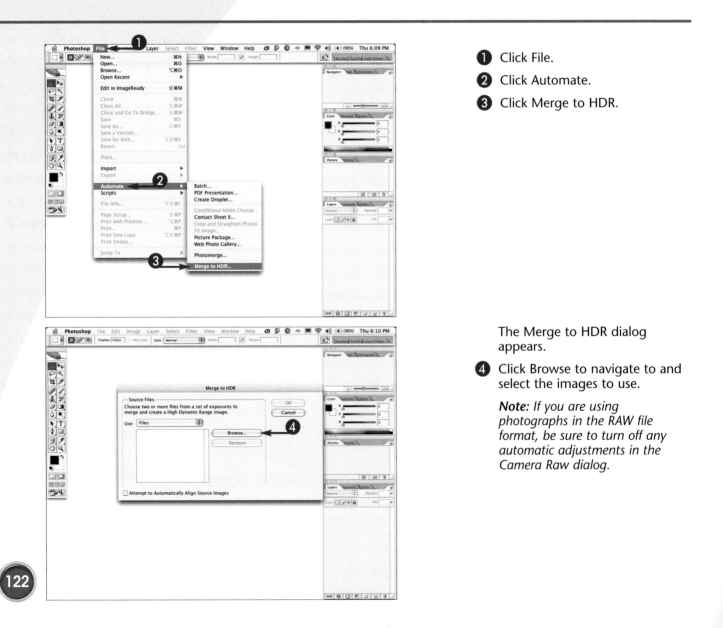

1 Click File.

2 Click Automate.

3 Click Merge to HDR.

The Merge to HDR dialog appears.

4 Click Browse to navigate to and select the images to use.

Note: If you are using photographs in the RAW file format, be sure to turn off any automatic adjustments in the Camera Raw dialog.

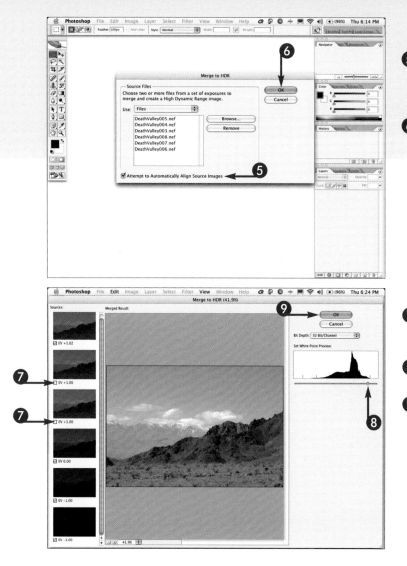

The files are listed in the data field.

⑤ Click the Attempt to Automatically Align Source Images check box (☐ change to ☑).

⑥ Click OK.

Photoshop opens and attempts to merge and align the photos.

55
DIFFICULTY LEVEL

The Merge to HDR dialog appears.

⑦ Click to deselect some of the source images on the left until the preview photo looks good.

⑧ Click and drag the Set White Point Preview slider to fit your image.

⑨ Click OK.

Photoshop merges the selected files into a new document named Untitled HDR.

TIPS

Caution!
When you take photos to be merged to HDR in Photoshop, use a tripod and take at least four to seven photos. You should also vary the shutter speed for the different exposures by at least one f-stop.

Did You Know?
The Merge to HDR command works best on photos in which nothing is moving. The aperture and ISO of the images to be merged should be the same in each photo. Only the shutter speed should be different.

Attention!
You can only use some of Photoshop's tools and about 15 of the more than 100 filters when you have 32-bit images. You cannot use any layers until you convert the images down to 16-bit for editing and printing.

APPLY A SPLIT NEUTRAL DENSITY FILTER
using Smart Objects

You may have photographed a scene with a dynamic sky, but the resulting photo did not reflect the drama you saw. The light in the sky or a reflection of water may have created a dynamic range larger than what the camera can capture. Photographers sometimes use a split neutral density filter on the lens to capture a large dynamic range. Using a tripod, you can also take multiple exposures of the same scene and combine the images using Photoshop's Merge to HDR command. However, if your digital camera can

save photos in the RAW file format, you can effectively simulate a neutral density filter or a multi-exposure photograph to create an image with a large dynamic range using a new feature in Photoshop CS2. You can import the original Raw file from the Bridge and place it as a Smart Objects layer. Then import and place the photo on another layer, edit the Camera Raw settings for color range and tone, and add a mask to combine the Smart Objects layers.

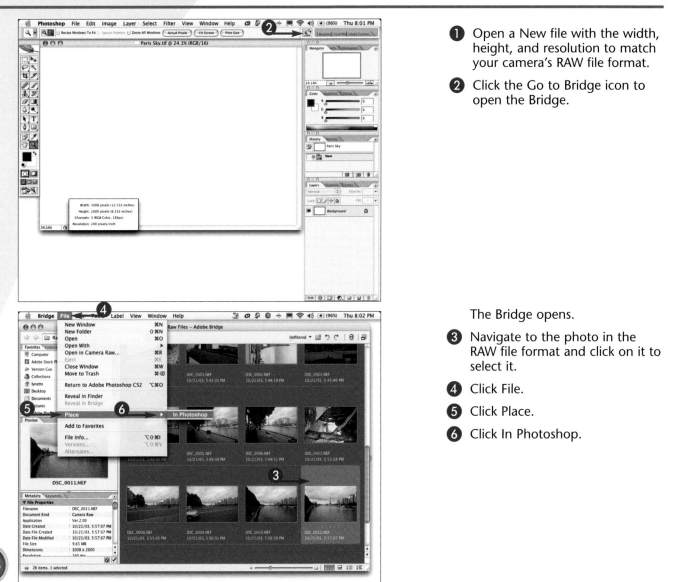

① Open a New file with the width, height, and resolution to match your camera's RAW file format.

② Click the Go to Bridge icon to open the Bridge.

The Bridge opens.

③ Navigate to the photo in the RAW file format and click on it to select it.

④ Click File.

⑤ Click Place.

⑥ Click In Photoshop.

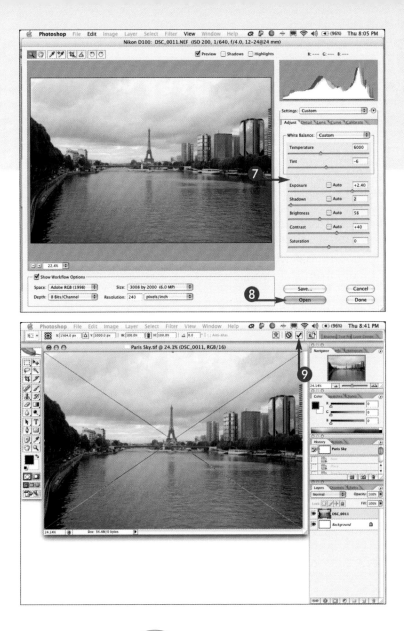

The Photoshop Raw dialog appears.

⑦ Click and drag the sliders to simulate the best exposure for the foreground.

⑧ Click Open to place the photo as a Smart Object.

The photo opens in Photoshop but is not yet committed as a placed Smart Object.

⑨ Click the Commit button in the Options bar.

TIPS

Important!

Creating the correct file size makes the project much easier. Start by opening the Bridge to check the width, height, and resolution of your RAW image. Type the same values when you create the new document. Set the Color Mode in the New dialog to RGB and the bit depth to match the RAW bit depth of your photo.

Did You Know?

You can place another Photoshop file or an Adobe Illustrator file as a Smart Object. A Smart Object acts as a container for the other file and retains all the source data of the original image so you can edit and scale the layer nondestructively. You can also change layer styles, opacity, and blend modes of Smart Objects.

APPLY A SPLIT NEUTRAL DENSITY FILTER
using Smart Objects

Smart Objects layers do increase the file size as you work on an image. However, they add unparalleled flexibility to the digital editing process. Using Smart Objects layers gives you more control and more options than simply applying various adjustment layers, filters, and masks to improve the photo. You can also fine-tune the adjustments and continue to edit the colors in the image, even after importing it. As long as the layer remains a Smart Objects layer, you can return to the linked Raw file, adjust the

settings in the Raw dialog, and import the photo with these new settings. You can edit one or both of the Smart Objects layers to enhance the photo and create multiple variations. You can also change the gradient on the mask to create even more alternatives. After making changes to the Raw photos and importing them again, click on the gradient mask thumbnail in the Layers palette to select it. Then drag a different gradient in the image to alter the blended photo.

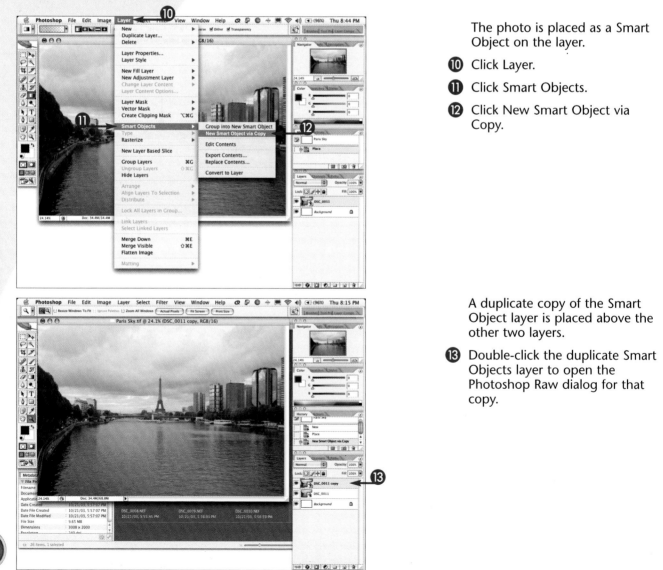

The photo is placed as a Smart Object on the layer.

⑩ Click Layer.

⑪ Click Smart Objects.

⑫ Click New Smart Object via Copy.

A duplicate copy of the Smart Object layer is placed above the other two layers.

⑬ Double-click the duplicate Smart Objects layer to open the Photoshop Raw dialog for that copy.

The Photoshop Raw dialog appears.

⓮ Click and drag the sliders to simulate the best exposure for the sky.

⓯ Click Done to change the colors of that Smart Object.

The image appears dark to match the settings for the sky.

⓰ Click the Add Layer Mask icon to add a layer mask to the top layer.

⓱ Press D to return the foreground and background colors to the default.

⓲ Click the Gradient tool.

⓳ Click the Linear Gradient icon in the Options bar.

⓴ Press Shift and click and drag from just above the horizon to just below the horizon in the image.

The gradient on the mask allows the properly exposed sky from the top Smart Objects layer to be seen on the Smart Objects photo layer with the well-exposed foreground.

TIPS

Try This!

You can drag the Gradient tool a short distance to create a short gradient and therefore a more abrupt transition between the layers. Dragging a longer line creates a smoother transition between the sky and the foreground.

Did You Know?

You can edit the Raw settings anytime to change the colors in the image. Double-click on the layer thumbnail to open the Photoshop Raw dialog. Make changes to the settings and click Done. Photoshop automatically updates the image.

Important!

Be sure to duplicate the Smart Object layer using New Smart Object via Copy. That way the Smart Objects are not linked and the subsequent changes to the exposure or any other settings do not affect the original Smart Object.

ADJUST DEPTH OF FIELD
with a Lens Blur filter

You can draw the attention of the viewer into the main subject of an image by controlling the depth of field, or defining the part of the image that is in focus and blurring other areas. Photographers control the depth of field by changing the aperture setting on the camera. A small opening results in a greater depth of field with more of the image in focus. A larger aperture creates an image with less depth of field and only the center of the image in focus. You can use Photoshop's blur filters to selectively adjust

the depth of field in your digital images. Use the Lens Blur filter and a white-to-black gradient on an Alpha channel to create a smooth transition from the focused areas to the out-of-focus areas in the photo. Click on one area in the image to set the main focal point. Areas with the same level of gray in the Alpha channel as the selected area are now in focus. All other areas are blurred depending on the level of gray in the Alpha channel.

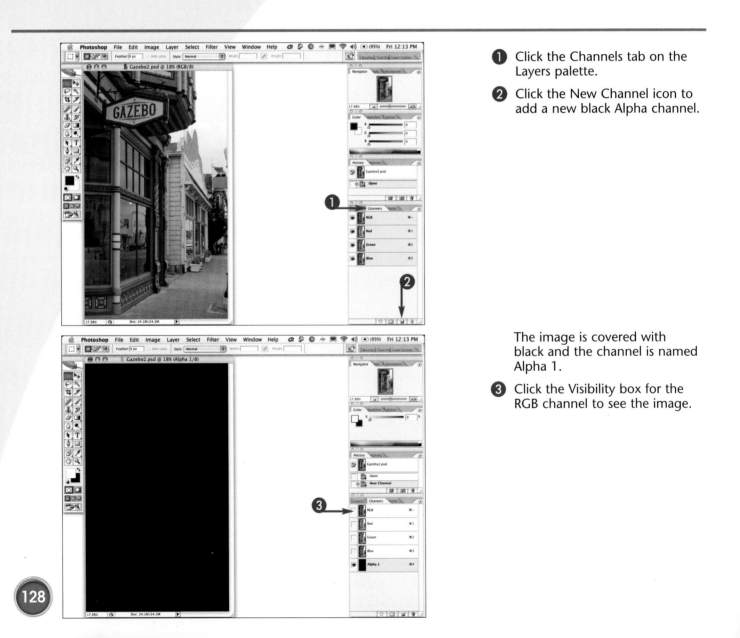

① Click the Channels tab on the Layers palette.

② Click the New Channel icon to add a new black Alpha channel.

The image is covered with black and the channel is named Alpha 1.

③ Click the Visibility box for the RGB channel to see the image.

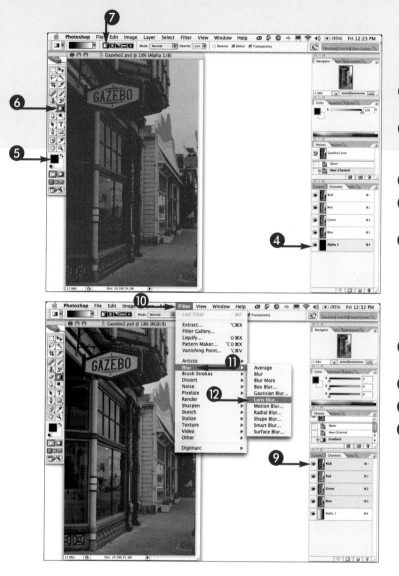

DIFFICULTY LEVEL

All the channels are visible and a red mask covers the image.

④ Click the Alpha 1 channel to highlight it.

⑤ Click D to select the default foreground and background colors.

⑥ Click the Gradient tool.

⑦ Click the Linear gradient in the Options bar.

⑧ Hold the Shift key and click and drag in the image from the background toward the foreground.

The red mask area appears as a red gradient.

⑨ Click the RGB channel to highlight it.

⑩ Click Filter.

⑪ Click Blur.

⑫ Click Lens Blur.

TIPS

More Options!

You can create a selection in the image and click Select ➪ Save Selection. Type a name in the data field in the Save Selection dialog. Click OK. Hide the visibility of the new channel, click the RGB channel in the Layers palette, and then click the Layers tab. Apply the Lens Blur, and everything in the selection remains in focus.

Try This!

You can also create a channel with two selections, one for the main subject and the second for an area slightly farther in the background. Fill the first selection with white and the second with a light gray. Apply the Lens Blur with this channel as the source. Your image now has areas with three distinct levels of focus.

ADJUST DEPTH OF FIELD
with a Lens Blur filter

Photoshop includes other blur filters. All the blur filters can soften or blur either a selected area or the entire image. These filters smooth the transitions between areas of contrast from hard edges or shaded areas by averaging the pixels that are juxtaposed to any lines or edges in an image. The Lens Blur filter works best for creating or simulating depth of field in a photo because it uses a Depth Map to determine the position of the pixels to blur. You can set the specific area to start blurring the focus in the image

by specifying the Source for the Depth Map. Using the Lens Blur filter with a separate Alpha channel or a layer mask as the Source allows you to specify exactly what is in sharp focus and how much depth of field to apply. The Lens Blur filter also allows you to determine the shape of the Iris to control how the blur appears. By changing the Shape, Curvature, or Rotation of the Iris in the dialog, you control the look of the Lens Blur.

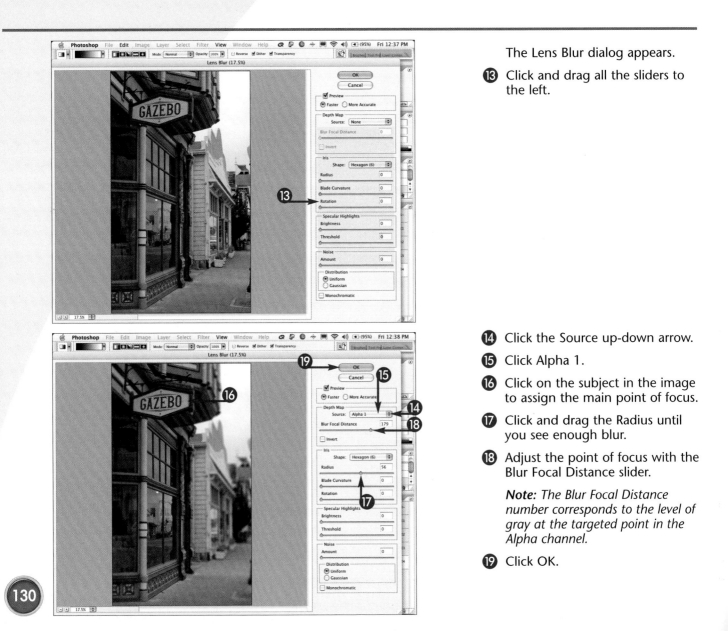

The Lens Blur dialog appears.

⑬ Click and drag all the sliders to the left.

⑭ Click the Source up-down arrow.

⑮ Click Alpha 1.

⑯ Click on the subject in the image to assign the main point of focus.

⑰ Click and drag the Radius until you see enough blur.

⑱ Adjust the point of focus with the Blur Focal Distance slider.

Note: *The Blur Focal Distance number corresponds to the level of gray at the targeted point in the Alpha channel.*

⑲ Click OK.

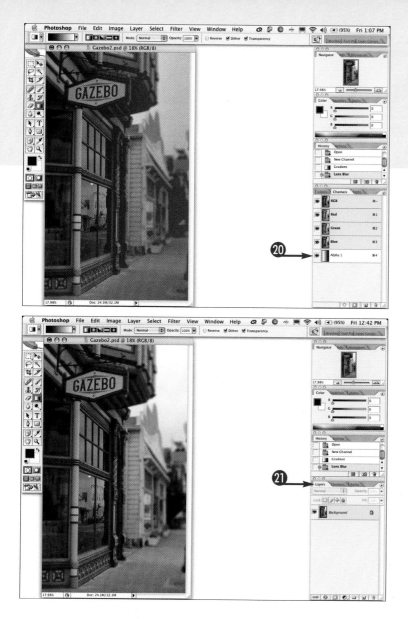

The Lens Blur filter is applied to the image.

⑳ Deselect the Visibility icon on the Alpha 1 channel to hide the red mask.

㉑ Click the Layers tab in the Layers palette.

The main subject in the image is sharp and the rest of the image gradually blurs out of focus.

TIPS

Attention!

Film grain and noise are removed when the Blur filter is applied. You can replace some of the noise and make the image look more realistic. First, zoom in to see the image at 100 percent. Click and drag the Amount slider in the Noise section of the Lens Blur dialog until the image appears less changed, and click OK.

Did You Know?

Applying a Lens Blur rather than a Gaussian Blur preserves more of the geometric shapes in the original image. Highlights in the image also reflect the Shape setting that is chosen in the Iris section of the Lens Blur Filter dialog. You can smooth the edges of the iris and rotate it by changing the Blade Curvature and Rotation settings.

CREATE A SILHOUETTE
for a custom design

Many advertising layouts are designed with a silhouetted person or object against a plain, colored background. You can easily design a similar advertising piece by making a selection in a photograph and using that selection in a background document. The silhouette design can be very effective as not only an advertising piece, but also a greeting card or an original logo.

Not all objects in a photograph can be used as a silhouette. The subject needs to have a detailed

enough shape when contrasted against a background to not only stand out but also be recognizable. People or objects that are angled or positioned parallel to the plane of the photograph often work best. The size of the object is not important because you can transform and resize the silhouetted item to fit your design. You can use just one silhouette or combine any number of objects from various photos and place these on any colored background. Just add some text to complete the layout or logo.

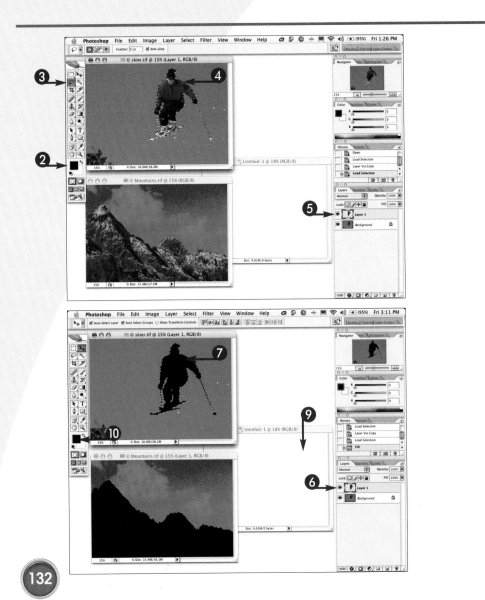

① Open the photos with the objects for the silhouettes and a new blank document with the width, height, and resolution set for the custom layout.

② Click D to set the foreground color to black.

③ Click the Lasso tool.

④ Click and drag a detailed selection around the person or object in the first photo.

⑤ Press ⌘-J (Ctrl+J) to put the selected area on its own separate layer.

⑥ ⌘-Click (Ctrl+Click) on the Layer 1 thumbnail to target the selection.

⑦ Click Option-Delete (Alt+Backspace) to fill the selection with black.

⑧ Repeat Steps **3** to **7** for the second photo.

⑨ Click the blank document to select it.

⑩ Click the Foreground color in the toolbar.

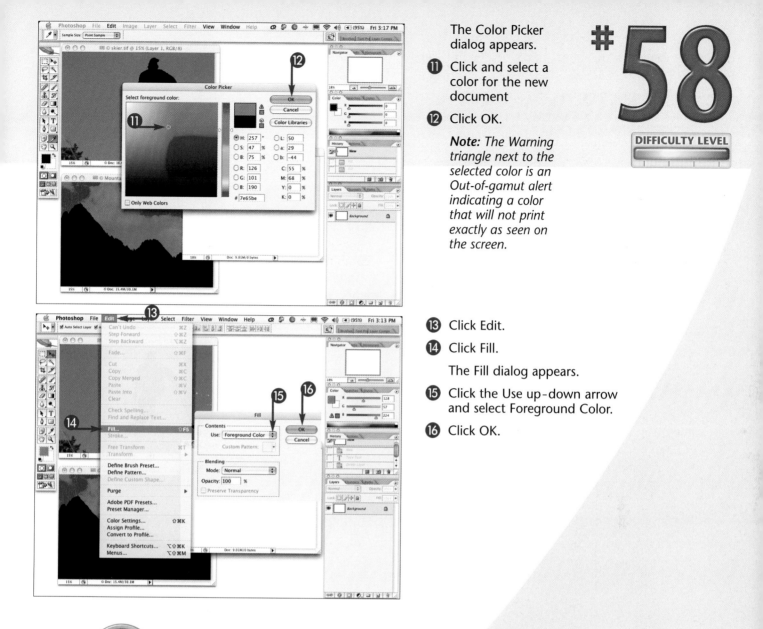

The Color Picker dialog appears.

⑪ Click and select a color for the new document

⑫ Click OK.

Note: The Warning triangle next to the selected color is an Out-of-gamut alert indicating a color that will not print exactly as seen on the screen.

⑬ Click Edit.

⑭ Click Fill.

The Fill dialog appears.

⑮ Click the Use up-down arrow and select Foreground Color.

⑯ Click OK.

DIFFICULTY LEVEL

Desktop Trick!

Instead of clicking the Edit menu and selecting Fill, press ⌘-A (Ctrl+A) to select the new document. Then press Option-Delete (Alt+Backspace) to fill the new document with the foreground color.

Did You Know?

You can view all the open documents at once by clicking Window ⇨ Arrange and selecting Tile Horizontally or Tile Vertically. Clicking Window ⇨ Arrange ⇨ Cascade makes the documents align to occupy the least amount of space.

Did You Know?

Pressing Control-Tab (Ctrl+Tab) allows you to cycle through all open documents. You can select the one you need to work on without clicking and dragging the others out of the way in the document window.

CREATE A SILHOUETTE
for a custom design

The silhouette technique can be used in a variety of ways. It can be the main part of the design, or a secondary element in the overall piece. A wedding thank-you note for example, might have a small silhouette of the couple kissing on the inside or back of the card.

You can make variations to the silhouette and the background depending on the purpose of the piece. Highlighting specific areas such as a bracelet or a belt adds dimension and focus to the silhouette. Select

these areas as the first step. Jump the selections to a separate layer and fill them with white. Then continue creating the silhouetted form. Place the highlights layer above the silhouette layer and merge these two layers. For a more subtle overall effect, apply a gradient to the background piece instead of using a solid color. Place the most important part of the silhouette over the lightest part of the gradient. As the gradient gets lighter, the silhouette stands out more due to the increased contrast.

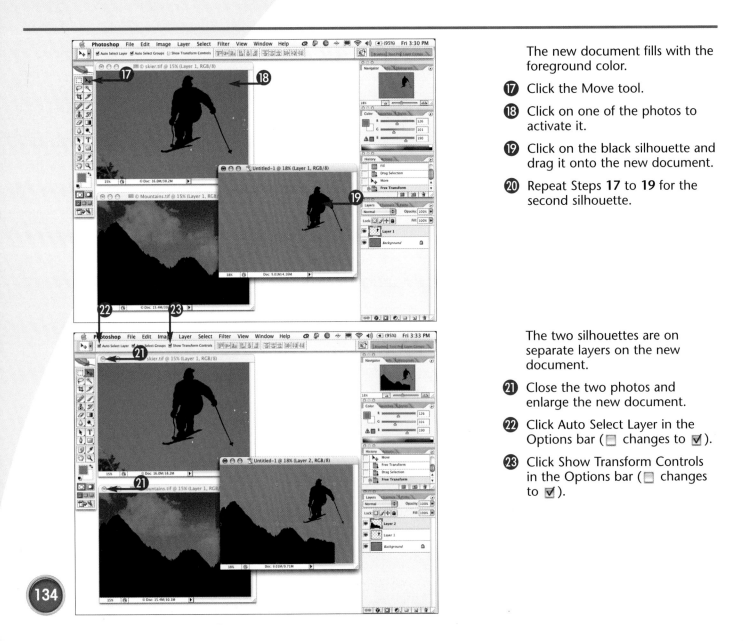

The new document fills with the foreground color.

17 Click the Move tool.

18 Click on one of the photos to activate it.

19 Click on the black silhouette and drag it onto the new document.

20 Repeat Steps **17** to **19** for the second silhouette.

The two silhouettes are on separate layers on the new document.

21 Close the two photos and enlarge the new document.

22 Click Auto Select Layer in the Options bar (☐ changes to ☑).

23 Click Show Transform Controls in the Options bar (☐ changes to ☑).

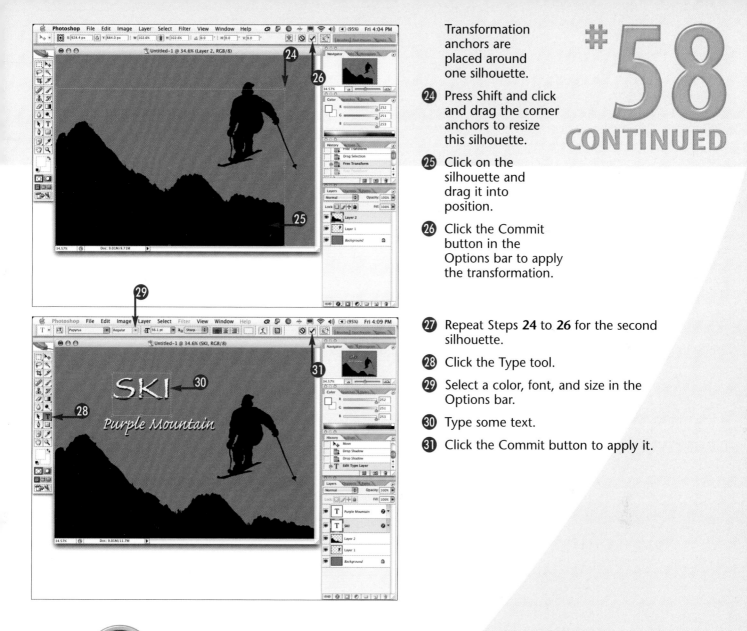

Transformation anchors are placed around one silhouette.

㉔ Press Shift and click and drag the corner anchors to resize this silhouette.

㉕ Click on the silhouette and drag it into position.

㉖ Click the Commit button in the Options bar to apply the transformation.

㉗ Repeat Steps **24** to **26** for the second silhouette.

㉘ Click the Type tool.

㉙ Select a color, font, and size in the Options bar.

㉚ Type some text.

㉛ Click the Commit button to apply it.

TIPS

Desktop Trick!
Pressing ⌘-T (Ctrl+T) brings up the Transformation controls. You can press Return (Enter) instead of clicking the Commit button in the Options bar to apply the transformation. You can press Esc to cancel the transformation.

Did You Know?
Selecting the Auto Select Layer and the Auto Select Groups check boxes in the Options bar allows you to click on an item in a multilayered document and automatically select the layer that contains the item.

Add It Automatically!
Selecting the Show Transform Controls check box in the Options bar makes the Transformation anchors appear. You can then click and drag on the corner anchors to resize without clicking the Edit menu and selecting Free Transform.

ERASE ITEMS IN PERSPECTIVE
with Vanishing Point

You can use the Clone Stamp tool, the Patch tool, or either of the Healing Brushes to erase unwanted items in a photo. If the areas are natural as in a sky or grass, cloning and patching is easy. If the area being patched or cloned includes architectural elements and perspective, removing them becomes more difficult. Use the Vanishing Point filter in Photoshop CS2 to help you remove items in an image while maintaining perspective.

The Vanishing Point filter depends on the perspective plane you draw and how it lines up with the

perspective of the item in the image. Use the Grid tool in the Vanishing Point dialog to carefully define the perspective plane. Zoom in to be as precise as possible. Then sample the first area you want to clone or copy from using the Stamp tool. Use short strokes when you erase the areas and resample several times to keep the look natural. By applying the Vanishing Point to a separate layer, you can adjust any areas once you are back in the main Photoshop window.

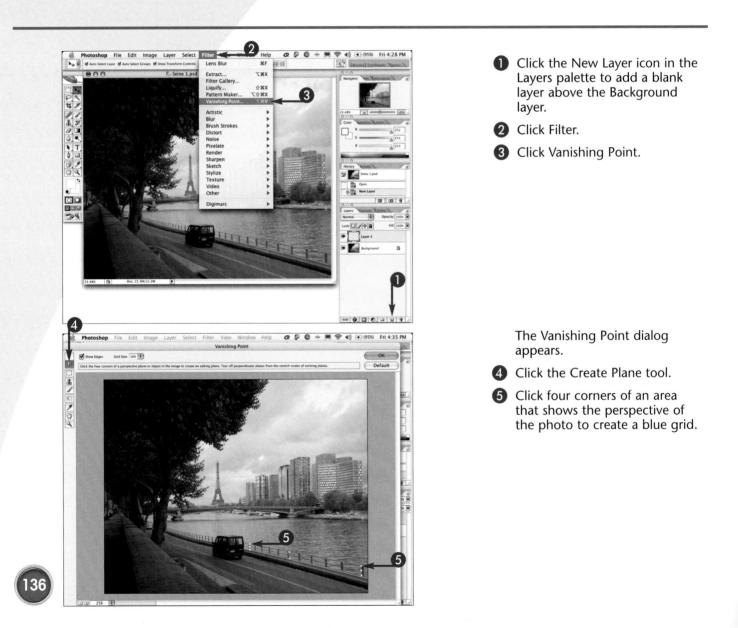

① Click the New Layer icon in the Layers palette to add a blank layer above the Background layer.

② Click Filter.

③ Click Vanishing Point.

The Vanishing Point dialog appears.

④ Click the Create Plane tool.

⑤ Click four corners of an area that shows the perspective of the photo to create a blue grid.

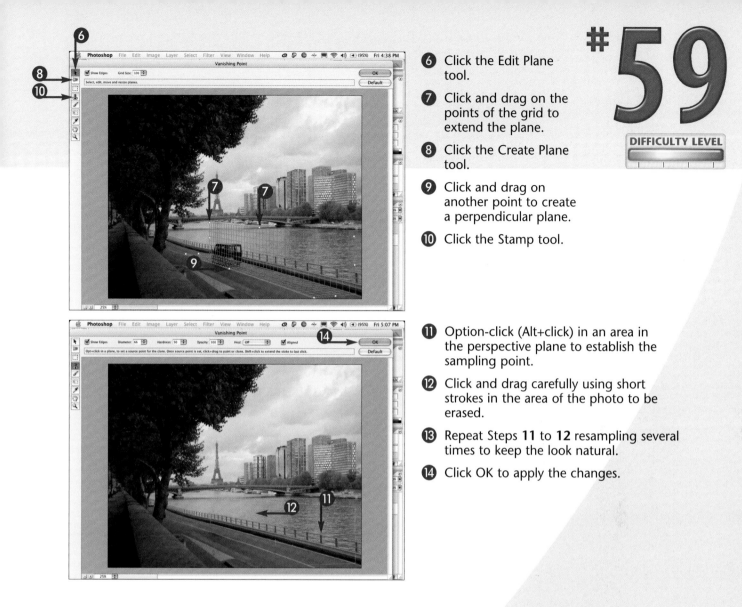

6 Click the Edit Plane tool.

7 Click and drag on the points of the grid to extend the plane.

8 Click the Create Plane tool.

9 Click and drag on another point to create a perpendicular plane.

10 Click the Stamp tool.

11 Option-click (Alt+click) in an area in the perspective plane to establish the sampling point.

12 Click and drag carefully using short strokes in the area of the photo to be erased.

13 Repeat Steps 11 to 12 resampling several times to keep the look natural.

14 Click OK to apply the changes.

TIPS

Caution!
If your grid is yellow or red, use the Edit Plane tool to adjust the anchor points until the grid turns blue. You can also press Option (Alt), which changes the Cancel button to Reset. Click Reset to start over.

Important
When erasing with the Clone Stamp tool, Option-click on a straight line in the area to be sampled. Then click along the same line in the area to be removed to help align the parts you will be cloning.

Did You Know?
You can use the Stamp tool options to choose a Heal mode. Click the Heal up-down arrow and select On to blend the cloned strokes with the texture of the sampled image. Select Luminance to blend the cloned strokes with the lighting of the surrounding pixels.

BECOME A DIGITAL ARCHITECT
with Vanishing Point

The Vanishing Point Filter helps Photoshop recognize the third dimension of objects so you can manipulate the items and maintain the perspective in the image. Using the Grid tool, you create a grid over a rectangular area and extend the grid by pulling on the anchor points. You can turn the corners of buildings, and the grid goes around the corner in perspective. Once the grid or perspective plane is defined, you can change the look of the image by copying objects from one area of the image to

another, or adding items from other images while keeping the perspective in the original photo. You can expand a building to make it look taller than it is. You can add windows and siding to design a new structure, or even add signs on any building.

To be effective, you must be accurate when creating the first grid. If the grid is blue, Vanishing Point has recognized the perspective plane. If it is red or yellow, you can adjust the anchor points until the grid turns blue.

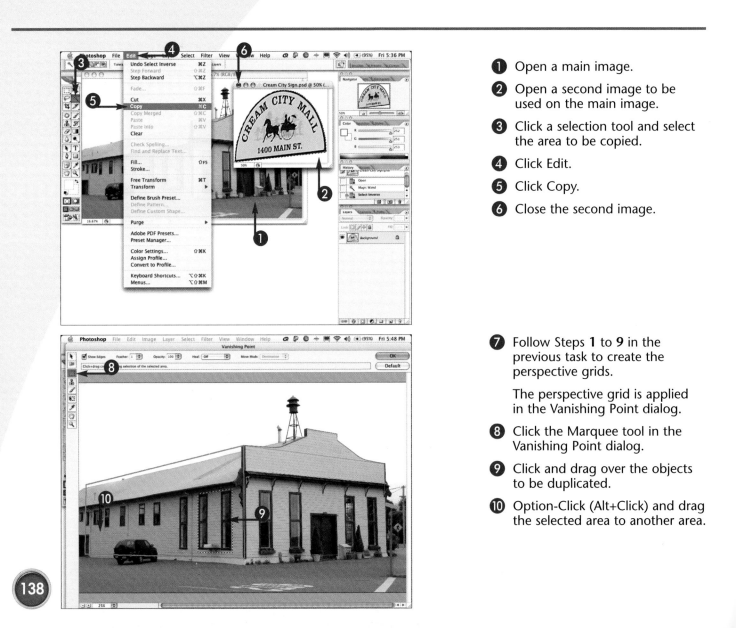

1. Open a main image.

2. Open a second image to be used on the main image.

3. Click a selection tool and select the area to be copied.

4. Click Edit.

5. Click Copy.

6. Close the second image.

7. Follow Steps **1** to **9** in the previous task to create the perspective grids.

   The perspective grid is applied in the Vanishing Point dialog.

8. Click the Marquee tool in the Vanishing Point dialog.

9. Click and drag over the objects to be duplicated.

10. Option-Click (Alt+Click) and drag the selected area to another area.

The objects are duplicated in perspective in the new area.

⑪ Click the Edit Plane tool and extend the perspective plane if necessary.

⑫ Press ⌘-V (Ctrl+V) to paste the item from the clipboard.

⑬ Click and drag the item to the new location.

⑭ Press ⌘-T (Ctrl+T) to bring up the Transformation anchors.

⑮ Move the cursor outside the corner anchors and click and drag to rotate the item.

⑯ Press and hold Shift as you click the Transformation anchor points to size the item.

⑰ Click OK to apply the additions in perspective.

TIPS

Did You Know?

Once you are in the Vanishing Point dialog, you can use the Zoom tool to enlarge the area you want to select. To zoom in as you are placing or adjusting the anchor points, press and hold X.

Important!

You can increase the size of the building beyond the boundaries of the existing photo. First, increase the canvas size by clicking Image ➪ Canvas Size and adding width or height to one side of the existing image.

Caution!

When you plan to copy an item or a layer from one photo to paste into another in perspective, be sure to copy the item first to save it to the clipboard *before* you choose the Vanishing Point filter.

Chapter 7

Designing with Text Effects

If a picture is worth a thousand words, then a picture with words has powers that are even more persuasive. Although Photoshop CS2 is not a page layout application, you can add text to photographs for added impact or to create an original design. You can also add special text effects to give personality to the words or even use the words alone to create the design.

With Photoshop, you can apply effects to text in more creative ways and more quickly than is possible using traditional tools. Not only can you see the result instantly, you also have complete creative freedom to make changes without wasting any paper or ink. By combining layer styles, patterns, colors, and fonts, you can create type with just the right look for your project. You can use text on images and make the words appear as part of the photograph or, conversely, make the photo appear as part of the text.

When you type in Photoshop the text is placed on a Type layer as vectors, or mathematically defined shapes that describe the letters, numbers, and symbols of a typeface. You can scale or resize the words, edit the text, and apply many layer effects to the text while preserving the crisp edges. Some commands and tools, however, require the type to be converted to a normal layer filled with pixels. The filter effects and painting tools, and the perspective and distort commands, can only work once the type has been rasterized or turned into pixels. Once the type layer has been converted, the text is no longer editable.

Top 100

PAINT TEXT TITLES
for a unique design

You can create a title for an album page or customize a line of text by simply painting the letters with different colors. You can match the title colors to an image or give the letters a strong contrast to an underlying photo. You can paint all the letters together or paint each one individually, making a very colorful title. You can also use a gradient to paint the text for a different effect.

You can type text in black or any color and then change the color globally by highlighting the text and selecting a different color in the Options bar.

However, to change the colors of the letters individually you must use painting tools, such as the Brush or Gradient tools, effectively changing the colors of the pixels. Type the text, then edit and resize it, or change the font. Then rasterize the type that turns the text into pixels before using the painting tools. Select a color from the Color Picker or anywhere else on your desktop and use any of the painting tools to fill the letters.

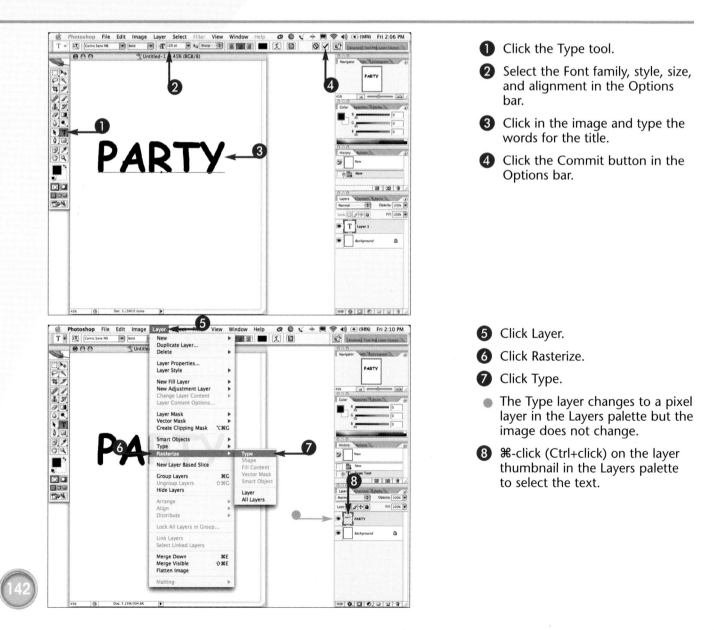

① Click the Type tool.

② Select the Font family, style, size, and alignment in the Options bar.

③ Click in the image and type the words for the title.

④ Click the Commit button in the Options bar.

⑤ Click Layer.

⑥ Click Rasterize.

⑦ Click Type.

● The Type layer changes to a pixel layer in the Layers palette but the image does not change.

⑧ ⌘-click (Ctrl+click) on the layer thumbnail in the Layers palette to select the text.

The letters are individually outlined by a selection marquee.

⑨ Click the Brush tool.

⑩ Click the Foreground Color box in the toolbar.

The Color Picker appears.

⑪ Click in the Color Picker to select another foreground color.

⑫ Click OK to close the Color Picker.

⑬ Paint over a letter or part of a letter with the brush to change the color.

⑭ Repeat Steps **10** to **13** to change each letter's color.

61

DIFFICULTY LEVEL

TIPS

Desktop Trick!

With the Type tool selected, pressing Return (Enter) moves the cursor to the next line and pressing Enter (Ctrl+Enter) applies the type or any transformations. Once the text is rasterized, pressing Return (Enter) applies any transformations.

Try This!

Type some text with the Type tool. Before clicking the Commit button, press and hold ⌘ (Ctrl) to bring up the transformation anchor points. Click and drag the anchors while pressing ⌘ (Ctrl) to transform the type.

More Options!

You can select the Gradient tool and a colored gradient from the Gradient Editor in the Options bar. Click and drag across the selected letters to create a variegated color fill. Each time you drag, the fill style changes.

Create a
CUSTOM WATERMARK
to protect your images

If you upload your proofs to a Web site for client approval or if you sell your digital artwork online, you want people to see the images but not to use the files without your permission. You can add a custom watermark with a transparent look to any image to protect it and still keep the image visible.

A custom watermark can be as simple as your name and the copyright symbol. After typing your name on a Type layer and adding a large copyright symbol as a Shape layer, you can add any kind of bevel or embossed style to your personalized watermark. You can even copy the two layers to another photo to apply the same custom watermark. To give a transparent look to each layer, you lower the Fill opacity, which only affects the fill pixels leaving the beveled areas appearing like a glass overlay. You can also use the same technique to give a transparent look to any text, shape, or other layer on any image.

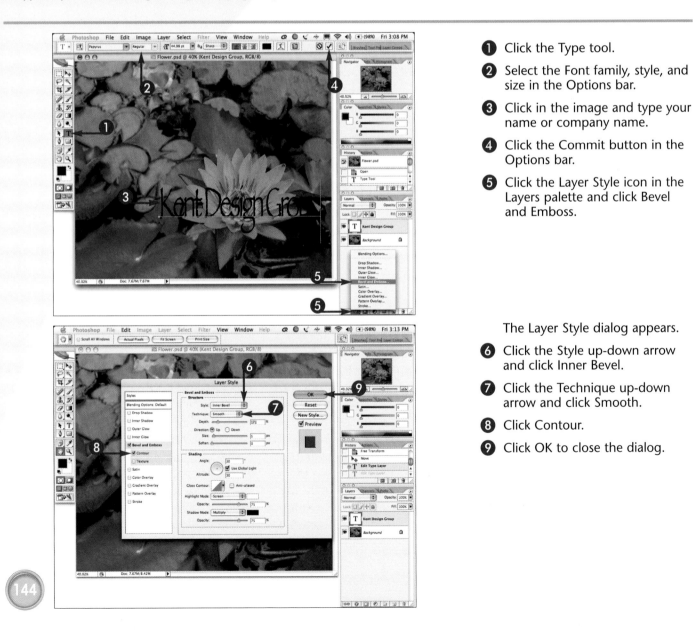

① Click the Type tool.

② Select the Font family, style, and size in the Options bar.

③ Click in the image and type your name or company name.

④ Click the Commit button in the Options bar.

⑤ Click the Layer Style icon in the Layers palette and click Bevel and Emboss.

The Layer Style dialog appears.

⑥ Click the Style up-down arrow and click Inner Bevel.

⑦ Click the Technique up-down arrow and click Smooth.

⑧ Click Contour.

⑨ Click OK to close the dialog.

62

DIFFICULTY LEVEL

⑩ Click and hold the Rectangle tool and then click the Custom Shape Tool.

⑪ Click the Shape down-arrow in the Options bar and click the copyright symbol.

⑫ Click and drag in the photo to create a copyright symbol.

You can press Shift to constrain the shape.

⑬ Press Option (Alt) and click the Layer Style icon in the Type layer.

⑭ Drag a copy of the Layer Style icon to the Shape layer to copy the effect.

The same emboss style is applied to the copyright symbol.

⑮ Click the Type layer to select it.

⑯ Double-click in the Fill data field and type **0**.

⑰ Click the Shape layer and repeat Step **16**.

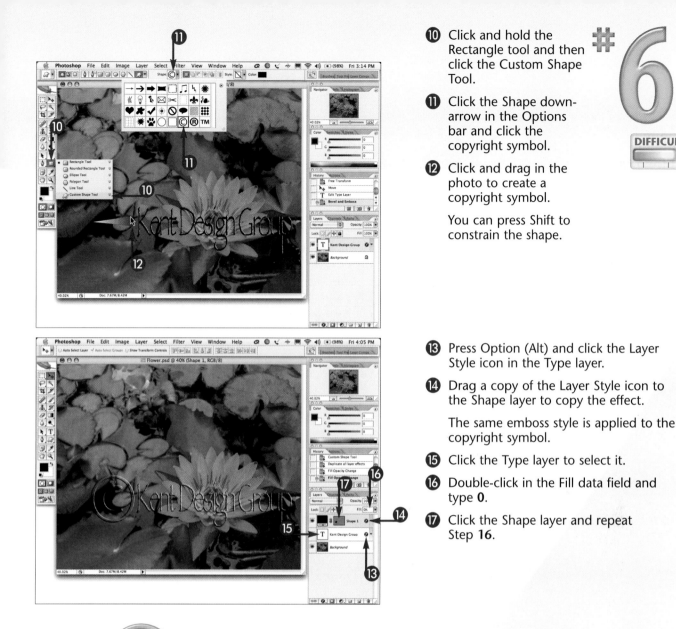

TIPS

Caution!

There are three options in the Options bar for the Custom Shape tool. When you select the Shape tool for the copyright symbol, make sure the Shape Layer icon is highlighted in the Options bar rather than the Paths or Fill Pixels icon.

Did You Know?

The Layers palette includes two types of sliders. The Opacity slider affects the visibility of both the filled pixels and the layer style. The Fill slider only affects the transparency of the filled pixels without changing any style that is applied.

Desktop Trick!

Double-click the Type thumbnail in the Layers palette to select and highlight all the type on that layer. Double-click in the blank space next to the name of a layer to bring up the Layer Style dialog.

WARP TYPE
for a fun effect

You can create many different effects with type by warping the letters into various shapes. If you warp text using the Warp command found under the Edit and Transform menu after rasterizing the Type layer, or turning the layer into pixels, the letters lose their sharp edges and appear fuzzy. Using the Warp Text feature of Photoshop gives text a completely new look and helps it remain sharp-edged and editable.

Once you type the text, click the Create Warped Text icon in the Options bar. You can select from a variety of warp styles and use the sliders to alter the look.

You can control the direction of the warp as well as the perspective of the letters. Because the warp style is an attribute of the Type layer, you can change the style at any time by reselecting the layer with the Type tool and opening the Warp Text dialog. As long as the text is on an editable Type layer, you can apply any layer styles before or after warping the text.

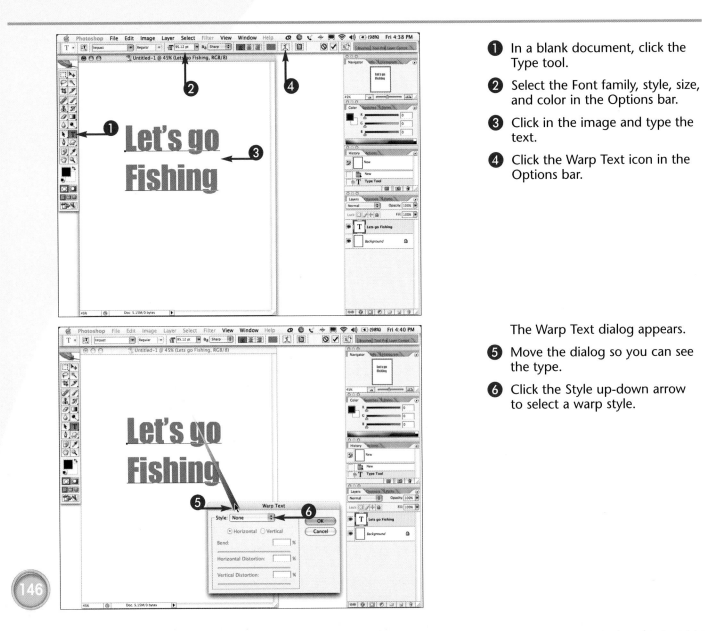

① In a blank document, click the Type tool.

② Select the Font family, style, size, and color in the Options bar.

③ Click in the image and type the text.

④ Click the Warp Text icon in the Options bar.

The Warp Text dialog appears.

⑤ Move the dialog so you can see the type.

⑥ Click the Style up-down arrow to select a warp style.

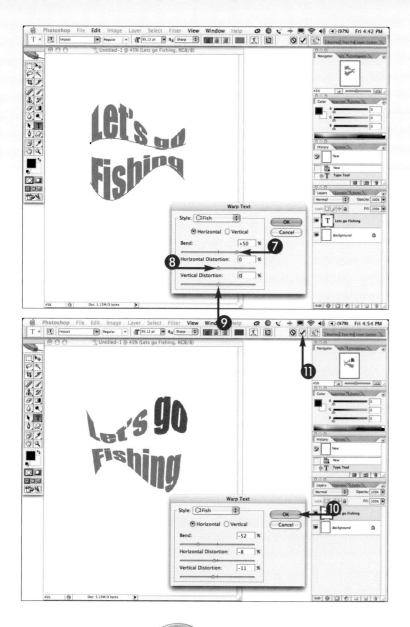

The text in the image changes to match the style selected.

63

DIFFICULTY LEVEL

⑦ Click and drag the Bend slider to change the amount of warp.

⑧ Click and drag the Horizontal Distortion slider to adjust the direction of the effect.

⑨ Click and drag the Vertical Distortion slider to change the effect.

⑩ Click OK to commit the warp.

⑪ Click the Commit button to apply the text.

TIPS

Did You Know?

You can change the color of the text after you warp it. Select the Type tool and click and drag across the text to highlight it. Click the foreground color in the Toolbar, select another color from the Color Picker, and click OK to close the dialog. Click the Commit button in the Options bar.

More Options!

To see the color of the type as you change it, highlight the type. Then press ⌘-H (Ctrl+H), the keyboard shortcut to Hide Extras. The type remains selected but the highlighting is not visible. When you select another foreground color in the Color Picker, you instantly see the color on your text.

ADD PERSPECTIVE TO TYPE
and keep it sharp

When you warp a Type layer, the letters always bend the shape to some degree, even if you set the Bend slider to 0. Using the Perspective function found under the Edit and Transform menu more accurately gives the illusion of text disappearing into the distance. However, this function is unavailable for a Type layer. If you rasterize the layer and turn the letters into pixels to use the Perspective transformation, the characters blur as you change the angles. However, you can add realistic perspective to type and preserve the crisp edges by converting the Type layer to a Shape layer.

Converting type to shapes changes the Type layer into a layer with a colored fill and a linked vector mask showing the outline of the letters. The outline is actually a temporary path and appears in the Paths palette as well. The text is no longer editable, but you can alter the vector mask, add layer styles, and use all the transformation tools to change the look.

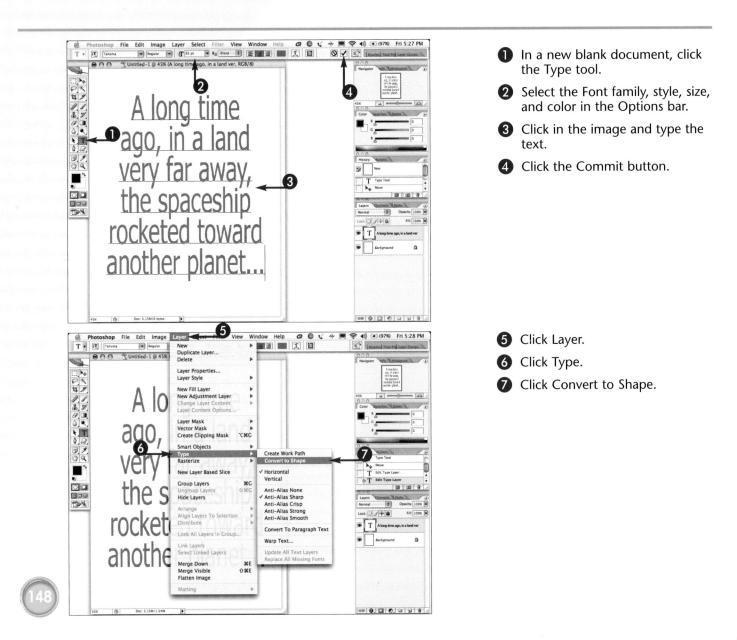

① In a new blank document, click the Type tool.

② Select the Font family, style, size, and color in the Options bar.

③ Click in the image and type the text.

④ Click the Commit button.

⑤ Click Layer.

⑥ Click Type.

⑦ Click Convert to Shape.

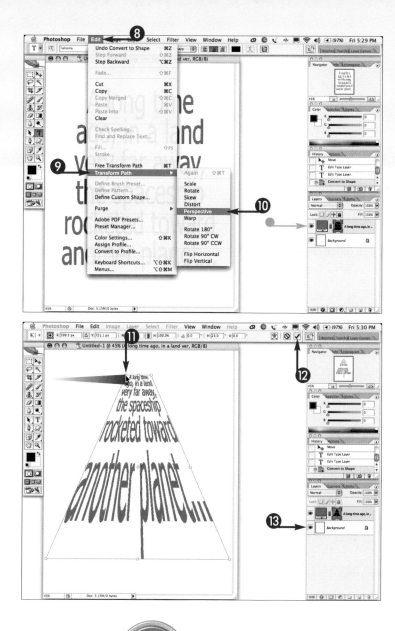

● The Type layer in the Layers palette changes to a fill and vector mask.

⑧ Click Edit.

⑨ Click Transform Path.

⑩ Click Perspective.

The Text has a bounding box with anchor points.

⑪ Click one of the top corner anchors and drag toward the center top anchor.

The text appears to be lying down on a perspective plane.

⑫ Click the Commit button in the Options bar.

⑬ Click the Background layer to see the text without the mask outline.

TIPS

More Options!
You can also click one of the top or bottom corner anchors and drag straight up or straight down to create a vertical perspective. The letters seem to disappear into the distance in a vertical position.

Desktop Trick!
When you need to select the Type tool to edit type, double-click the T in the Type layer thumbnail in the Layers palette. The type on the layer is highlighted and the Type tool is selected.

Try This!
You can edit Type without changing back to the Type tool. Click the Type layer in the Layers palette. Click Window ➪ Character to open the Character palette. Make any changes to the text directly in the palette.

Make your
TEXT FOLLOW ANY PATH

You can make text move along an angled line or curve and swoop in any direction to create an original design. By creating an angled path with the Pen tool or a curved path with the Freeform Pen tool, you can place the Type tool cursor on the path and type the text. The text flows along the path, starting from the insertion point. Another option is to create a shape using the Shape tool and place the text around the edges of the shape. You can also use any object

in a photograph to create the path. When you add the text, it flows along the edges of the object in the photo, creating a sophisticated design.

You can use any selection tool to select around the object. Convert the selection to a complex working path using the selections in the Paths palette pop-up menu. The text remains on a Type layer so you can change or add words or style and color the letters.

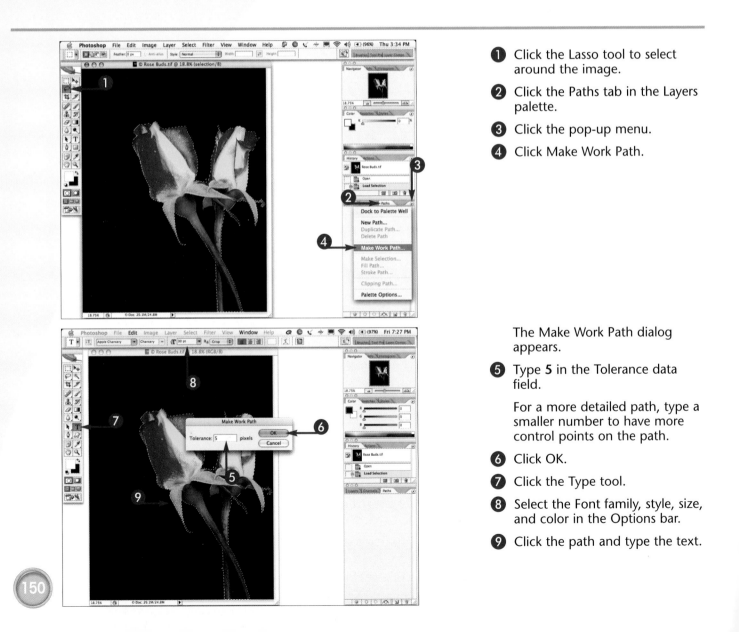

① Click the Lasso tool to select around the image.

② Click the Paths tab in the Layers palette.

③ Click the pop-up menu.

④ Click Make Work Path.

The Make Work Path dialog appears.

⑤ Type **5** in the Tolerance data field.

For a more detailed path, type a smaller number to have more control points on the path.

⑥ Click OK.

⑦ Click the Type tool.

⑧ Select the Font family, style, size, and color in the Options bar.

⑨ Click the path and type the text.

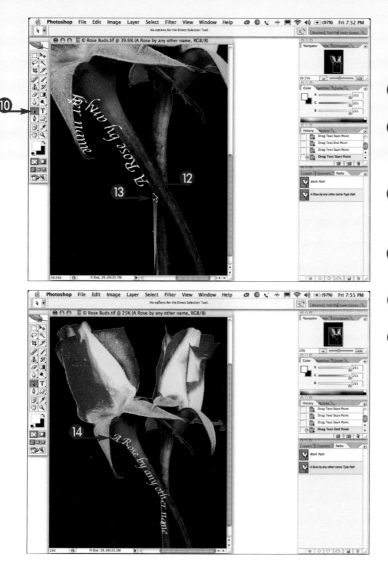

The text follows the path and a Type path appears in the Paths palette.

10 Click the Direct Selection tool.

11 Press ⌘-Spacebar (Ctrl+Spacebar) and click the image to zoom in.

12 Click the small X at the beginning of the text.

The cursor changes to an I-beam with a small black arrow.

13 Drag along the path to reposition the text.

14 Drag the cursor across the path to put the text on the other side of the path.

15 Press Option-Spacebar (Alt+Spacebar) to zoom out.

65

DIFFICULTY LEVEL

![TIPS]

Did You Know?

A small X indicates the beginning of the text on a path and a small O indicates the end of the text. If the text is center-aligned, a small diamond shape designates the center.

Try This!

On sharp curves, letters may appear on top of each other. Click Window and then Character to open the Character palette. Select the letters and adjust the tracking in the Character palette, or click between the letters and adjust the kerning.

Desktop Trick!

To adjust kerning, click between two letters and press Option (Alt) and the right or left arrow. To adjust tracking, select a group of letters and press Option (Alt) and the right or left arrow.

FILL ANY SHAPE WITH TEXT
to create unique effects

In Photoshop, you can type text in several ways. Any text that is typed is placed on a Type layer, retaining its vector-based outlines so you can scale, skew, or rotate it to fit your design. With the Type tool selected, place the cursor anywhere in an image and type the text, or type the text so it flows along the edge of a path. You can also type text as a paragraph, either horizontally or vertically, by controlling the flow of the characters within a bounding box. You first use the Type tool to drag

diagonally and define a bounding area, then click and type the text. Typing text as a paragraph is useful for creating brochures, scrapbooks, or various design projects. The bounding box is not limited to the rectangular shape created by dragging the Type tool. You can also drag out any shape using the Custom Shape tool and a shape from the Custom Shape Picker. You can then fill the shape with paragraph text to create unique visual effects.

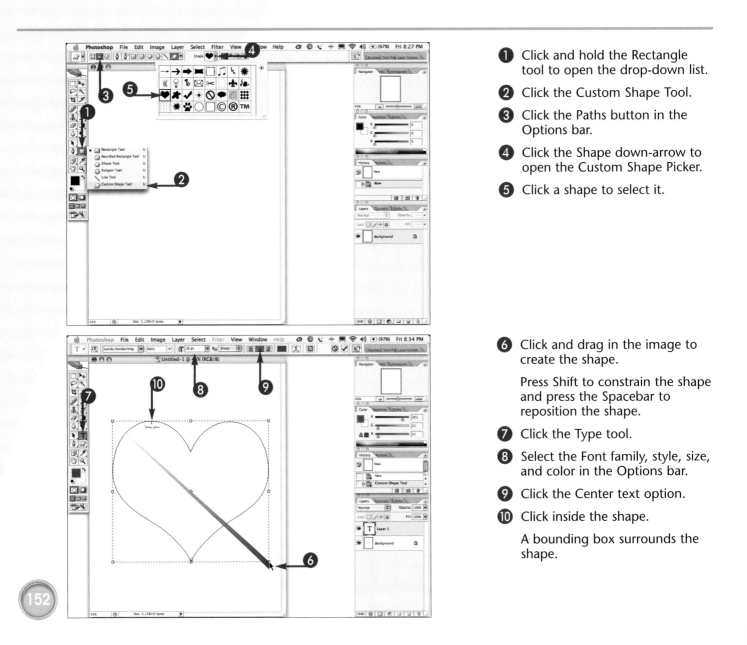

① Click and hold the Rectangle tool to open the drop-down list.

② Click the Custom Shape Tool.

③ Click the Paths button in the Options bar.

④ Click the Shape down-arrow to open the Custom Shape Picker.

⑤ Click a shape to select it.

⑥ Click and drag in the image to create the shape.

   Press Shift to constrain the shape and press the Spacebar to reposition the shape.

⑦ Click the Type tool.

⑧ Select the Font family, style, size, and color in the Options bar.

⑨ Click the Center text option.

⑩ Click inside the shape.

   A bounding box surrounds the shape.

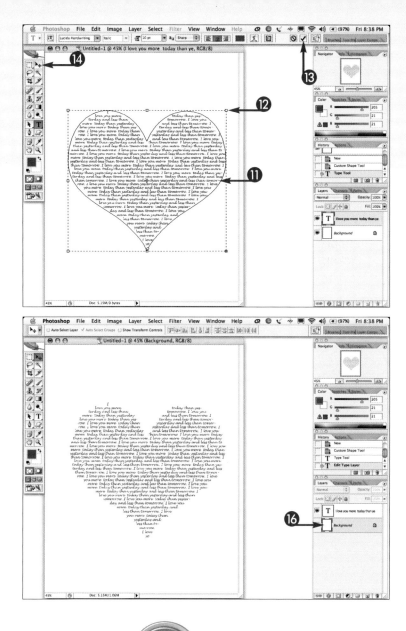

⑪ Type the text until the shape is full.

⑫ Click and drag the anchor points around the shape to alter the form.

⑬ Click the Commit button in the Options bar.

⑭ Click the Move tool.

⑮ Click and drag in the shape to reposition it on the page.

⑯ Click the Background layer in the Layers palette to view the text without the outline of the shape.

66

DIFFICULTY LEVEL

TIPS

Did You Know?
You can access more custom shapes by clicking the down-arrow on the Custom Shape Picker in the Options bar. Select All from the choices in the menu and click Append to add these to the current set. You can also use the Pen tool to create an original path to use as the bounding box for text.

More Options!
You can copy text from another document and paste it into the shape. Select the text in the other document and then press ⌘-C (Ctrl+C) to copy. Click the Photoshop document. Use the Type tool to click in the shape. Press ⌘-V (Ctrl+V) to paste the text.

Create eye-catching
PHOTO-FILLED TITLES

You can easily create mood-inspiring or memory-evoking titles for a photo or album page by making a photograph fill the letters. Photoshop CS2 includes two kinds of Type tools: the Horizontal and Vertical Type tools, and the Horizontal and Vertical Type Mask tools. When you use the Type Mask tools, Photoshop automatically creates a selection in the shape of the letters. However, using the regular Type tools gives you more control over the design and makes it easier to see the area of the photo that will be cut out by the letters.

Filling text or any other object with a photograph or other image is one of the many collage techniques in Photoshop. You type text and use a Clipping Mask to clip the photograph so that it only shows through the letters. Because the letters are on an editable Type layer, you can change the text even after the letters are filled with the image. You can also add a drop shadow or emboss to the Type layer to make the letters stand out.

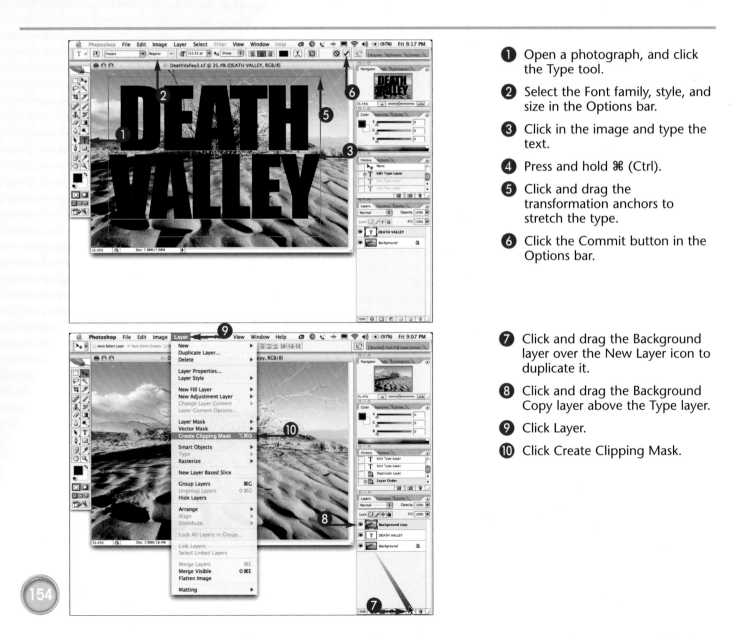

① Open a photograph, and click the Type tool.

② Select the Font family, style, and size in the Options bar.

③ Click in the image and type the text.

④ Press and hold ⌘ (Ctrl).

⑤ Click and drag the transformation anchors to stretch the type.

⑥ Click the Commit button in the Options bar.

⑦ Click and drag the Background layer over the New Layer icon to duplicate it.

⑧ Click and drag the Background Copy layer above the Type layer.

⑨ Click Layer.

⑩ Click Create Clipping Mask.

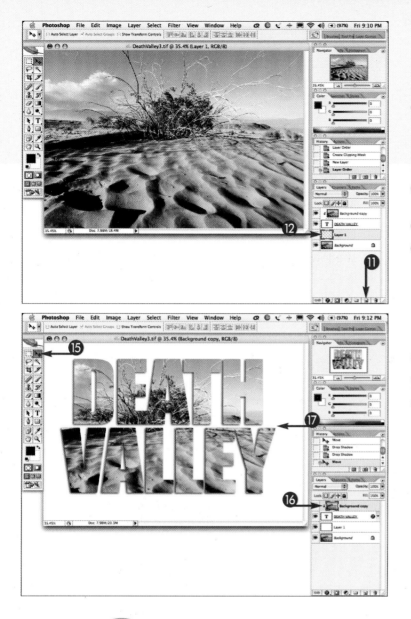

The Background Copy layer is indented with an arrow in the Layers palette but the image does not change.

⓫ Click the New Layer icon in the Layers palette to create a new blank layer named Layer 1.

⓬ Click and drag the new blank layer below the Type layer.

⓭ Press D to reset the default colors.

⓮ Click ⌘-Delete (Ctrl+Backspace) to fill the layer with white.

The photo fills the letters on a white background.

⓯ Click the Move tool.

⓰ Click the Background Copy layer.

⓱ Click and drag in the image to move the photo into position inside the letters.

TIPS

More Options!

You can also change the type attributes using the Character palette. Click Window ➪ Character to open the palette. Place the cursor over any of the settings to activate the scrubby sliders. Move the cursor to change the settings.

Attention!

Be sure to highlight the Background copy layer, which must be above the Type layer, when you create the clipping mask. Changing the stacking order of the layers after a clipping mask has been applied can remove the clipping mask.

Desktop Tricks!

You can create a clipping mask using two different keyboard shortcuts. Press Option (Alt) and click between the two layers in the Layers palette or press ⌘-Option-G (Ctrl+Alt+G).

BLEND TEXT
into a photograph creatively

When you type on a photograph, you can reduce the opacity of the Type layer to make the letters fade into the image in a uniform manner. For a more interesting effect, use the blending Options in the Layer Style dialog to give the illusion of the text disappearing behind different elements in the photograph. You can make the letters disappear behind clouds or trees, blend parts of the letters into a mountain, or create a variety of different effects using the colors from the underlying layer and the Blending Options for the text layer.

The Layer Style dialog includes Blending Options sliders for both the active layer and the underlying layer. The sliders determine which pixels appear through the active layer and which are hidden, based upon the brightness of the pixels. You can make the text blend even more smoothly with the underlying photo by splitting the sliders and in effect partially blending some of the pixels in the tonal range.

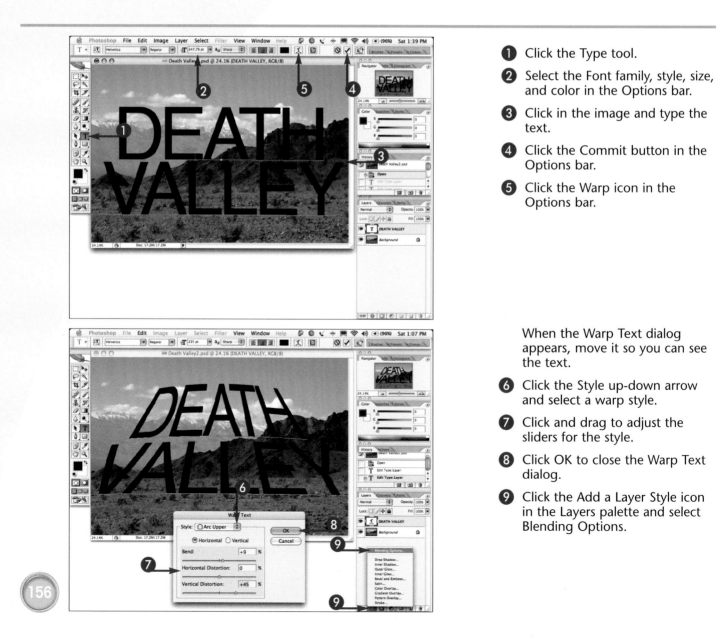

1. Click the Type tool.

2. Select the Font family, style, size, and color in the Options bar.

3. Click in the image and type the text.

4. Click the Commit button in the Options bar.

5. Click the Warp icon in the Options bar.

When the Warp Text dialog appears, move it so you can see the text.

6. Click the Style up-down arrow and select a warp style.

7. Click and drag to adjust the sliders for the style.

8. Click OK to close the Warp Text dialog.

9. Click the Add a Layer Style icon in the Layers palette and select Blending Options.

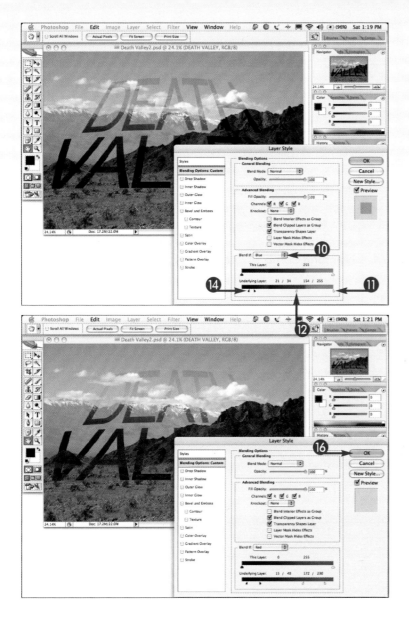

Move the Layer Style dialog to see the photo.

#68

DIFFICULTY LEVEL

⑩ Click the Blend If up-down arrows to select the first color.

⑪ Click and drag the Underlying Layer's white slider.

⑫ Press Option (Alt) and click and drag to separate the slider halves.

⑬ Click and drag the slider halves until the image blends with the text.

⑭ Repeat Steps **11** to **13** using the black slider for the Underlying Layer.

⑮ Repeat Steps **10** to **14** for other underlying colors until the text blends with the elements in the photograph.

⑯ Click OK.

Did You Know?

Splitting the white highlight or the black shadow sliders for the underlying layer defines a range of partially blended or composite pixels and softens the transitions as the text is blended with the background photo.

Try This!

You can also view the Layer Style dialog by clicking Layer ⇨ Layer Style ⇨ Blending Option or by double clicking in the empty space next to the layer name in the Layers palette.

More Options!

You can add a Bevel or Emboss or any of the other Layer Styles to the letters at anytime. Open the Layer Styles dialog and click any of the styles to see the effect.

Create an amazing
COLORED SHADOW

When you apply a drop shadow to text in an image using the Layer Style drop shadow, the default shadow is gray. Actual shadows of text or other objects are usually not gray. Shadows generally reflect the colors of the objects they cover. You could select another color for the shadow in the Layer Style dialog; however, the shadow would have an unnatural and uniform color. You can apply a drop shadow with the same colors that occur in the real world by using a selection and a Brightness/Contrast adjustment. Then, by linking the shadow layer to the

text layer, you can reposition the text in the image and the shadow follows, automatically adjusting itself for colors in the image below.

You can use the same technique to add a realistic shadow to any object in an image. Add depth to natural light shadows under a tree, or increase the shadow of a person in a sunlit photo. The greater the number of colors and textures affected by the shadow, the more natural your colored shadow appears.

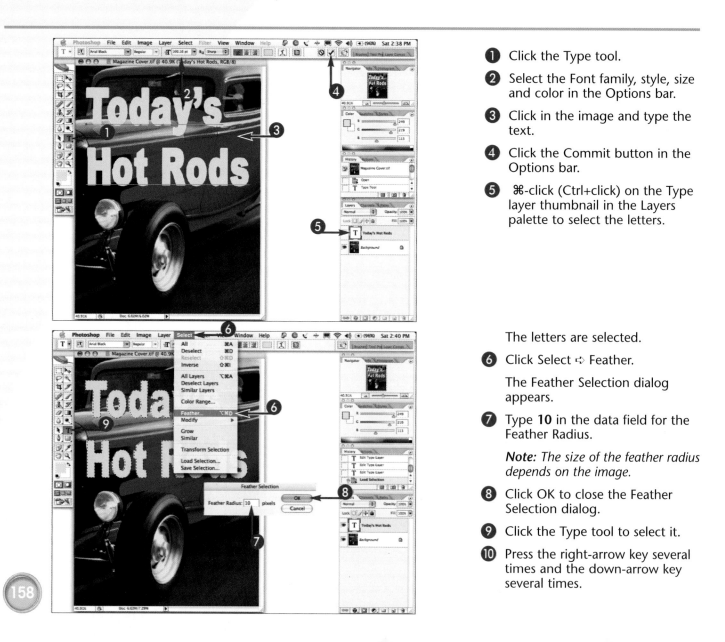

① Click the Type tool.

② Select the Font family, style, size and color in the Options bar.

③ Click in the image and type the text.

④ Click the Commit button in the Options bar.

⑤ ⌘-click (Ctrl+click) on the Type layer thumbnail in the Layers palette to select the letters.

The letters are selected.

⑥ Click Select ➪ Feather.

The Feather Selection dialog appears.

⑦ Type **10** in the data field for the Feather Radius.

Note: The size of the feather radius depends on the image.

⑧ Click OK to close the Feather Selection dialog.

⑨ Click the Type tool to select it.

⑩ Press the right-arrow key several times and the down-arrow key several times.

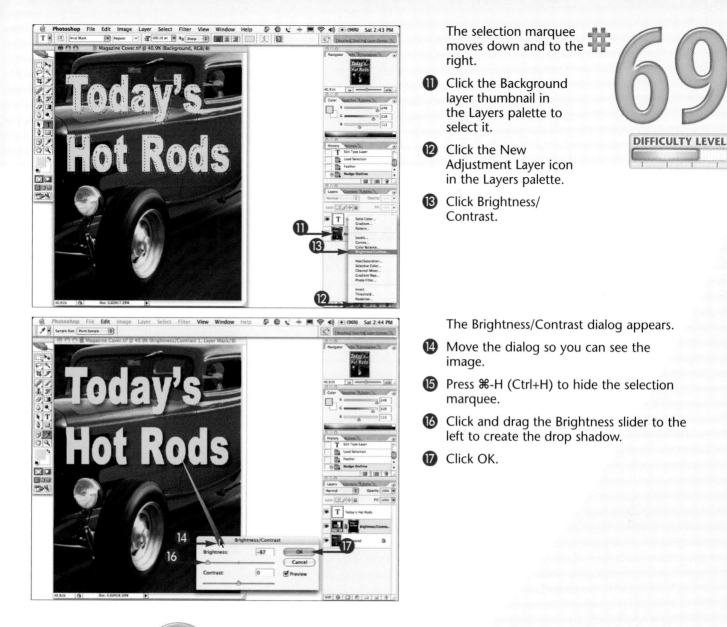

The selection marquee moves down and to the right.

⑪ Click the Background layer thumbnail in the Layers palette to select it.

⑫ Click the New Adjustment Layer icon in the Layers palette.

⑬ Click Brightness/Contrast.

The Brightness/Contrast dialog appears.

⑭ Move the dialog so you can see the image.

⑮ Press ⌘-H (Ctrl+H) to hide the selection marquee.

⑯ Click and drag the Brightness slider to the left to create the drop shadow.

⑰ Click OK.

TIPS

More Options!

Press Shift and click the Type layer and the Adjustment layer in the Layers palette to select them both. Then click the Link Layers icon in the Layers palette to link the layers for the text and the shadow together. Click the Move tool and reposition the text. The shadow follows the text around the image.

Desktop Trick!

You can quickly change the alignment of type using keyboard shortcuts. Click in the type and press Shift-⌘-L (Shift+Ctrl+L) to align left; press Shift-⌘-R (Shift+Ctrl+R) to align right; and press Shift-⌘-C (Shift+Ctrl+C) to align center.

WEAVE TEXT AND GRAPHICS
for intriguing designs

You can create a design using type as the central element by changing the letter styles and size, adding layer effects, warping the text, or adding perspective. You can also make the individual letters interweave and interact with each other to add more interest to any project. You can make the colors reverse with the background where the letters overlap creating new design elements. Add a shape to the text, make the letters intertwine with the shape, and you can create eye-catching logos or page titles.

When you convert a Type layer to a shape, the text is no longer editable. However, you can still move individual letters. You can transform, warp, and resize one letter at a time or a group of letters. You can also add layer styles to the grouped design elements and change the look completely. Because the letters and shapes are all on one layer, the color and any layer styles you use are applied to all the elements on the layer. Flatten the layers as a final step in creating the design.

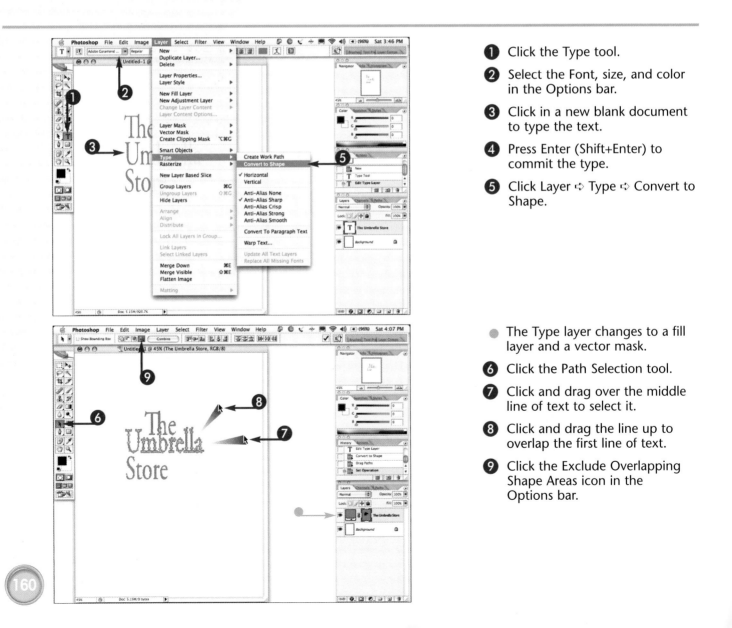

① Click the Type tool.

② Select the Font, size, and color in the Options bar.

③ Click in a new blank document to type the text.

④ Press Enter (Shift+Enter) to commit the type.

⑤ Click Layer ➪ Type ➪ Convert to Shape.

● The Type layer changes to a fill layer and a vector mask.

⑥ Click the Path Selection tool.

⑦ Click and drag over the middle line of text to select it.

⑧ Click and drag the line up to overlap the first line of text.

⑨ Click the Exclude Overlapping Shape Areas icon in the Options bar.

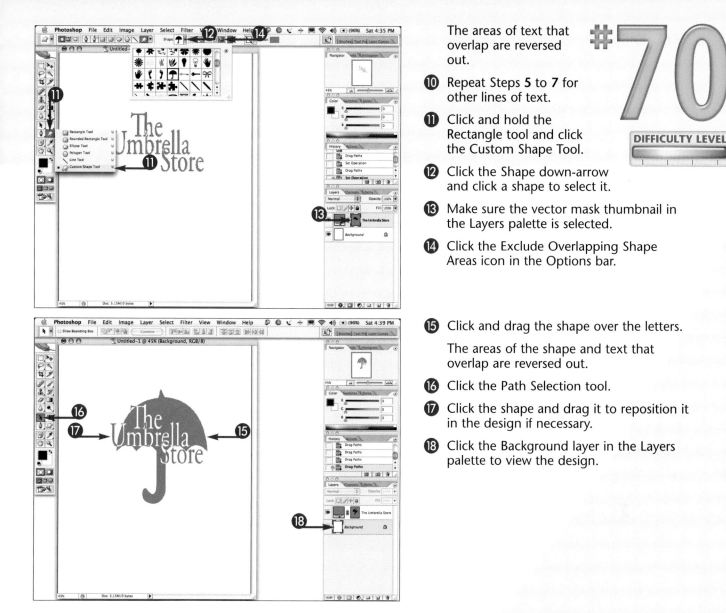

The areas of text that overlap are reversed out.

⑩ Repeat Steps **5** to **7** for other lines of text.

⑪ Click and hold the Rectangle tool and click the Custom Shape Tool.

⑫ Click the Shape down-arrow and click a shape to select it.

⑬ Make sure the vector mask thumbnail in the Layers palette is selected.

⑭ Click the Exclude Overlapping Shape Areas icon in the Options bar.

⑮ Click and drag the shape over the letters.

The areas of the shape and text that overlap are reversed out.

⑯ Click the Path Selection tool.

⑰ Click the shape and drag it to reposition it in the design if necessary.

⑱ Click the Background layer in the Layers palette to view the design.

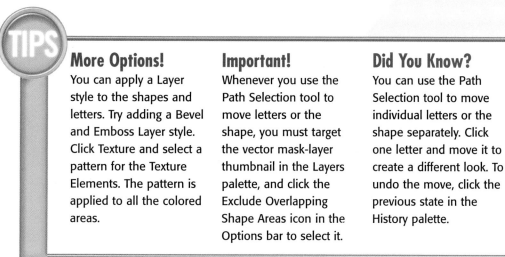

TIPS

More Options!

You can apply a Layer style to the shapes and letters. Try adding a Bevel and Emboss Layer style. Click Texture and select a pattern for the Texture Elements. The pattern is applied to all the colored areas.

Important!

Whenever you use the Path Selection tool to move letters or the shape, you must target the vector mask-layer thumbnail in the Layers palette, and click the Exclude Overlapping Shape Areas icon in the Options bar to select it.

Did You Know?

You can use the Path Selection tool to move individual letters or the shape separately. Click one letter and move it to create a different look. To undo the move, click the previous state in the History palette.

Creating Digital Artwork from Photographs

You can use Photoshop to replicate traditional art materials and techniques and see immediate results on your screen. If you have spent years in art school working with traditional materials, you can find a whole new source of creativity as you experiment with different techniques. Even if you have never tried art in any form or claim you cannot even draw a straight line, you can use Photoshop to draw line art, sketch a person or a building, create a painted portrait, or paint with oils and watercolors. You can experiment and try all sorts of projects without wasting any paper products or paints. You can vary colors, mix media, copy, trace, or draw freehand, and even erase the results before anyone else can see your attempts!

The key to creating digital artwork is to combine different layers, effects, filters, masks, and blend modes. The results not only vary with the methods used, each style of photograph as well as the subject matter affects the overall look of the finished piece. You can vary methods to make your work more efficient and at the same time expand your creative horizons. With so many options and choices, artistic experimentation with Photoshop can be very addictive. You may spend a lot more time with the art projects than you ever thought you would.

The ten tasks and techniques described in this chapter are only a taste of what is possible.

Top 100

Give any photo a
SKETCHED LOOK

You can make a photo appear to be sketched onto the page, giving a traditional photograph an entirely new look. Create a title page for an album or a Web gallery, or use the technique as the final touch to a painted image. The image appears to be applied to the paper using charcoal, soft pencils, or a paintbrush, leaving the edges and brush marks visible. Starting with any image, you add a new layer filled with white. You then use the Eraser tool to erase through the white to reveal areas of the image on the underlying layer. Using this technique on a slightly grainy photo even intensifies the effect. You can use any of Photoshop's brushes and change them as you continue sketching the photo onto the page. The greater the number and opacity of the brush strokes, the more of your photograph appears on the white layer. You can vary the style of the strokes by altering the attributes of the eraser from the Brushes palette.

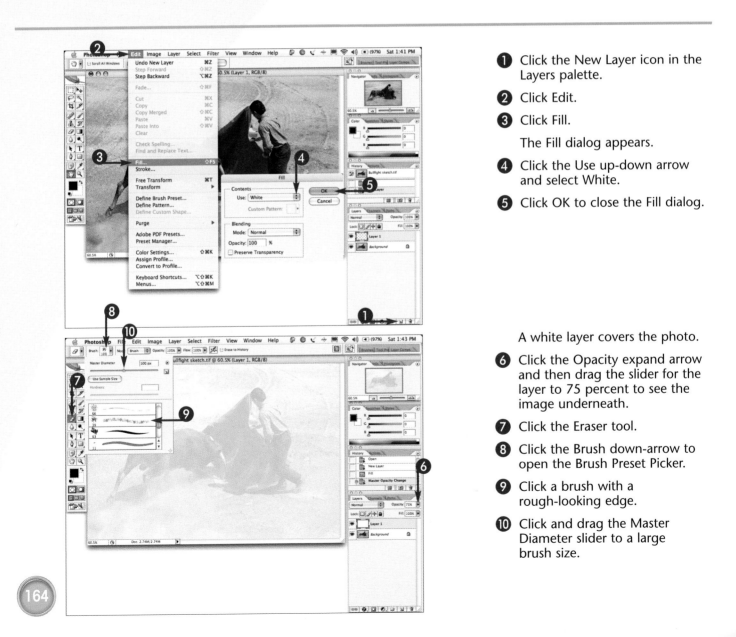

1 Click the New Layer icon in the Layers palette.

2 Click Edit.

3 Click Fill.

   The Fill dialog appears.

4 Click the Use up-down arrow and select White.

5 Click OK to close the Fill dialog.

A white layer covers the photo.

6 Click the Opacity expand arrow and then drag the slider for the layer to 75 percent to see the image underneath.

7 Click the Eraser tool.

8 Click the Brush down-arrow to open the Brush Preset Picker.

9 Click a brush with a rough-looking edge.

10 Click and drag the Master Diameter slider to a large brush size.

⑪ Click and drag across the image using several broad strokes.

⑫ Click the Brush drop-down arrow to open the Brush Preset Picker.

⑬ Click and drag the Master Diameter slider to a smaller brush size.

⑭ Click and drag across the image to add more brush strokes.

⑮ Click the Opacity expand arrow and drag the slider for the layer to 100 percent.

⑯ Repeat Steps **8** to **11** applying broad strokes until the image looks sketched-in.

TIPS

More Options!

You can add more brushes to the selection in the Brush Picker. Click the Brush down-arrow and then click the Brush Picker down-arrow. Click any of the choices from the bottom section, such as Dry Media Brushes. Click Append in the dialog that appears to add the dry media brushes to the existing list.

Customize It!

You can view brushes by name instead of the stroke thumbnail. Click the Brush expand arrow and then click the Brush Picker down-arrow. Click Small List or Large List to view the brushes by name and thumbnail. You can return to the default brush set by selecting Reset brushes from the same menu.

Add a quick
QUADRANT COLOR SCHEME

You can quickly apply a quadrant color look to any image using the action included with Adobe Photoshop CS2 and turn an ordinary photograph into an interesting advertising piece. The colored quadrants can become shaded text backgrounds or can simply hide uncorrected colors in a photograph. You can add text to some areas while maintaining the image in muted tones as a background. Other times the client may supply an image that requires major color correction or overpowers the message.

You can also use this technique to see how using different duo tones might affect the image.

Photoshop Actions are a series of recorded steps that you play to apply the effect to an image. The Quadrant Color action can be found in the Image Effects action set listed on the Actions palette tab pull-down menu. You can use the quadrant colors as they appear or you can add an adjustment layer to fine-tune the colors in the quadrants.

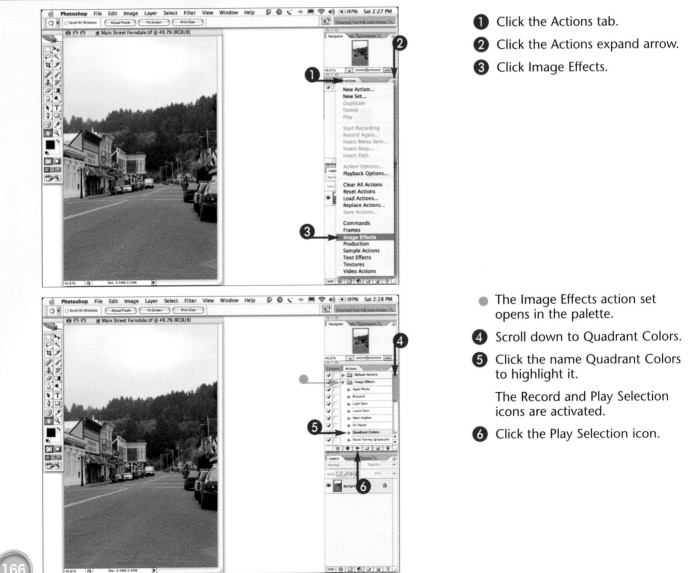

① Click the Actions tab.

② Click the Actions expand arrow.

③ Click Image Effects.

● The Image Effects action set opens in the palette.

④ Scroll down to Quadrant Colors.

⑤ Click the name Quadrant Colors to highlight it.

The Record and Play Selection icons are activated.

⑥ Click the Play Selection icon.

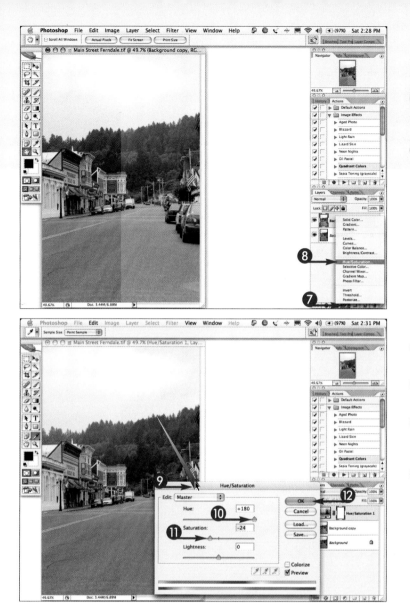

The action creates a background copy layer and applies the quadrant colors.

7 Click the New Adjustment Layer icon in the Layers palette.

8 Click Hue/Saturation.

The Hue/Saturation dialog appears.

9 Move the dialog so you can see the image.

10 Click and drag the Hue slider in either direction to change the color scheme.

11 Click and drag the Saturation slider to change the intensity of the colors in the quadrants.

12 Click OK to apply the adjustment.

TIPS

Remove It!

Pressing ⌘-Option-Z (Ctrl+Alt+Z) multiple times only steps backward through an action. Instead, take a snapshot using the History palette's Create a New Snapshot icon before running an action. You can then undo the action by reselecting the snapshot in the History palette. Or simply drag the Background copy to the Layer palette trash.

Did You Know?

Clicking in the empty box next to the check mark in front of an action toggles the dialogs for the steps in the action on or off. When the toggle is on, the action stops at each step so you can select your own settings. Click the box again to return the action to the automatic setting.

Create a digital
PEN AND INK DRAWING

You can create the look of a pen and ink drawing from a photograph using a variety of methods in Photoshop. Often the method you use depends on the subject matter of the original photograph. Photoshop includes many filters such as Find Edges, which finds areas of contrast and outlines these; however, the filter applies the colors in the image to the edges. By using a black-and-white gradient map first to create a high-contrast grayscale image and then applying the Smart Blur filter in the Edges Only

mode, you get a black image with white lines. You can then invert the image to get black lines on a white background. Finally, apply a filter such as Minimum with a 1-pixel radius to thicken the lines.

You must adjust the image size before applying Photoshop filters for artistic results because the filters are always applied at a fixed brush size. Start by changing the image size on a copy of the image. Try a setting of 1000 pixels for the largest dimension in the Image Size dialog.

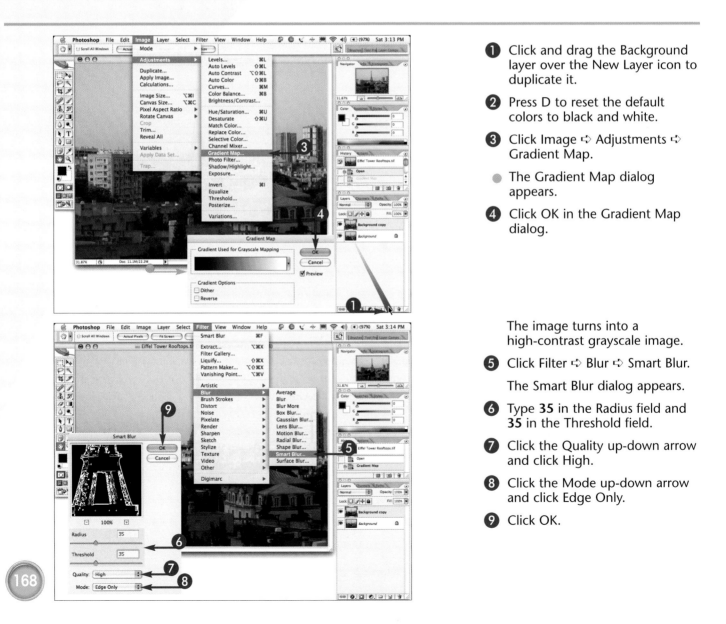

① Click and drag the Background layer over the New Layer icon to duplicate it.

② Press D to reset the default colors to black and white.

③ Click Image ⇨ Adjustments ⇨ Gradient Map.

● The Gradient Map dialog appears.

④ Click OK in the Gradient Map dialog.

The image turns into a high-contrast grayscale image.

⑤ Click Filter ⇨ Blur ⇨ Smart Blur.

The Smart Blur dialog appears.

⑥ Type **35** in the Radius field and **35** in the Threshold field.

⑦ Click the Quality up-down arrow and click High.

⑧ Click the Mode up-down arrow and click Edge Only.

⑨ Click OK.

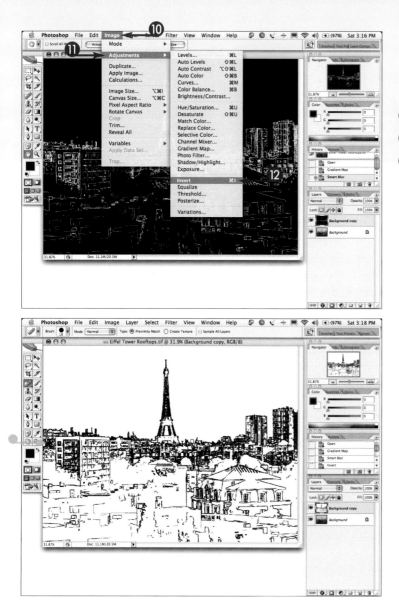

A progress bar appears as the Smart Blur is applied, and the image turns black with white outlines.

⑩ Click Image.

⑪ Click Adjustments.

⑫ Click Invert.

DIFFICULTY LEVEL

● The drawing appears as black lines on a white background.

Did You Know?

You can make the lines thicker and darker by clicking Filter ➪ Other ➪ Minimum. Set the Radius to 1 pixel. For heavier lines try clicking Filter ➪ Artistic ➪ Smudge Stick. Make sure to reduce the Stroke Length to 0.

More Options!

You can get better results using a high-contrast image or by increasing the contrast in the original image. After the grayscale conversion, click Image ➪ Adjustments ➪ Levels. Click and drag the outside sliders slightly toward the center to increase the contrast.

More Options!

Put the drawing on a separate layer. Use the Magic Wand tool and click a white area. Click Select ➪ Similar to select all the white. Then click Select ➪ Inverse. Press ⌘-J (Ctrl+J) to put the black lines on a new layer.

Give a photograph a
WOODCUT LOOK

A traditional woodcut is an engraving made by cutting areas into a block of wood using gouges and knives. The surface is then inked and printed on paper or another material. The uncut areas are raised to receive the ink in a process similar to that of a rubber stamp. A woodcut often has thicker black lines than other types of engravings, depending on the style and skill of the artist. Sometimes the areas that are not inked on the paper show the color of the paper and other times those areas are painted or

inked as well. You can give a photograph a woodcut look using Photoshop to add a unique creative element to any design. You use the High Pass filter to create a grayscale image enhancing the high-contrast areas. Then using the Threshold command, you turn the grayscale layer into a very high-contrast black and white and set the layer mode to Color Burn, allowing only the black lines to show through on the background image.

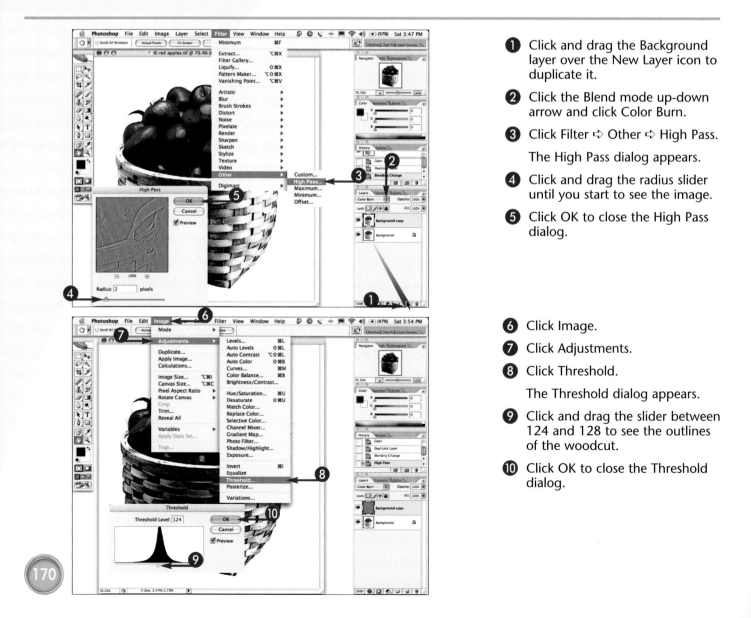

① Click and drag the Background layer over the New Layer icon to duplicate it.

② Click the Blend mode up-down arrow and click Color Burn.

③ Click Filter ⇨ Other ⇨ High Pass.

The High Pass dialog appears.

④ Click and drag the radius slider until you start to see the image.

⑤ Click OK to close the High Pass dialog.

⑥ Click Image.

⑦ Click Adjustments.

⑧ Click Threshold.

The Threshold dialog appears.

⑨ Click and drag the slider between 124 and 128 to see the outlines of the woodcut.

⑩ Click OK to close the Threshold dialog.

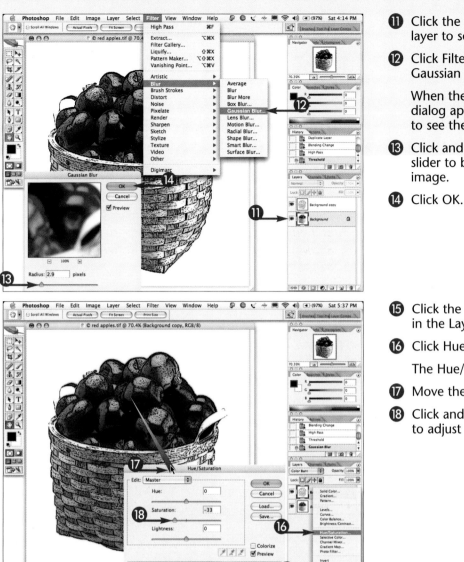

⑪ Click the Background layer to select it.

⑫ Click Filter ➪ Blur ➪ Gaussian Blur.

When the Gaussian Blur dialog appears, move it to see the main image.

⑬ Click and drag the slider to blur the main image.

⑭ Click OK.

⑮ Click the New Adjustment Layer icon in the Layers palette.

⑯ Click Hue/Saturation.

The Hue/Saturation dialog appears.

⑰ Move the dialog to see the image.

⑱ Click and drag the Saturation slider to adjust the look.

TIPS

Change It!

You can get a quicker but different woodcut look by using the Stamp filter instead of Steps **3** to **10**. Click Filter ➪ Sketch ➪ Stamp. Set the Light and Dark balance to about 4 and the Smoothness to about 3.

More Options!

The High Pass filter retains edge details wherever there are sharp color contrasts and reduces the rest of the image to a flat grayscale. You can create a woodcut with less detail by lowering the setting of the High Pass filter.

Did You Know?

Setting the Threshold below 128 reduces the strength of the woodcut lines. The Threshold command changes images to high-contrast black and white, in which pixels with gray values above 128 turn white and pixels below 128 turn black.

Design your own
KALEIDOSCOPE

The repetitive patterns and colors of a kaleidoscope mesmerize both children and adults with their colors and shapes that bend and blend. You can create your own kaleidoscope design starting with a portion of a photograph. You can use the kaleidoscope as an element in a page design or create a custom pattern to fill a border or picture frame. Start by selecting a triangular area in your photograph and copying it onto a new larger document. Duplicate the triangle layer and use the Transformation command to flip

the duplicate on its horizontal axis. Move the second triangle to align with the first triangle. You combine the two triangle shapes onto one layer, duplicate that layer, flip it on the vertical axis, and move it to create a diamond shape. Repeat these steps until you have two diamond shapes lining up on the points. Duplicate this new layer and transform the duplicate layer at 90 degrees to create one larger diamond. You can then crop, resize, or define a selection of the combined image as a pattern.

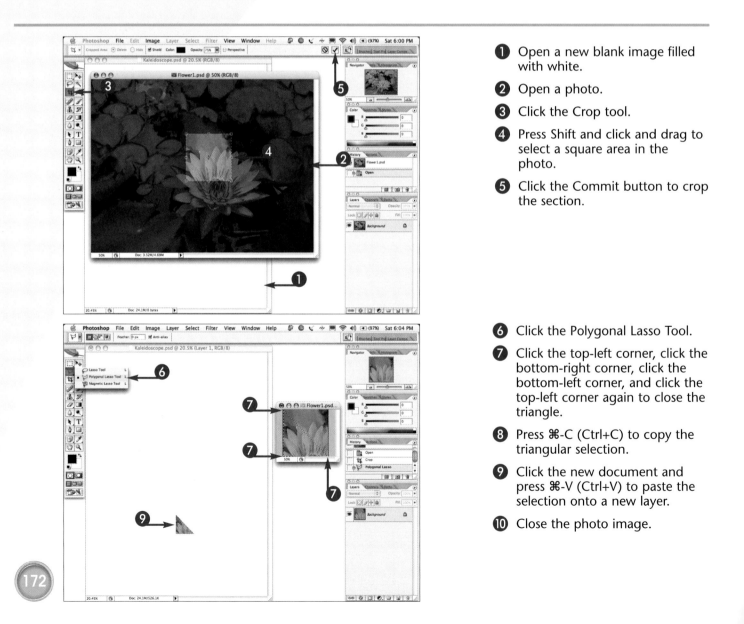

1 Open a new blank image filled with white.

2 Open a photo.

3 Click the Crop tool.

4 Press Shift and click and drag to select a square area in the photo.

5 Click the Commit button to crop the section.

6 Click the Polygonal Lasso Tool.

7 Click the top-left corner, click the bottom-right corner, click the bottom-left corner, and click the top-left corner again to close the triangle.

8 Press ⌘-C (Ctrl+C) to copy the triangular selection.

9 Click the new document and press ⌘-V (Ctrl+V) to paste the selection onto a new layer.

10 Close the photo image.

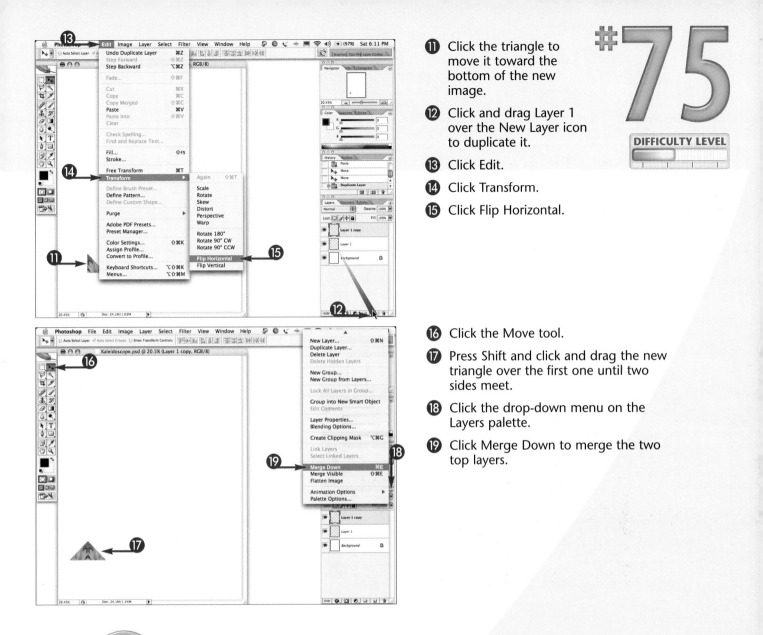

⑪ Click the triangle to move it toward the bottom of the new image.

⑫ Click and drag Layer 1 over the New Layer icon to duplicate it.

⑬ Click Edit.

⑭ Click Transform.

⑮ Click Flip Horizontal.

⑯ Click the Move tool.

⑰ Press Shift and click and drag the new triangle over the first one until two sides meet.

⑱ Click the drop-down menu on the Layers palette.

⑲ Click Merge Down to merge the two top layers.

#75

DIFFICULTY LEVEL

TIPS

Did You Know?
Turn on the grid to help you line up the pieces. Click View ➪ Show ➪ Grid. Or just press ⌘-' (Ctrl+'). Make sure that View ➪ Snap To ➪ Grid is checked.

Desktop Trick!
To see the document in full on the screen, double-click the Hand tool on the toolbar or click Fit Screen in the Options bar. To zoom to 100 percent, double-click the Zoom tool in the toolbar.

Attention!
The kaleidescope image can become quite large. Resize it by clicking Image ➪ Image Size. With the Constrain Proportions check box selected, change the width to a smaller size. Click the Resample Image up-down arrow and select Bicubic Sharper. Click OK.

Design your own
KALEIDOSCOPE

You can actually make a large variety of kaleidoscopes using only one colorful photograph. Every time you select a triangular shape from a different area in the photo, the resulting pattern will be different. You can even use the same triangle and by reversing the order of the transformations, first applying Flip Vertical and then Flip Horizontal, you can totally change the look of the kaleidoscope. Using a selection of a complete object, such as a flower, rather than a portion of the object and a portion of the background, gives your kaleidoscope a more circular look.

By starting with a photo that has the color scheme of your design, you can create an imaginative border or pattern that always blends with the page. Keep the shape on its own layer and add a drop shadow, bevel, or other layer effect. You can use the Elliptical Marquee tool to select a circular portion. Add a stroke or a bevel to the circle and you have the start of a unique Web page button.

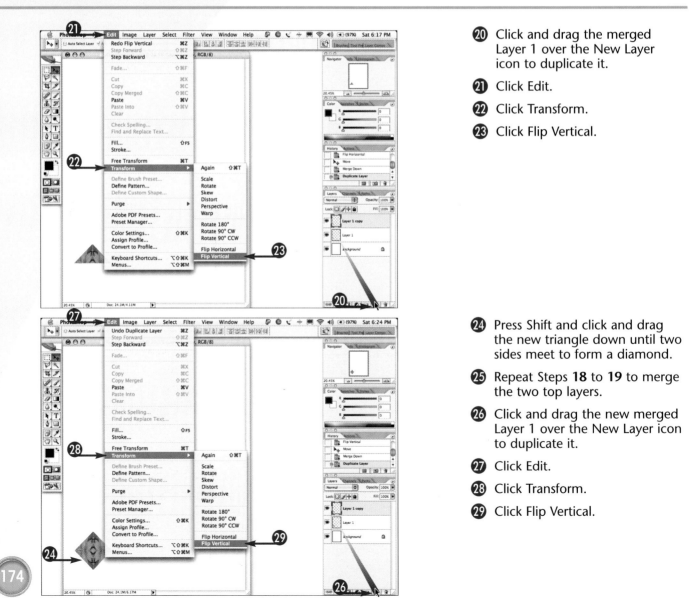

⑳ Click and drag the merged Layer 1 over the New Layer icon to duplicate it.

㉑ Click Edit.

㉒ Click Transform.

㉓ Click Flip Vertical.

㉔ Press Shift and click and drag the new triangle down until two sides meet to form a diamond.

㉕ Repeat Steps **18** to **19** to merge the two top layers.

㉖ Click and drag the new merged Layer 1 over the New Layer icon to duplicate it.

㉗ Click Edit.

㉘ Click Transform.

㉙ Click Flip Vertical.

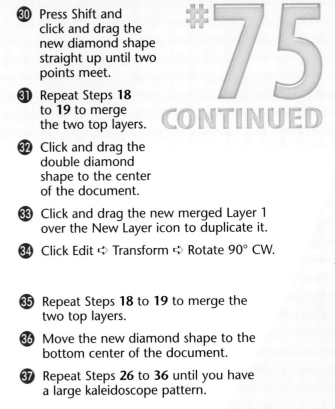

30 Press Shift and click and drag the new diamond shape straight up until two points meet.

31 Repeat Steps **18** to **19** to merge the two top layers.

32 Click and drag the double diamond shape to the center of the document.

33 Click and drag the new merged Layer 1 over the New Layer icon to duplicate it.

34 Click Edit ➪ Transform ➪ Rotate 90° CW.

35 Repeat Steps **18** to **19** to merge the two top layers.

36 Move the new diamond shape to the bottom center of the document.

37 Repeat Steps **26** to **36** until you have a large kaleidoscope pattern.

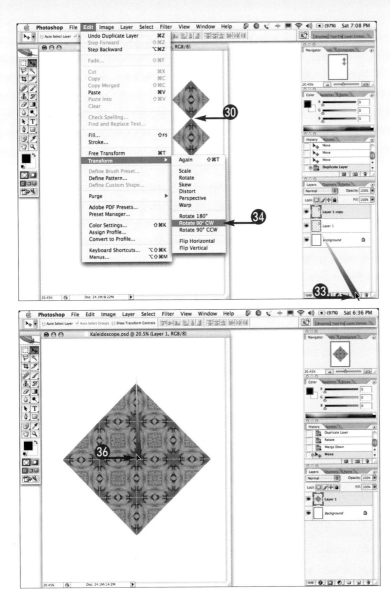

TIP

More Options!

After making a kaleidoscope, you can turn it into a pattern and save it to fill other selections or documents. Click the Rectangular Marquee tool. Press Shift to constrain it to a square, and click and drag over a square section of the kaleidoscope. Click Edit and click Define Pattern. Name the pattern in the dialog that appears and click OK. To use the pattern, make a selection in a new document. Click Edit ➪ Fill. Click the Use up-down arrow and click Pattern. Click the Custom Pattern thumbnail and scroll to your pattern in the Pattern Picker. Click OK to close the Fill dialog. The selection fills with a repeating pattern of your custom kaleidoscope.

POSTERIZE A PHOTO
for a Warhol-style image

Photoshop includes a Posterize command that automatically posterizes an image by mapping the Red, Green, and Blue channels to the number of tonal levels you set. The Poster Edges filter creates a different look, more like an etching than a posterized print. To create a posterized image more reminiscent of the Andy Warhol style of the 1960s and '70s, you can instead use three adjustment layers in succession. Use a Channel Mixer Adjustment layer to convert the photo to a grayscale image. Then apply a

Posterize Adjustment layer, specifying a number of levels that correspond to the number of colors in the final image. More levels make the image less stylized as it adds many more colors. Finally, use a Gradient Map Adjustment layer to map any color to each of the levels of gray. You can edit any of the adjustment layers to change the colors or levels until you get the look you want. For the best result, select a photo with a main subject on a plain background, or extract the subject and place it on a black background.

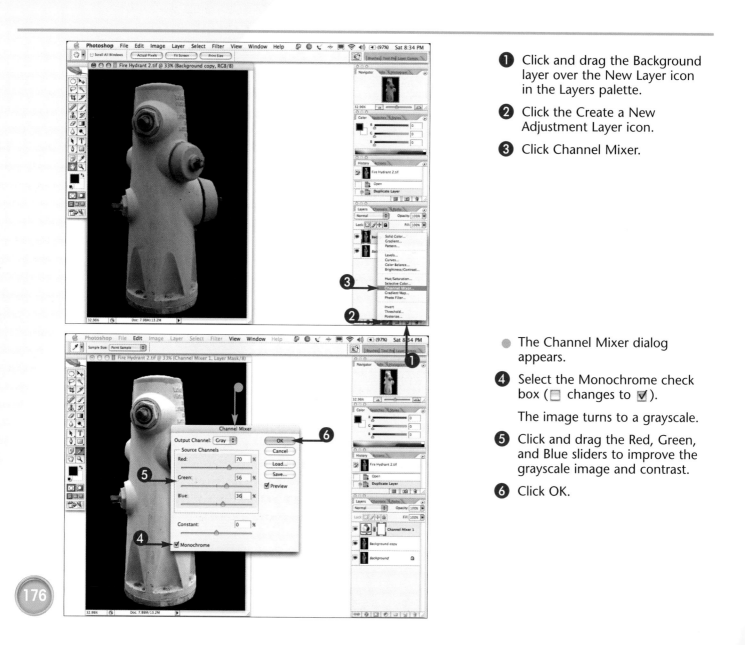

① Click and drag the Background layer over the New Layer icon in the Layers palette.

② Click the Create a New Adjustment Layer icon.

③ Click Channel Mixer.

● The Channel Mixer dialog appears.

④ Select the Monochrome check box (☐ changes to ☑).

The image turns to a grayscale.

⑤ Click and drag the Red, Green, and Blue sliders to improve the grayscale image and contrast.

⑥ Click OK.

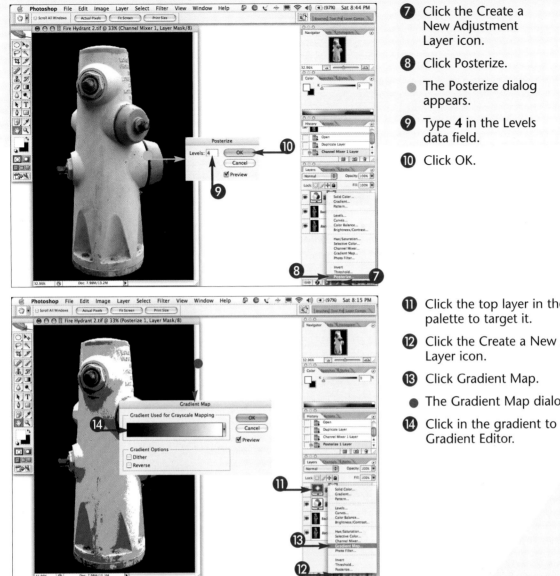

7 Click the Create a New Adjustment Layer icon.

8 Click Posterize.

● The Posterize dialog appears.

9 Type **4** in the Levels data field.

10 Click OK.

11 Click the top layer in the Layers palette to target it.

12 Click the Create a New Adjustment Layer icon.

13 Click Gradient Map.

● The Gradient Map dialog appears.

14 Click in the gradient to open the Gradient Editor.

TIPS

Attention!

You get better results if you match the number of gray levels with the number of color stops in the gradient. To add more gray levels, double-click the Posterize thumbnail in the Layers palette and increase the number of levels. Then double-click the Gradient Map thumbnail and add more color stops.

Try This!

If you want a more realistically colored image, fill the color stops on the right in the Gradient Editor with the lightest colors you want in the image and the color stops on the left with the darkest colors. The greater the number of color stops and the more colors you use, the wilder the image appears.

POSTERIZE A PHOTO
for a Warhol-style image

You can create an image with multiple copies of the posterized photo using different colors. Click File and then click Save As to give this version another name. Save the image in a new, separate folder. Click the Gradient Map thumbnail in the Layers palette to open the dialog again.

Click in the gradient to open the Gradient editor. Change the colors for each of the four color stops, each time selecting the darkest colors for the leftmost color stops and the lightest colors for the

rightmost color stops. Click OK to close the Gradient Editor and again to close the Gradient Map dialog. Click Save As and give this second color version another name. Repeat this process until you have four different versions of the image.

Create a new blank document and make the grid visible. Then click File and click Place to place each of the four images on the page. You can flip any of the images horizontally to add more variety. Click Edit, click Transform, and then click Flip Horizontal.

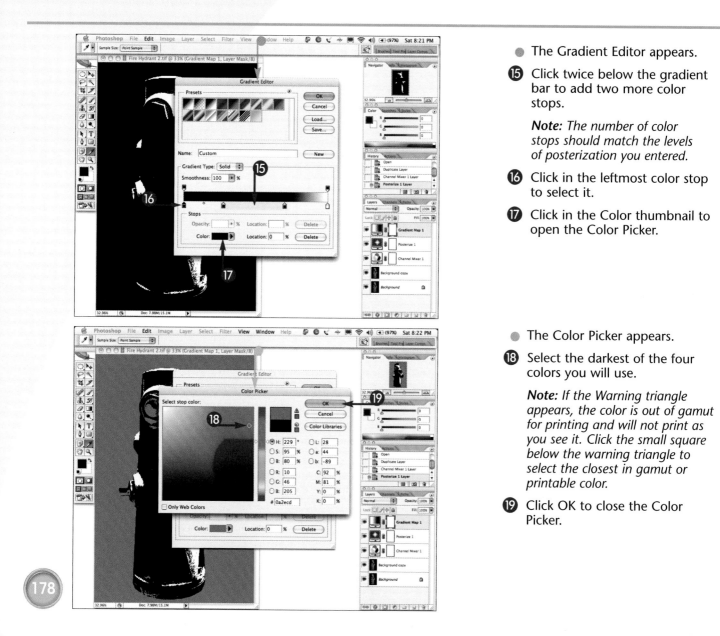

● The Gradient Editor appears.

⑮ Click twice below the gradient bar to add two more color stops.

Note: The number of color stops should match the levels of posterization you entered.

⑯ Click in the leftmost color stop to select it.

⑰ Click in the Color thumbnail to open the Color Picker.

● The Color Picker appears.

⑱ Select the darkest of the four colors you will use.

Note: If the Warning triangle appears, the color is out of gamut for printing and will not print as you see it. Click the small square below the warning triangle to select the closest in gamut or printable color.

⑲ Click OK to close the Color Picker.

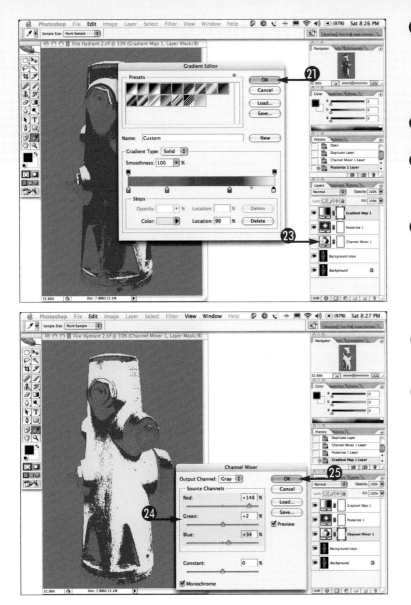

20 Repeat Steps **16** to **19** selecting each of the other three color stops to change the color.

21 Click OK to close the Gradient Editor.

22 Click OK to close the Gradient Map dialog in the open dialog underneath.

23 Double-click the Channel Mixer thumbnail in the Layers palette.

The Channel Mixer dialog appears.

24 Click and drag the Red, Blue, and Green sliders to adjust the areas of color.

25 Click OK.

TIPS

Customize It!
You can adjust the gray areas individually by using the Dodge and Burn tools on the Background copy layer, making some areas lighter and others darker. Click the Dodge or Burn tool and click and drag over light or dark areas to adjust them. You can lower the Exposure setting in the Options bar to lessen the change.

More Options!
Instead of using a Gradient Map, you can merge the Background copy with the Channel Mixer layer and the Posterize Adjustment layers. Then add colors individually to gray areas. Select the first gray area using the Magic Wand with a Tolerance of 0. Click the foreground color and select a new color. Press Option-Delete (Alt+Backspace) to fill the selection.

CREATE AN ARTIST'S SKETCH
from a photograph

You can easily transform a photograph into a simple artist's sketch by applying the Filter Gallery on two separate layers and changing the layer modes. Start by reducing the image size. A 1- 2-megapixel image works well. The color of your sketch is determined by the foreground color in the Photoshop toolbar. In other words, if you want your final sketch to look like a charcoal sketch, set black as the foreground color. To give the illusion of a sketch done with reddish-brown Conte crayons, select a reddish-brown

foreground color in the toolbar before starting. As with every project in Photoshop, there are multiple ways you can achieve a similar effect. The sketch method works best when there is one main subject against a plain background. Each type of photo also gives you a slightly different effect.

This technique works well on low-resolution images and is a great way to use either small photos or ones that are not sharp enough to produce good photo prints.

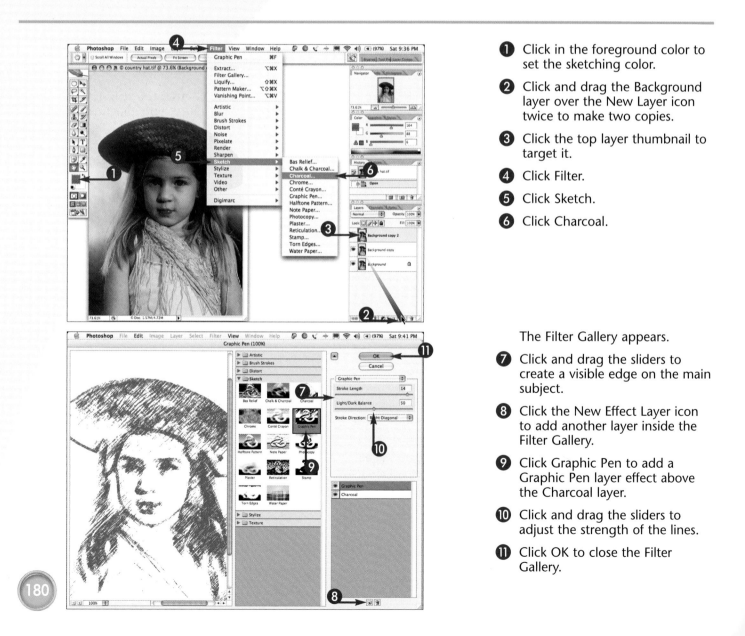

① Click in the foreground color to set the sketching color.

② Click and drag the Background layer over the New Layer icon twice to make two copies.

③ Click the top layer thumbnail to target it.

④ Click Filter.

⑤ Click Sketch.

⑥ Click Charcoal.

The Filter Gallery appears.

⑦ Click and drag the sliders to create a visible edge on the main subject.

⑧ Click the New Effect Layer icon to add another layer inside the Filter Gallery.

⑨ Click Graphic Pen to add a Graphic Pen layer effect above the Charcoal layer.

⑩ Click and drag the sliders to adjust the strength of the lines.

⑪ Click OK to close the Filter Gallery.

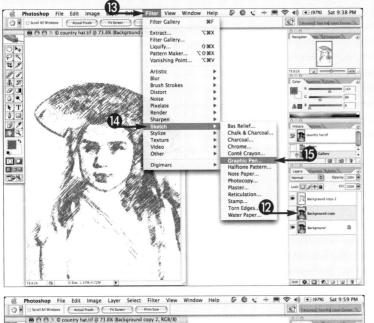

⑫ Click the middle copy to target it.

⑬ Click Filter.

⑭ Click Sketch.

⑮ Click Graphic Pen.

When the Filter Gallery appears, make no changes.

⑯ Click OK to close the Filter Gallery.

⑰ Click the top layer in the Layers palette to target it.

⑱ Click the Layer Blend mode up-down arrow and click Screen.

⑲ Click the Opacity expand arrow and move the slider to lower the opacity to about 60 percent or until the image looks like a pencil sketch.

TIPS

Customize it!

You can turn a color photo into a colored pencil sketch. Set the foreground color to black. Apply the filters and change the layer mode for both Background copies to Screen. The original colors appear as colored pencil lines.

More Options!

You can add many different layers and effects in the Filter Gallery dialog box in any combination. The sliders and other choices available for each individual filter change the look of each layer as well as the combination of layers.

Compose a
PHOTO COLLAGE

Artists and photographers have long been blending separate images into one combined finished piece. Artists might glue disparate items onto a background, hence the word collage from the French for gluing. Photographers might combine exposures on one piece of film or combine several images in the darkroom in a photo montage, a word taken from the French for mounting or assembling. Photoshop adds many new and easier techniques for creating such artistic composites. Instead of worrying about image registrations or unexpected interactions of shapes

and forms, you can now visually combine multiple images into one by blending pixels. Starting with a basic Photoshop collage technique, you can apply so many variations that the piece can be used for everything from advertising to fine art.

You start with one image as the background and drag other photographs and artwork onto it in separate layers. You resize and adjust the position of each layer and add masks to blend images together. Add gradients and paint on the masks, or even add masks to masks for more variations.

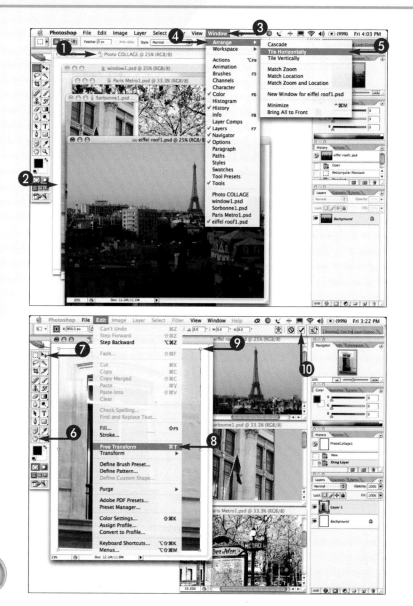

① Create a new blank document the size of your desired collage.

② Open all the images for the collage.

③ Click Window.

④ Click Arrange.

⑤ Click Tile Horizontally or Tile Vertically depending on the size of your monitor to see all the open images at once.

The images are tiled across the screen.

⑥ Click the Blank new document and double-click the Hand tool to make it fit the screen.

⑦ Click the Move tool, drag the first image onto the collage, and then close the first image.

⑧ Click Edit ➪ Free Transform to bring up the transformation anchors.

⑨ Click and drag on the corner anchors to size the image.

⑩ Click the Commit button in the Options bar.

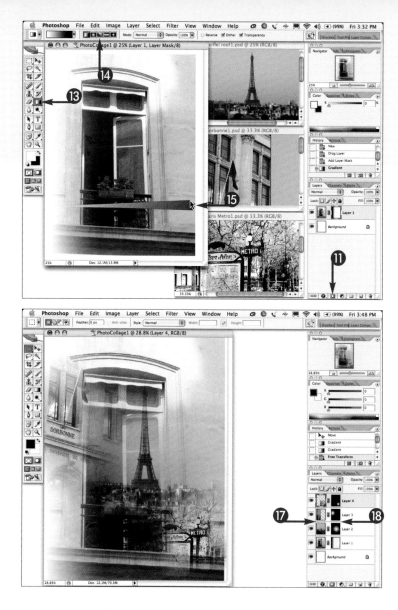

DIFFICULTY LEVEL

⓫ Click the Layer Mask icon in the Layers palette to add a mask to the layer.

⓬ Press D to reset the foreground and background colors.

⓭ Click the Gradient tool.

⓮ Click one of the gradient styles in the Options bar.

⓯ Click and drag the Gradient tool across the image to blend it with the background.

⓰ Repeat Steps **7** to **15** until all the images are layers in the collage.

⓱ Click each layer to adjust the placement of the image.

⓲ Click the layer mask thumbnail and then click and drag a different gradient to change the look.

TIPS

Important!

Make sure all your photos for the collage are set to the same color space or convert them to Adobe RGB as you place them. Also check the bit depth and resolution of the images and change these as needed.

Did You Know?

You can organize your layers into groups by clicking the New Group icon in the Layers palette and dragging layers into the group. You can add masks and other attributes to multiple layers simultaneously by adding these to the group.

Caution!

The number of additional layers, effects, and layer sets you can add to an image is limited by your computer's memory. Close any unnecessary files and applications, making as much RAM available as possible for Photoshop to process the collage.

Turn a photo into a
HAND-PAINTED OIL PAINTING

You can use the Filter Gallery and various Photoshop filters to turn any photograph into an image that has a painterly look. However, filters are applied evenly to the active layer of an image and therefore do not appear hand painted. By applying a filter to a layer and then using brush strokes of varied size to paint the filtered image onto a new layer, you can create an oil painting that appears to be painted one stroke at a time. After applying an Artistic filter, you select the total image and define a pattern. Then select

the Pattern Stamp tool with the Impressionist option as your paintbrush and the image as the pattern, and brush the image on a new blank layer. You should always start with a large brush and paint in more open areas of the photograph. Reduce the brush size and continue painting in the details. To emphasize a few edges and capture some finer detail, continue to paint with the Pattern Stamp tool, deselecting the Impressionist option.

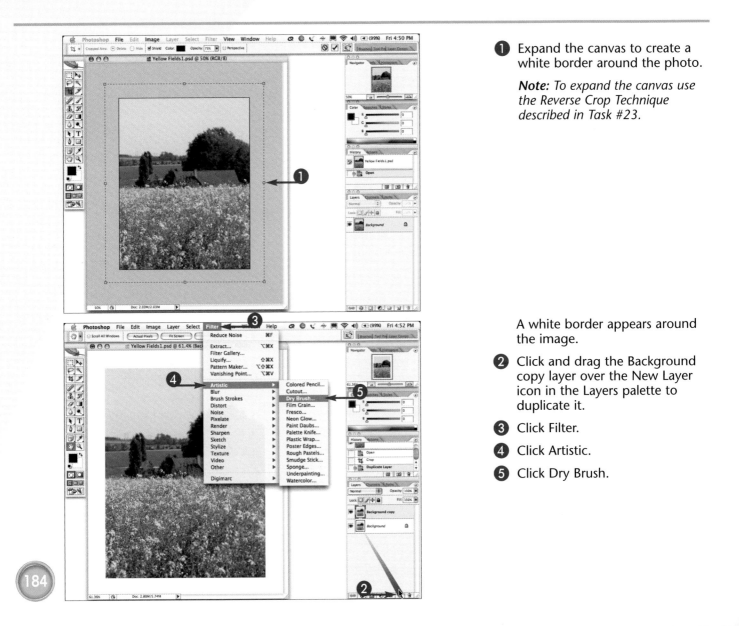

① Expand the canvas to create a white border around the photo.

Note: *To expand the canvas use the Reverse Crop Technique described in Task #23.*

A white border appears around the image.

② Click and drag the Background copy layer over the New Layer icon in the Layers palette to duplicate it.

③ Click Filter.

④ Click Artistic.

⑤ Click Dry Brush.

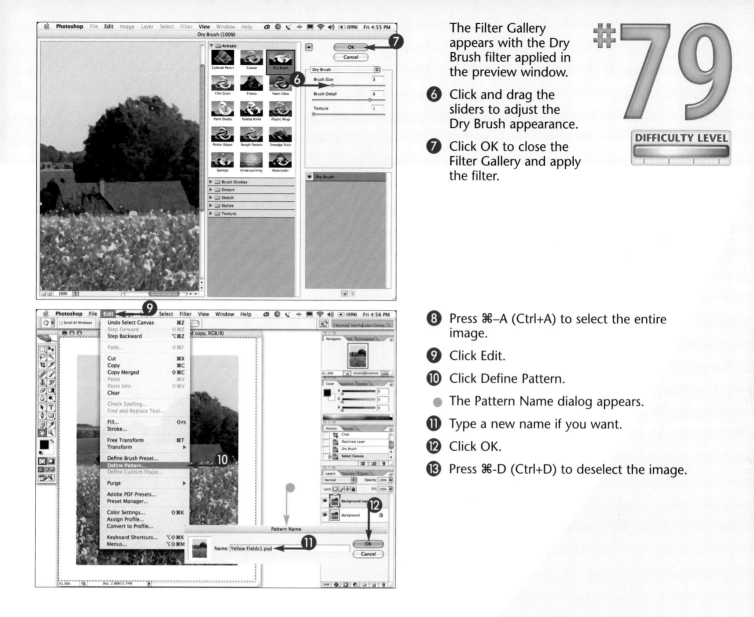

The Filter Gallery appears with the Dry Brush filter applied in the preview window.

6 Click and drag the sliders to adjust the Dry Brush appearance.

7 Click OK to close the Filter Gallery and apply the filter.

8 Press ⌘–A (Ctrl+A) to select the entire image.

9 Click Edit.

10 Click Define Pattern.

● The Pattern Name dialog appears.

11 Type a new name if you want.

12 Click OK.

13 Press ⌘-D (Ctrl+D) to deselect the image.

TIPS

Caution!
Take your time to make the image appear hand painted. Change the brush size often. Start with large brushes and make them smaller as you paint in details, deselecting the impressionist option to emphasize the finest details.

More Options!
If you have a Wacom digitizing tablet, you can choose a larger brush and set the Shape Dynamics of the brush to Pen Pressure. Press lightly with the Stylus to produce small strokes and press harder to produce larger strokes.

Attention!
When you first start painting with a large brush and the Impressionist option selected, click the brush rather than dragging it like a true paintbrush. The effect appears more natural by spreading the paint unevenly.

Turn a photo into a
HAND-PAINTED OIL PAINTING

You can completely cover the layer to create a separate painting or use the newly painted layer in combination with the underlying Dry Brush filtered layer, depending on the look you want. Turn the Visibility icon for the Background layers off and on as you work so you can see the image you are painting.

If you decide to use the top painted layer alone when you have finished painting, you can add a canvas-colored layer as a background to fill in around the edges for a realistic look. Click the New Layer icon in the Layers palette. Drag the new blank layer

underneath the top painted layer. Click Edit and then Fill. Click the Use up-down arrow and click Color. When the Color Picker appears, select a color for the canvas, such as Red 248, Green 242, and Blue 224. Click OK to close the Color Picker. Click OK again to close the Fill dialog and fill the layer.

Duplicate the top painted layer and apply the Texturizer filter with a canvas texture as a final touch. Before applying the Texturizer filter, click the Layers palette arrow and select Merge Down to merge the top painted layer with the colored fill layer.

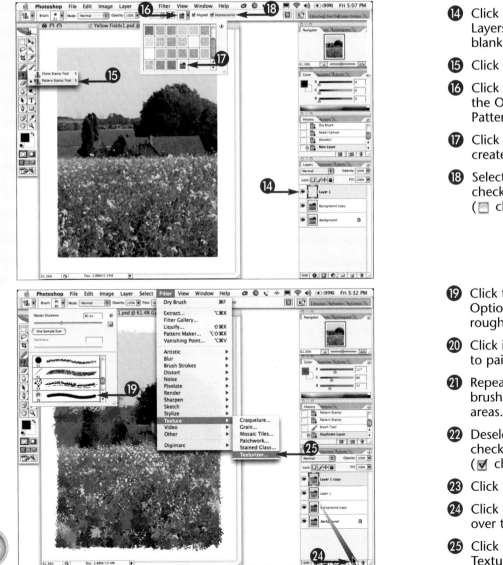

⑭ Click the New Layer icon in the Layers palette to add a new blank layer.

⑮ Click the Pattern Stamp Tool.

⑯ Click the Pattern thumbnail in the Options bar to open the Pattern Picker.

⑰ Click the pattern you just created of the image.

⑱ Select the Impressionist check box in the Options bar (☐ changes to ☑).

⑲ Click the Brush thumbnail in the Options bar and click a large rough-edged brush.

⑳ Click in the layer multiple times to paint the image.

㉑ Repeat Step **19**, reducing the brush size to paint more detailed areas.

㉒ Deselect the Impressionist check box in the Options bar (☑ changes to ☐).

㉓ Click to paint some final details.

㉔ Click and drag the painted layer over the New Layer icon.

㉕ Click Filter ➪ Texture ➪ Texturizer.

The Filter Gallery Texturizer dialog appears.

㉖ Click the Texture up-down arrow and click Canvas.

㉗ Increase the scaling if necessary to make the texture fit the image.

㉘ Click OK to close the Filter Gallery and Texturizer dialog.

● The Canvas texture is applied to the finished painting.

TIP

Try This!

Click the Pattern Stamp tool and click the Brush thumbnail in the Options bar opening the Brush Picker presets. Click the Brush Picker presets down-arrow and select Large List to view the brushes by name. Click the pull-down menu again and click Wet Media Brushes. When the dialog appears, click Append to add the brushes to the current set. Click the brush called Dry Brush on Towel. Open the Brush Presets by clicking on the Brushes palette tab. Click Brush Tip Shape. Click the circular shape and move the dots to change the shape into an oval. Click and drag on the arrow in the circle to change the direction to fit your brush stroke style. Paint using your custom brush.

Paint a
DIGITAL WATERCOLOR

You can create a digital watercolor from a photograph and make it appear like a traditionally painted image on watercolor paper. Traditional watercolor paintings have transparent colors and loosely defined shapes with the surface of the paper often showing through the paint to give the image more personality. You start by duplicating the Background layer and applying a Photoshop filter from the Filter Gallery to the Background copy. Duplicate the Background copy and apply a blur to soften the edges and blend the colors. Add a blank

layer over the other layers, fill it with white, and use it as a background to paint through. Using the eraser and one of the chalk-styled brushes, erase through the white layer to reveal as much of the filtered layer below as you want. When your painting looks good, merge the two top layers and duplicate the merged copy. Then apply a texture filter to create the watercolor paper look. The final step is to lighten the image by setting the layer blend mode to Screen and brighten the watercolor paints.

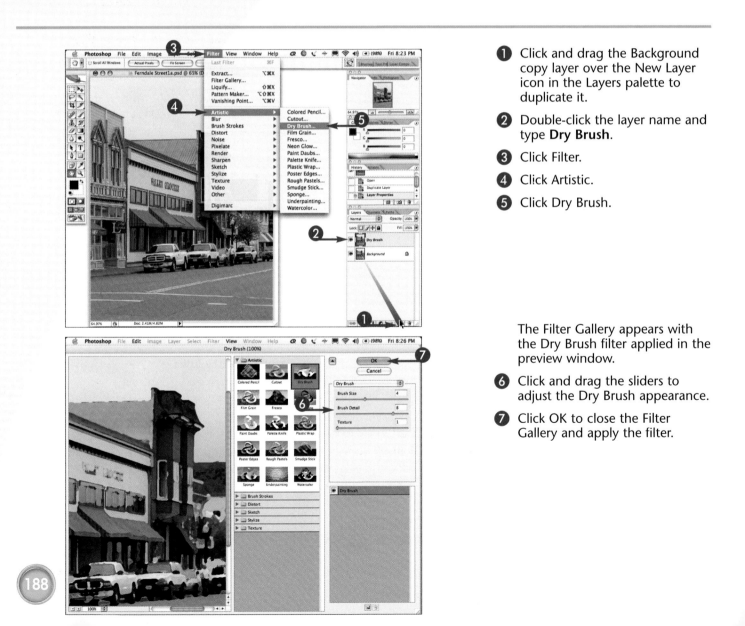

① Click and drag the Background copy layer over the New Layer icon in the Layers palette to duplicate it.

② Double-click the layer name and type **Dry Brush**.

③ Click Filter.

④ Click Artistic.

⑤ Click Dry Brush.

The Filter Gallery appears with the Dry Brush filter applied in the preview window.

⑥ Click and drag the sliders to adjust the Dry Brush appearance.

⑦ Click OK to close the Filter Gallery and apply the filter.

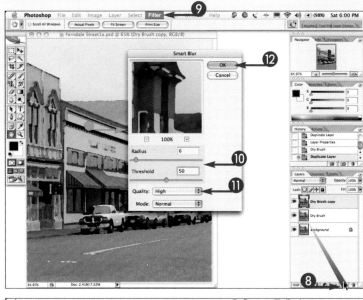

8 Click and drag the Dry Brush layer over the New Layer icon to duplicate it.

9 Click Filter ⇨ Blur ⇨ Smart Blur.

● The Smart Blur dialog appears.

10 Click and drag the Radius slider to 6 and the Threshold slider to 50.

11 Click the Quality up-down arrow and select High. Leave Mode set at Normal.

12 Click OK to close the dialog and apply the filter.

13 Click the New Layer icon in the Layers palette.

14 Click the Opacity expand arrow and lower the slider to 50 percent.

15 Press D to reset the default foreground and background colors.

16 Press ⌘-Delete (Ctrl+Backspace) to fill the layer with white.

TIPS

Try This!

You can make the paper look more like watercolor paper by using an off-white color to fill the top layer. After creating a new blank layer in Step **13**, click Edit ⇨ Fill. The Fill dialog opens. Click the Use up-down arrow and click Color to make the Color Picker appear. Type **250** for the Red data field, **246** for the Green data field, and **239** for the Blue data field to select a color for the watercolor paper. Click OK to close the Color Picker and click OK again to close the Fill dialog. Erase carefully over just the objects you want to show as painted on the image. Areas left blank show through as the watercolor paper.

Paint a DIGITAL WATERCOLOR

Photoshop actually includes a Watercolor filter in the Filter Gallery. This filter generally adds too much black to replicate a traditional watercolor. A true watercolor palette includes only a gray and no black paint at all.

Because watercolors not only have soft edges but also minimal transitions of color tones, you get the best results by applying the Reduce Noise or the Median filter to the photo before starting to create the painting. These filters are found in the Filter menus under Noise. By applying a filter first, you

eliminate some of the color changes and sharp edges that make a photograph look like a photograph. With a limited color palette, the Dry Brush filter creates a more-painterly image. Then using the Smart Blur filter after the Dry Brush has been applied blends the paints to complete the effect.

Traditional watercolor paintings often leave rough edges around the borders and even some blank areas in the painting, so do not completely paint away all the white in the top layer.

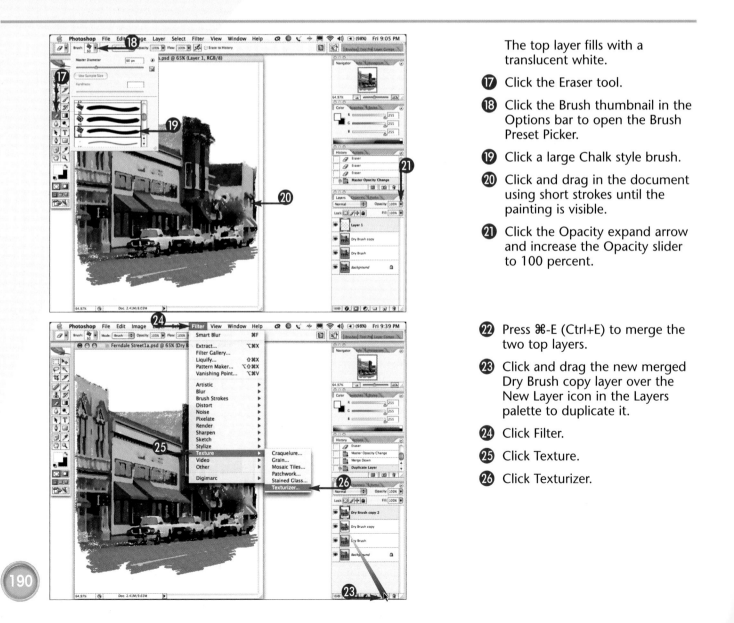

The top layer fills with a translucent white.

⑰ Click the Eraser tool.

⑱ Click the Brush thumbnail in the Options bar to open the Brush Preset Picker.

⑲ Click a large Chalk style brush.

⑳ Click and drag in the document using short strokes until the painting is visible.

㉑ Click the Opacity expand arrow and increase the Opacity slider to 100 percent.

㉒ Press ⌘-E (Ctrl+E) to merge the two top layers.

㉓ Click and drag the new merged Dry Brush copy layer over the New Layer icon in the Layers palette to duplicate it.

㉔ Click Filter.

㉕ Click Texture.

㉖ Click Texturizer.

The Filter Gallery appears with the Texturizer filter.

㉗ Click the Texture up-down arrow and click Sandstone.

㉘ Click and drag the Scaling and Relief sliders to look like rough watercolor paper.

㉙ Click OK to close the Filter Gallery dialog.

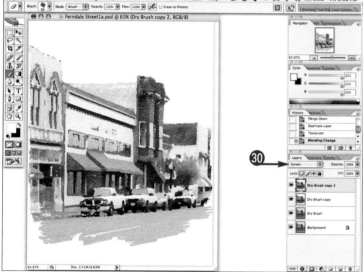

The filter is applied to the top layer.

㉚ Click the Layer Blend mode up-down arrow on the Layers palette and click Screen to lighten the painting like a traditional watercolor.

TIPS

Did You Know?

The paint strokes appear more realistic if you click and drag in the document using short strokes in the same direction as the objects in the image. Paint vertical objects with vertical strokes and horizontal items with horizontal strokes.

Change It!

With the Eraser tool selected, click the Brushes tab to open the Brushes palette. Click the word Texture in the Brush Presets to highlight it. Make changes to the scale, depth, or pattern to add texture to your brush.

Important!

Photoshop's Artistic filters are applied at a fixed size and work best on files smaller than 5MB. Always view your photo at 100 percent to see the effect, and wait for the effect to process when changing adjustment sliders.

Giving Your Images a Professional Presentation

Presentation is so important that even an average photo can appear good when properly displayed or framed. For professional designers, a powerful presentation can help keep an art director happy. For photographers, an elegant display can make all the difference in keeping a client or securing a new one. From the family snapshots to your portfolio, Photoshop makes it easy to show your images in a professional manner.

You can add frames to enhance any image with minimal effort using the one-click frame actions included with Photoshop. You can also create your own frames, change the frame colors and borders, and add a visual matte to the photo. You can create a traditional contact sheet of all the photos in one client folder or on one CD. Using Photoshop's PDF Presentation command, you can easily prepare a custom slide show with professional transitions, save it as a PDF document, and send it to friends or clients as an e-mail attachment. You can create custom backgrounds to display your images or for a novel effect, place your images into a traditional slide template. Photoshop can help you apply an artistic edge to a photo using a sequence of filters from the Filter Gallery, or you can brush an artistic edge onto any images by hand using the Brush tool. You can even use the Picture Package feature to prepare a design layout using different photos for each page. With Photoshop, you can display all your images with a professional touch.

Top 100

Add traditional
PHOTO CORNERS WITH ONE CLICK

You can add interest and give a finished look to your photographs by adding photo corners to your digital images. You can add these corners easily and quickly using an Action from the Actions palette in Photoshop. An Action is a prerecorded set of commands that are automatically performed in the same sequence when you click the Play icon.

Photoshop allows you to record your own actions and provides a number of predefined actions that are installed with the application. When you first open

Photoshop and click the Actions palette tab, you find a folder of Default Actions. Click the Actions palette expand arrow to reveal seven other Actions folders. Click the Frames name to load the Frames actions and click the down-arrow next to the Frames folder to see all the actions in the set. Click the name of the type of photo frame style you want to apply and click the Play icon.

Actions are stored as ATN files in the Photoshop Actions folder in the Presets folder.

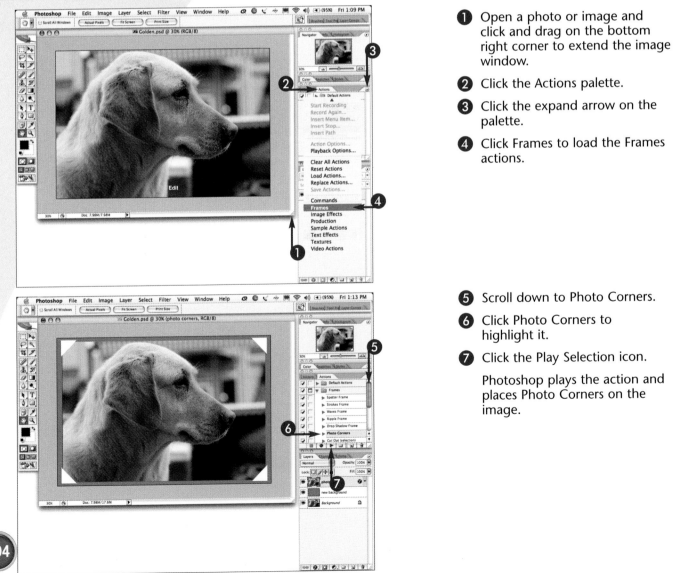

① Open a photo or image and click and drag on the bottom right corner to extend the image window.

② Click the Actions palette.

③ Click the expand arrow on the palette.

④ Click Frames to load the Frames actions.

⑤ Scroll down to Photo Corners.

⑥ Click Photo Corners to highlight it.

⑦ Click the Play Selection icon.

Photoshop plays the action and places Photo Corners on the image.

Make the
FRAME FROM A
PHOTOGRAPH

Rather than cropping the photo, you can transform the excess background into a frame for the central focus of the image. Making a frame from the photograph itself is a quick way to give a finished look to any image. Select the area of the photo you would otherwise crop using the Rectangular Marquee tool, then inverse the selection to create the frame. You can also vary the frame shape by using the Elliptical Marquee tool to create an oval frame. Jump

the selected area to its own layer above the Background and change the blend mode to Screen to lighten it. To separate the frame from the photo even more, stroke the borders of the new frame layer using the Layer Style dialog. The default Stroke color is red; however, you can change it to any color that fits your image. As a final touch, add a Drop Shadow and an Inner Shadow, and even a Bevel and Emboss look.

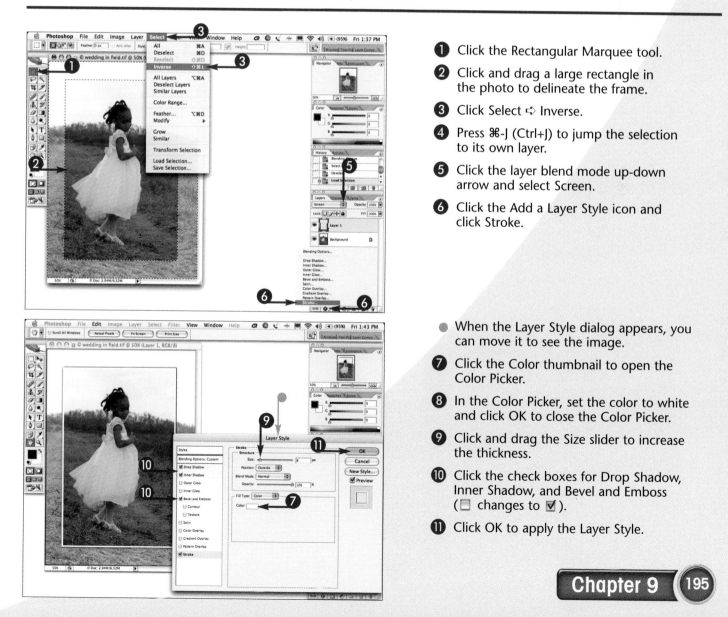

① Click the Rectangular Marquee tool.

② Click and drag a large rectangle in the photo to delineate the frame.

③ Click Select ➪ Inverse.

④ Press ⌘-J (Ctrl+J) to jump the selection to its own layer.

⑤ Click the layer blend mode up-down arrow and select Screen.

⑥ Click the Add a Layer Style icon and click Stroke.

● When the Layer Style dialog appears, you can move it to see the image.

⑦ Click the Color thumbnail to open the Color Picker.

⑧ In the Color Picker, set the color to white and click OK to close the Color Picker.

⑨ Click and drag the Size slider to increase the thickness.

⑩ Click the check boxes for Drop Shadow, Inner Shadow, and Bevel and Emboss (☐ changes to ☑).

⑪ Click OK to apply the Layer Style.

MAKE A CONTACT SHEET
of your photos

Your digital files are like digital negatives. Whether these are photos from a digital camera or scans of traditional prints and negatives, the first file downloaded or scanned is the original. You should always burn a CD of the originals before you enhance them or use them in projects. Then use the Contact Sheet II feature under Photoshop's Automate command to make a contact sheet to help you identify the images on the CD or other storage device. You can also make an index of all the images in one project folder using the same command.

From the Contact Sheet II dialog, select the location and the images to be included. You set the size of the document, the number of rows and columns, and the font and font size for the captions. The size of the thumbnails is determined by the number of rows and columns. Fewer columns and rows on a page allows for larger thumbnail images. Print the contact sheet on a color printer as a visual index to show a client or for your own reference.

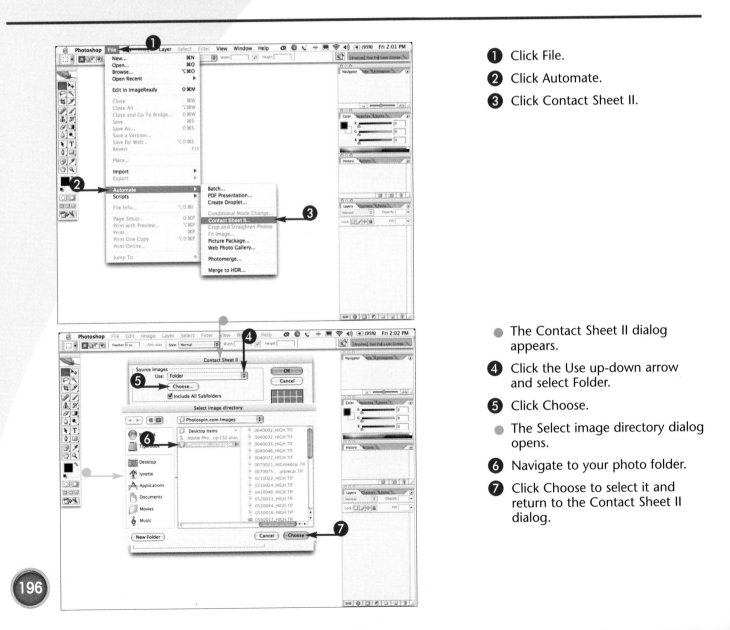

① Click File.

② Click Automate.

③ Click Contact Sheet II.

● The Contact Sheet II dialog appears.

④ Click the Use up-down arrow and select Folder.

⑤ Click Choose.

● The Select image directory dialog opens.

⑥ Navigate to your photo folder.

⑦ Click Choose to select it and return to the Contact Sheet II dialog.

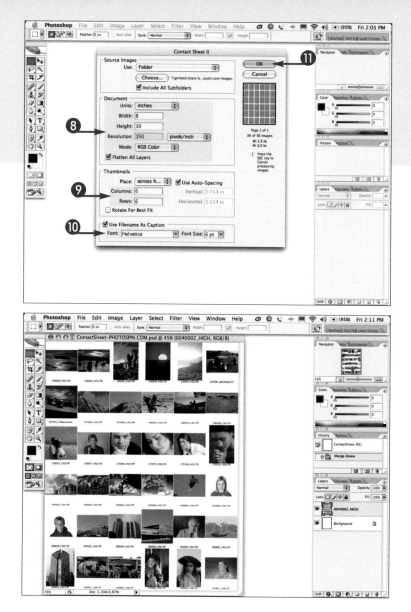

⑧ Type the settings for your desired printed contact sheet.

⑨ Type a number for the Columns and Rows of thumbnails to be printed.

⑩ Click the Font and Font Size down-arrows and select the font and size for the printed file name.

⑪ Click OK.

Photoshop builds the contact sheet.

TIPS

Caution!
By selecting Flatten All Layers the command flattens the individual photo layers into one so it prints more quickly. If you deselect the box, Photoshop creates a large, multilayered document that requires large amounts of RAM.

Did You Know?
A resolution of 150 dpi is sufficient because the thumbnails are so small the higher resolution would not be a visible improvement. In addition, the Contact Sheet II command runs much faster with low-resolution images.

More Options!
To make a contact sheet for a CD jewel case, type **4.5** inches for both the Width and Height. Type **5** in each data field for the number of rows and columns. Select 6-point type to fit the text under the thumbnail.

Create a
PDF SLIDE SHOW PRESENTATION

If you want to e-mail photos to friends or your portfolio to a prospective employer, or send a client some images for review, you can use Photoshop to help you create a slide show and save it as a PDF presentation ready to be attached to an e-mail or burned to a CD. The PDF Presentation command in Photoshop allows you to combine any type of images into either a multipage document or a slide show presentation. You determine the image quality depending on where it will be shown and set a level

of security so that the recipient cannot reproduce your images without your permission. You can even select from a number of slide transitions to give your presentation a professional look. You can select a complete folder to use as the source images, or use images that are already open. You select the amount of time each slide appears on-screen and decide if the slide show should stop after the last image or continue in a loop. Click Save, and Photoshop does all the work for you.

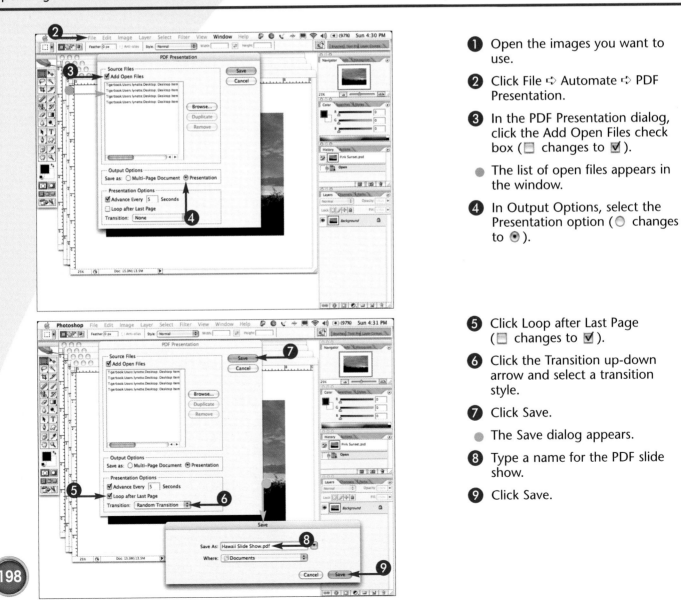

① Open the images you want to use.

② Click File ➪ Automate ➪ PDF Presentation.

③ In the PDF Presentation dialog, click the Add Open Files check box (☐ changes to ☑).

● The list of open files appears in the window.

④ In Output Options, select the Presentation option (○ changes to ◉).

⑤ Click Loop after Last Page (☐ changes to ☑).

⑥ Click the Transition up-down arrow and select a transition style.

⑦ Click Save.

● The Save dialog appears.

⑧ Type a name for the PDF slide show.

⑨ Click Save.

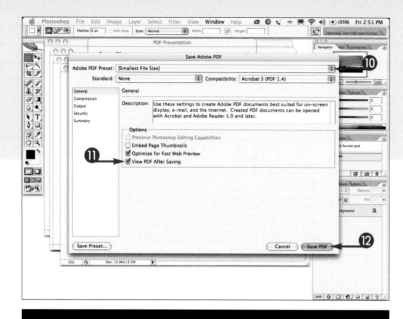

The Save Adobe PDF dialog appears.

⑩ Click the Adobe PDF Preset up-down arrow and select Smallest File Size.

⑪ Click the View PDF After Saving check box (☐ changes to ☑).

⑫ Click Save PDF.

Photoshop creates the PDF file, and launches Acrobat or Adobe Reader.

The PDF slide show begins.

You can press Esc to end the slide show.

TIPS

Customize It!
Change the transitions from Random Transition to one transition style. You can also change how many seconds each image appears on the screen by typing a different number of seconds in the data field in the Presentation Options. If you do not want the presentation to repeat in a continuous loop, deselect the Loop after Last Page check box (☑ changes to ☐).

Attention!
To protect the images from being reproduced without permission, click the Security category in the Save Adobe PDF dialog. In the Permissions section, select the Use a password check box (☐ changes to ☑). Type the password in the data field. Set the Printing Allowed and Changes Allowed selections to None. Click Save PDF and confirm the password in the dialog that appears.

Give a photo an
ARTISTIC EDGE

You can give any photo a more artistic look by adding an irregular edge using the Filter Gallery and the Brush Strokes filters. The Filter Gallery allows you to add multiple Effect Layers to combine the filters in different ways. After duplicating the Background layer, you add a new blank layer filled with white and place it below the Background copy. Using the Rectangular Marquee tool on the Background copy layer, you make a selection just inside the edge of the photo and then add a Layer

Mask to delineate the borders of the photo. The artistic edge starts from the selected area. Open the Filter Gallery and start adding different layers of Brush Stroke filters. The preview window of the Filter Gallery shows the edge effect in reverse. The white areas represent the photo area and the black areas represent what will be cut away. Every time you change the various sliders for the Brush Stroke filters, your edge effect changes in the preview window of the Filter Gallery.

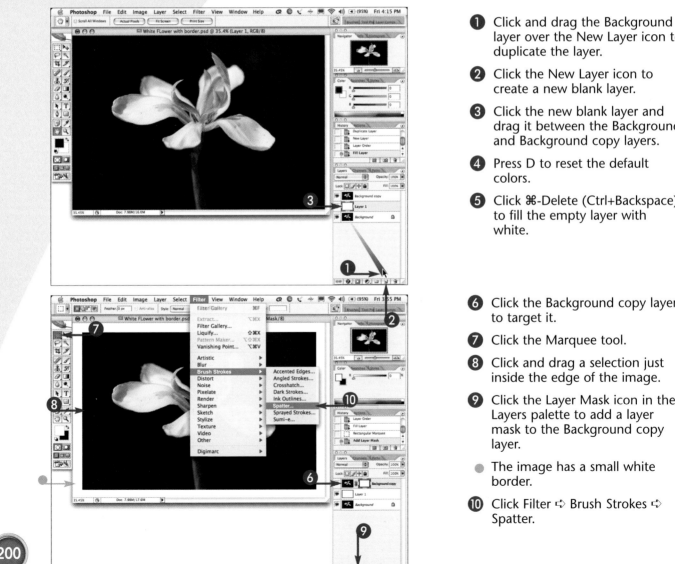

1. Click and drag the Background layer over the New Layer icon to duplicate the layer.

2. Click the New Layer icon to create a new blank layer.

3. Click the new blank layer and drag it between the Background and Background copy layers.

4. Press D to reset the default colors.

5. Click ⌘-Delete (Ctrl+Backspace) to fill the empty layer with white.

6. Click the Background copy layer to target it.

7. Click the Marquee tool.

8. Click and drag a selection just inside the edge of the image.

9. Click the Layer Mask icon in the Layers palette to add a layer mask to the Background copy layer.

● The image has a small white border.

10. Click Filter ➪ Brush Strokes ➪ Spatter.

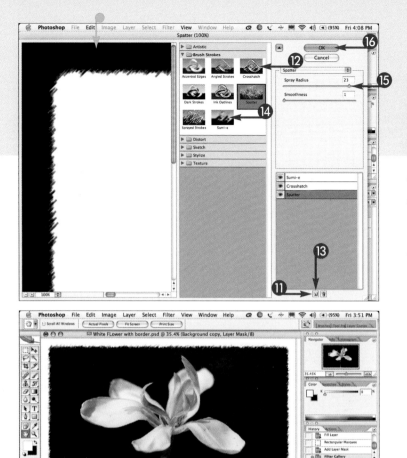

The Filter Gallery opens with the Spatter edge applied.

⑪ Click the New Effect Layer icon.

⑫ Click Crosshatch.

⑬ Click the New Effect icon again.

⑭ Click Sumi-e.

⑮ Click each Effect layer and adjust the sliders to get the desired edge.

⑯ Click OK to close the Filter Gallery and apply the edge.

The custom edge is applied to the photo.

TIPS

Did You Know?
Add as many Filter Effects layers as your computer's memory allows. Each one you add changes the style of the effect. Change the order of the layers in the Filter Gallery dialog and the overall effect changes, also.

More Options!
Darken the edge for a light image. Click the Layer Style icon in the Layers palette. Click Drop Shadow. Drag the Distance slider to 0. To darken it more, click Inner Shadow also and drag its Distance slider to 0.

Try This!
Click the Layer Style icon in the Layers palette. Click Stroke. Click the Color thumbnail and change the default color to black. Click the Position up-down arrow and click Inside. Move the Size slider to get the desired thickness of line.

Create a
CUSTOM SLIDE TEMPLATE

You can create a template that looks like a traditional photographic slide mount and use it to feature your photos when you print them or even use the photos mounted as slides in a PDF slide show. After you create the custom slide template, you can use it repeatedly with any image.

You can create a slide with any color or use a gray or off-white color similar to a traditional slide mount. Use the Rounded Rectangle tool to create the basic shape

and the Rectangular Marquee tool to cut out the photo viewing area. Apply a Drop Shadow from the Layer Styles dialog to give the illusion of a traditional slide mount. Save the template with both a white Background layer and the slide layer so you can sandwich an image between them for the final slide.

You can add text to the slide, fading it back so the text looks authentic, and make a slide template for each of your clients for a unique presentation.

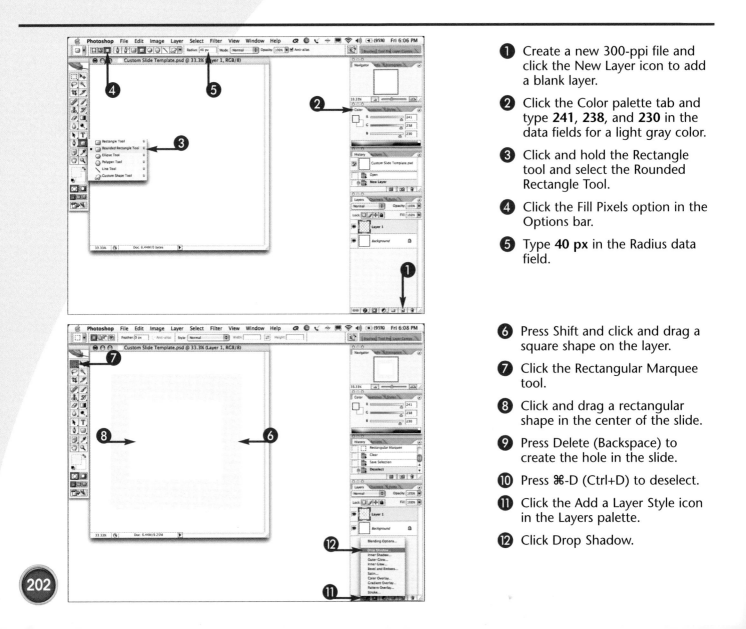

① Create a new 300-ppi file and click the New Layer icon to add a blank layer.

② Click the Color palette tab and type **241, 238,** and **230** in the data fields for a light gray color.

③ Click and hold the Rectangle tool and select the Rounded Rectangle Tool.

④ Click the Fill Pixels option in the Options bar.

⑤ Type **40 px** in the Radius data field.

⑥ Press Shift and click and drag a square shape on the layer.

⑦ Click the Rectangular Marquee tool.

⑧ Click and drag a rectangular shape in the center of the slide.

⑨ Press Delete (Backspace) to create the hole in the slide.

⑩ Press ⌘-D (Ctrl+D) to deselect.

⑪ Click the Add a Layer Style icon in the Layers palette.

⑫ Click Drop Shadow.

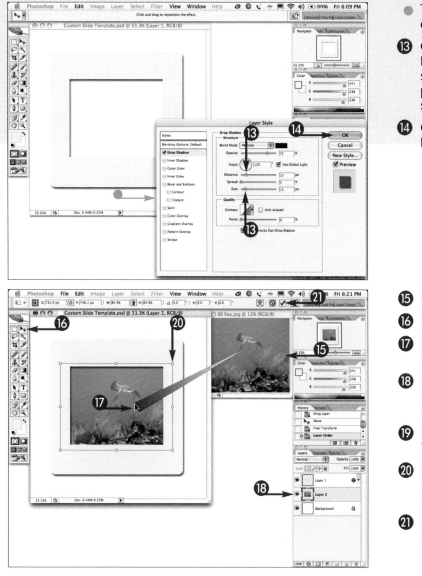

● The Layer Style dialog appears.

⑬ Click and drag the Distance and Size sliders to about 15 percent to give the slide depth.

⑭ Click OK to close the Layer Style dialog.

⑮ Open a photo.

⑯ Click the Move tool.

⑰ Click and drag the image on top of the slide template.

⑱ Click the Photo layer in the Layers palette and move it between the other two layers.

⑲ Press ⌘-T (Ctrl+T) to add Transformation anchors.

⑳ Press Shift and click and drag on the corner anchors to fit the image inside the slide.

㉑ Click the Commit button in the Options bar.

TIPS

Try This!
Add text to your slide. Click the Type tool and type the text above and below the opening in the center. Use all caps in a font such as Helvetica (Arial) for a realistic effect. Then lower the Opacity of the Type layer to 50 percent. Press ⌘-E (Ctrl+E) to merge the Type layer with the Slide layer.

Apply It!
To use your slide on multiple photos, drag the first photo on top of the slide file. Drag the photo layer between the slide and the Background layer. Adjust the photo using the Transformation anchors and flatten the layers. Click File ➪ Save As to save the filled slide with a new name. Repeat for each of the photos.

Create a custom
PARCHMENT BACKGROUND

You can scan images and use these as backgrounds for album pages or photo layouts. You can also create any number of different backgrounds starting with a new white document, adding colors or black and applying Photoshop filters and effects. The Clouds filter found under the Render filters is particularly useful for creating backgrounds because it changes the look of the image each time it is applied. You can make a white document look like an old piece of parchment by starting with a gradient

blend of light browns and white. When you apply the Clouds filter to the layer, the gradient changes to light-brown clouds. Add a Sepia brown photo filter and use a layer mask to apply the darker color only to the edges. Then vary the edges using the Liquify filter for an aged parchment look. Save the parchment background as a file and use it as a Background layer for different photographs. Use it as a base for any number of designs or as a background for text.

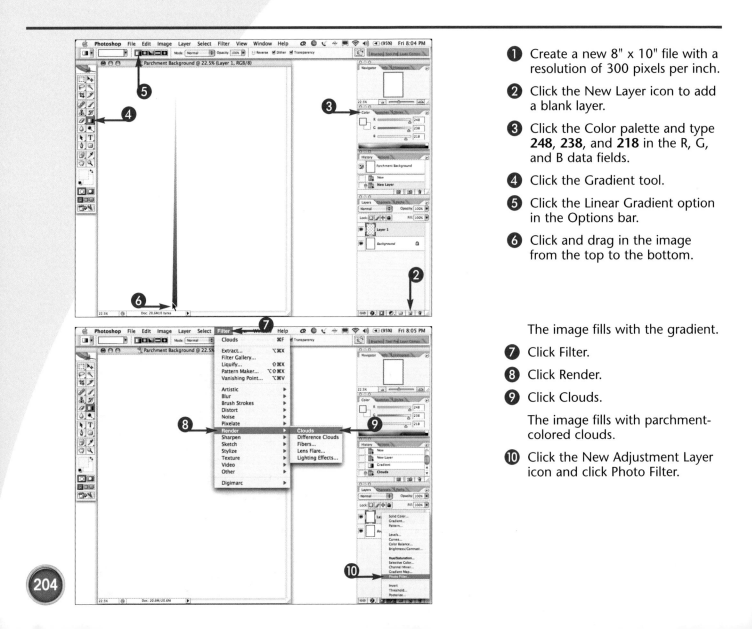

① Create a new 8" x 10" file with a resolution of 300 pixels per inch.

② Click the New Layer icon to add a blank layer.

③ Click the Color palette and type **248**, **238**, and **218** in the R, G, and B data fields.

④ Click the Gradient tool.

⑤ Click the Linear Gradient option in the Options bar.

⑥ Click and drag in the image from the top to the bottom.

The image fills with the gradient.

⑦ Click Filter.

⑧ Click Render.

⑨ Click Clouds.

The image fills with parchment-colored clouds.

⑩ Click the New Adjustment Layer icon and click Photo Filter.

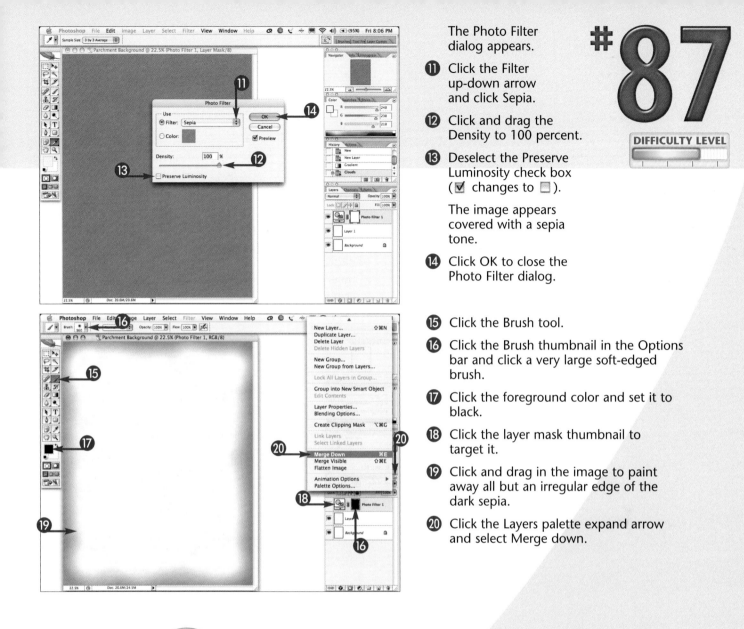

The Photo Filter dialog appears.

⑪ Click the Filter up-down arrow and click Sepia.

⑫ Click and drag the Density to 100 percent.

⑬ Deselect the Preserve Luminosity check box (☑ changes to ☐).

The image appears covered with a sepia tone.

⑭ Click OK to close the Photo Filter dialog.

⑮ Click the Brush tool.

⑯ Click the Brush thumbnail in the Options bar and click a very large soft-edged brush.

⑰ Click the foreground color and set it to black.

⑱ Click the layer mask thumbnail to target it.

⑲ Click and drag in the image to paint away all but an irregular edge of the dark sepia.

⑳ Click the Layers palette expand arrow and select Merge down.

#87

DIFFICULTY LEVEL

More Options!

You can add an irregular edge and make the parchment look old by adding some edge effects with the Liquify filter. Click Filter ➪ Liquify. Use the Forward warp tool and select a very large brush. Click each corner and drag just slightly toward the center. Repeat on several areas around the edges. Click OK to close the Liquify dialog. Then add a drop shadow to give a realistic look to the aged parchment. Click the Layer Style icon in the Layers palette and click Drop Shadow. When the Layer Style dialog opens, click and drag the Distance, Spread, and Size sliders to fit your design. Click OK to close the dialog and apply the Layer Style.

Create your own
CUSTOM EDGE

Custom edges add an artistic look to a photo. You can let a Photoshop filter draw an edge for you or you can create your own custom edge as a personal digital signature, using the Brush tool and any rough-edged brush. The default brush set that installs with Photoshop includes various rough-edged brushes. However, you can find many more in the brush sets listed in the drop-down menu on the Brush Preset Picker. To create a custom edge, you need to cut

the photo out of the Background layer and put it on a separate layer. Then drag over the photo using the Crop tool and extend the anchor points to enlarge the canvas. Click the Background layer in the Layers palette and select a rough-edged brush. Click and drag around the edges of the photo painting black strokes on the Background layer. Make sure the black edges extend underneath the photo and paint as much or as little of a visible edge as you want.

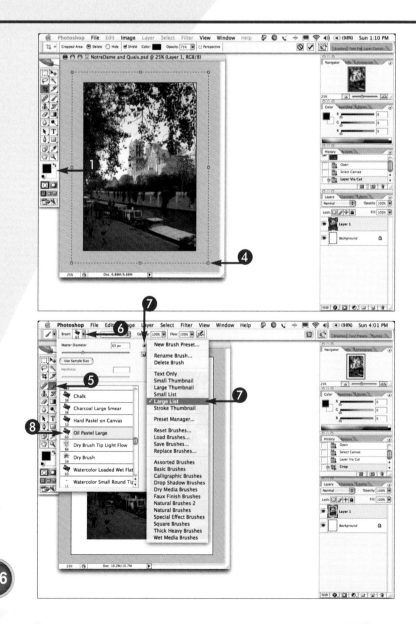

① Press D to reset the foreground and background colors to white and black.

② Press ⌘-A (Ctrl+A) to select the photo.

③ Press ⌘-Shift-J (Ctrl+Shift+J) to jump the image onto its own layer.

④ Click and drag the canvas to create a white border around the photo.

Note: To expand the canvas, use the Reverse Crop Technique described in Task #23.

A white border appears around the photo.

⑤ Click the Brush tool.

⑥ Click the Brush thumbnail in the Options bar to open the Brush Preset Picker.

⑦ Click the Brush Preset Picker expand arrow and select Large List.

⑧ Click a rough-edged brush, such as Oil Pastel Large.

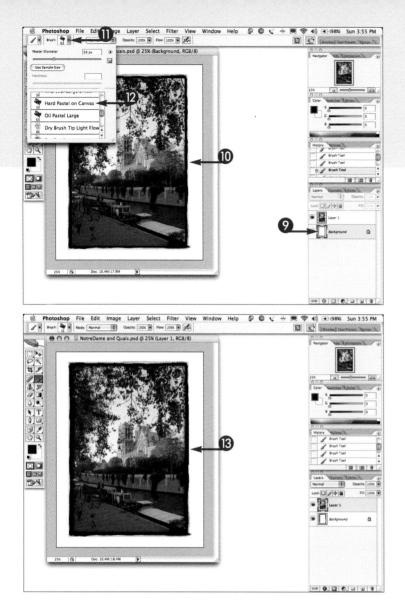

⑨ Click the Background layer to target it.

⑩ Click and drag along the edge of the photo, keeping part of the brush on the photo.

⑪ Click the Brush thumbnail in the Options bar to open the Brush Preset Picker.

⑫ Click another brush, such as Hard Pastel on Canvas.

⑬ Continue painting brush strokes on the Background layer going around the edge of the photo to add variety to the edge.

TIPS

Did You Know?

You can paint with different brush angles for more variety. Click the Brushes tab and click Brush Tip Shape. Click and drag on the Brush Roundness and Angle thumbnail to narrow the circle. Paint the vertical edges of the photo. Click the Brushes tab again and reverse the angle for the brush before painting the horizontal edges.

More Options!

Blend the photo softly into the custom edge. Click the top photo layer. Use the Rectangular Marquee tool to make a selection just inside the outside border of the photo. Click Select ➪ Inverse. Click Select ➪ Feather. Type **10** in the Feather Radius and click OK. Press Delete (Backspace) to soften the edge of the photo.

Make a photo look like a
GALLERY PRINT

You can give your photograph a professional finish by making it look like a gallery print. Gallery prints generally have wide white, black, or even gray borders. The photo is placed in the top portion of the border or frame area, allowing for the name of the gallery, name of the artist, and the name of the artwork to fit under the image in stylized type. You can make a gallery print using either a color or a grayscale photograph. After making a selection of the

photo and jumping it to its own layer, use the Canvas Size command under the Image menu to enlarge the canvas size by 3 inches all around the photo. Then use the Canvas size command again to add another inch below the photograph extending the area for the text. Adding a stroke around the photo and a second stroke just into the extended canvas gives a finished look to the gallery print. The strokes can be the same or different colors and pixel width.

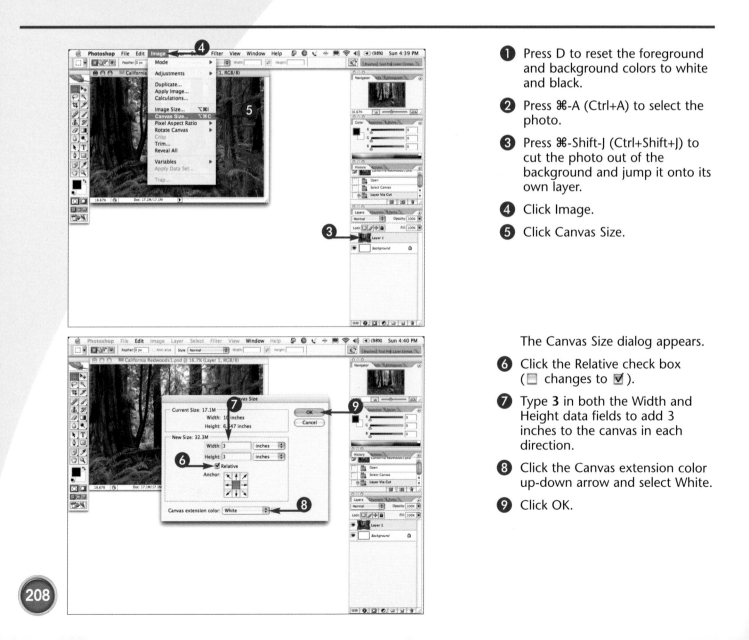

① Press D to reset the foreground and background colors to white and black.

② Press ⌘-A (Ctrl+A) to select the photo.

③ Press ⌘-Shift-J (Ctrl+Shift+J) to cut the photo out of the background and jump it onto its own layer.

④ Click Image.

⑤ Click Canvas Size.

The Canvas Size dialog appears.

⑥ Click the Relative check box (☐ changes to ☑).

⑦ Type **3** in both the Width and Height data fields to add 3 inches to the canvas in each direction.

⑧ Click the Canvas extension color up-down arrow and select White.

⑨ Click OK.

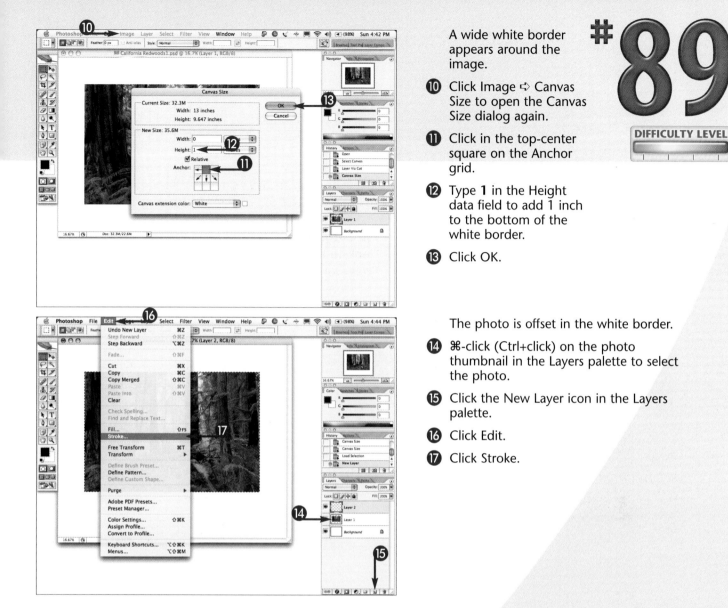

A wide white border appears around the image.

⑩ Click Image ➪ Canvas Size to open the Canvas Size dialog again.

⑪ Click in the top-center square on the Anchor grid.

⑫ Type 1 in the Height data field to add 1 inch to the bottom of the white border.

⑬ Click OK.

The photo is offset in the white border.

⑭ ⌘-click (Ctrl+click) on the photo thumbnail in the Layers palette to select the photo.

⑮ Click the New Layer icon in the Layers palette.

⑯ Click Edit.

⑰ Click Stroke.

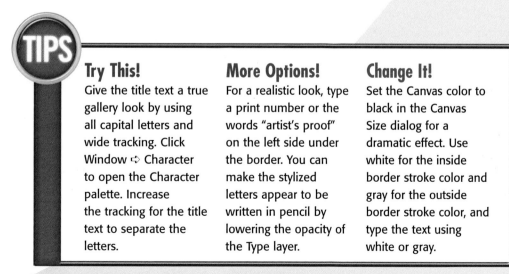

TIPS

Try This!
Give the title text a true gallery look by using all capital letters and wide tracking. Click Window ➪ Character to open the Character palette. Increase the tracking for the title text to separate the letters.

More Options!
For a realistic look, type a print number or the words "artist's proof" on the left side under the border. You can make the stylized letters appear to be written in pencil by lowering the opacity of the Type layer.

Change It!
Set the Canvas color to black in the Canvas Size dialog for a dramatic effect. Use white for the inside border stroke color and gray for the outside border stroke color, and type the text using white or gray.

Make a photo look like a
GALLERY PRINT

By placing the strokes on separate layers, you can adjust the opacity of the stroke to change the look of the gallery print. Select the photo on the layer to target it and add an empty layer. Using the selection and targeting the new layer, add a stroke around the photo to make it stand out. Still using the same selection, transform the selection to make it slightly wider and higher. Then add another empty layer to add another stroke just outside the first one.

Gallery prints often have the name of the gallery set in a serif-styled font in all capital letters. Widen the tracking of the letters to increase the space between the letters to add a realistic look. You can also use this space to type your name, your studio, or even the name of the image. Select a script font to sign your work under the outside stroke, and add a print number to complete the gallery print look.

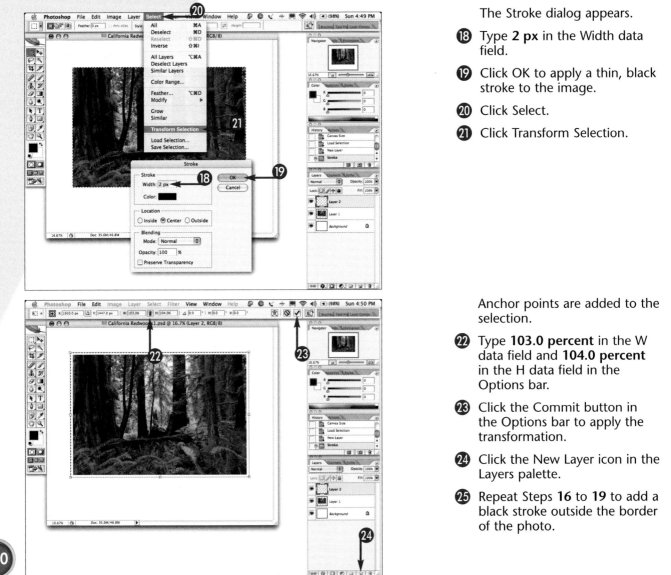

The Stroke dialog appears.

⑱ Type **2 px** in the Width data field.

⑲ Click OK to apply a thin, black stroke to the image.

⑳ Click Select.

㉑ Click Transform Selection.

Anchor points are added to the selection.

㉒ Type **103.0 percent** in the W data field and **104.0 percent** in the H data field in the Options bar.

㉓ Click the Commit button in the Options bar to apply the transformation.

㉔ Click the New Layer icon in the Layers palette.

㉕ Repeat Steps **16** to **19** to add a black stroke outside the border of the photo.

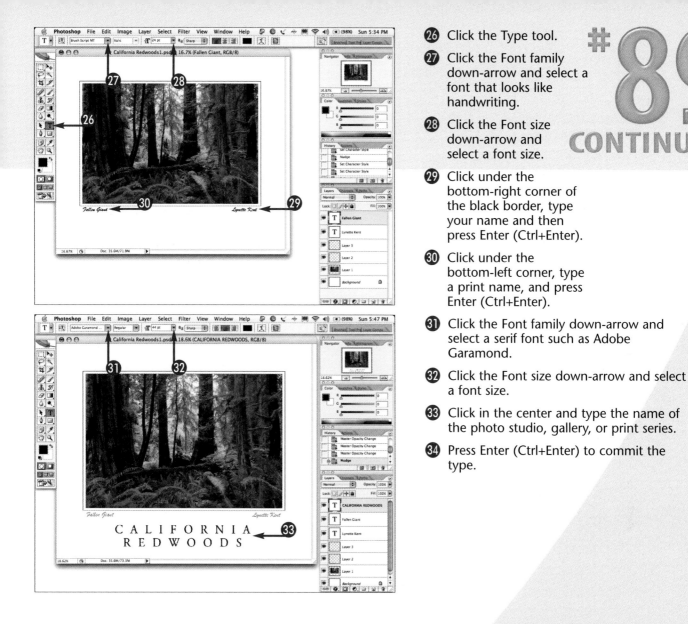

26 Click the Type tool.

27 Click the Font family down-arrow and select a font that looks like handwriting.

28 Click the Font size down-arrow and select a font size.

29 Click under the bottom-right corner of the black border, type your name and then press Enter (Ctrl+Enter).

30 Click under the bottom-left corner, type a print name, and press Enter (Ctrl+Enter).

31 Click the Font family down-arrow and select a serif font such as Adobe Garamond.

32 Click the Font size down-arrow and select a font size.

33 Click in the center and type the name of the photo studio, gallery, or print series.

34 Press Enter (Ctrl+Enter) to commit the type.

TIP

More Options!

The size of the stroke you apply to the borders depends on the size and resolution of the image. Use a thicker stroke for both the border of the photo and the outside border if the image is large or if you want to give the photo more of a framed look. You can also use different colors for the stroke for different effects. If the photo is light in color, try using a shade of gray to stroke the inner border instead of black. Because each stroke border is on its own layer, you can also lower the opacity of the layer if the color of the stroke appears too bold.

Use picture package for an
ADVERTISING LAYOUT

The Picture Package command helps photographers prepare multiple copies of an image on one page. You can also use this command to create a flexible design for a mailing piece or a portfolio presentation by customizing the layout or creating new layouts. This task, inspired by the inimitable Russell Brown, creative director at Adobe Systems, allows you to create a design that you can reuse with different photographs. You can quickly change a Picture Package into a portfolio or advertising piece for

different clients. Start with a background image, such as a page of letterhead or other layout with the logo or name of the company. Set the desired size of the piece and clear the layout of any existing Image Zones. An Image Zone is a placeholder for the photographs or other images that you add to the final piece. Start adding Image Zones for your design and move them into place. When the layout is complete, click Save to save your custom layout as a TXT file in Photoshop's Layouts folder in the Presets folder.

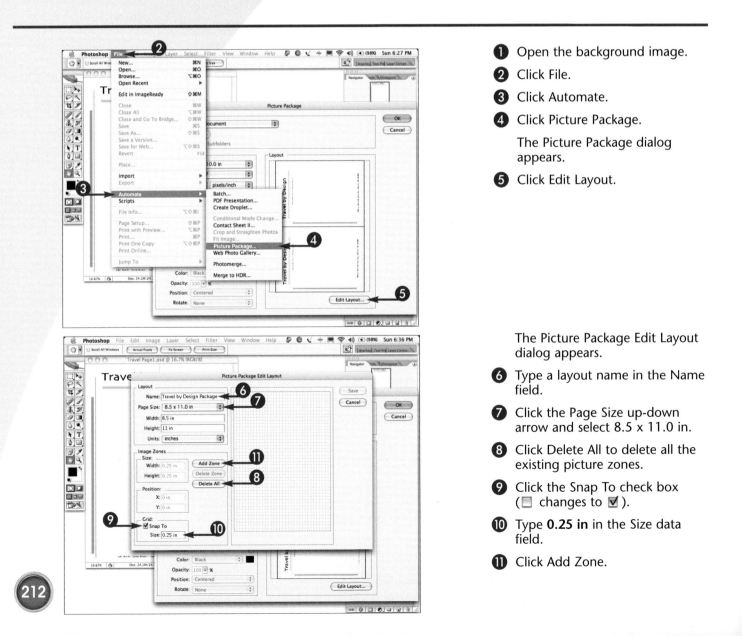

① Open the background image.

② Click File.

③ Click Automate.

④ Click Picture Package.

The Picture Package dialog appears.

⑤ Click Edit Layout.

The Picture Package Edit Layout dialog appears.

⑥ Type a layout name in the Name field.

⑦ Click the Page Size up-down arrow and select 8.5 x 11.0 in.

⑧ Click Delete All to delete all the existing picture zones.

⑨ Click the Snap To check box (☐ changes to ☑).

⑩ Type **0.25 in** in the Size data field.

⑪ Click Add Zone.

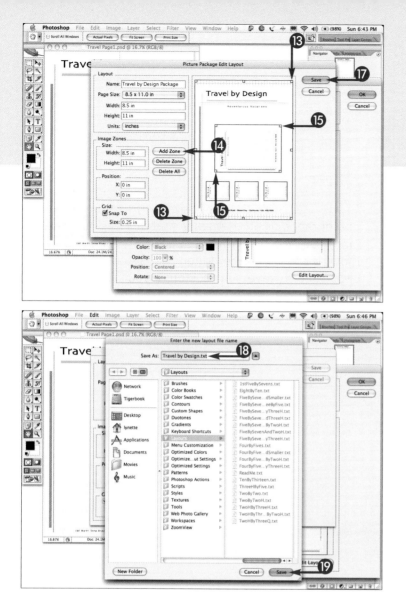

⑫ Click in the zone to select it.

⑬ Click and drag on the corner anchors to make it fit the space.

⑭ Click Add Zone again and position the zone for the first photograph.

⑮ Click and drag on the corner anchors of the new zone to resize it to fit the design.

⑯ Repeat Steps **14** to **15** to add additional photograph zones.

⑰ Click Save.

A dialog appears to save the layout.

⑱ Type the name of the new layout leaving the extension as .txt.

⑲ Click Save.

TIPS

Important!

Move the Image Zones and resize them for the type of images you intend to use. The shape of the Image Zone determines the orientation of the image. If the zone is a horizontal box, a horizontal image is placed appropriately in the zone. A vertical image is rotated counterclockwise when placed in a horizontal Image Zone.

Did You Know?

When you need more than one zone of the same size, you can create the first zone and duplicate it. Press Option (Alt) and click the first zone. Click Duplicate from the menu that appears. The duplicate zone will be in the top-left corner of your layout. Click and drag it into position on the layout.

Use picture package for an
ADVERTISING LAYOUT

You can resize the images any way you want to fit your design. Selecting the Snap To Grid option helps you line up the zones for a clean look. Set the grid to the minimum size of 0.25 inches to have the most flexibility when placing the Image Zones with the Snap To Grid feature turned on. To set a zone to a specific size, click Add Zone and click the new zone in the dialog. Click and drag the corner anchors until the width and height are close to the desired size. Then type the exact numbers in the size data fields

and press Tab after each entry to apply the dimensions to the zone.

Deselect the Flatten All Layers option in the Picture Package layout dialog to keep all the layers intact when Photoshop builds the page. You can then add Layer Styles or other layer changes to each layer individually. If you do not plan to add any Layer Styles, leave the Flatten All Layers check box selected. The finished file is much smaller.

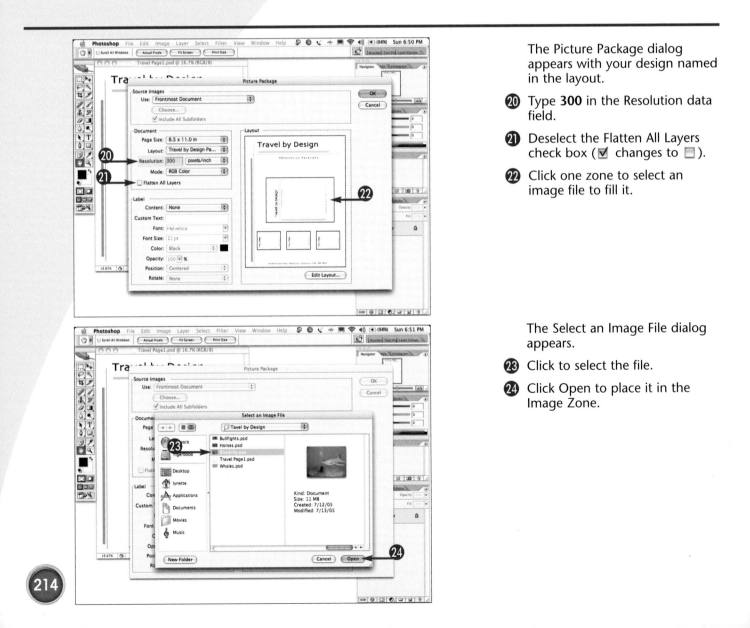

The Picture Package dialog appears with your design named in the layout.

⑳ Type **300** in the Resolution data field.

㉑ Deselect the Flatten All Layers check box (☑ changes to ☐).

㉒ Click one zone to select an image file to fill it.

The Select an Image File dialog appears.

㉓ Click to select the file.

㉔ Click Open to place it in the Image Zone.

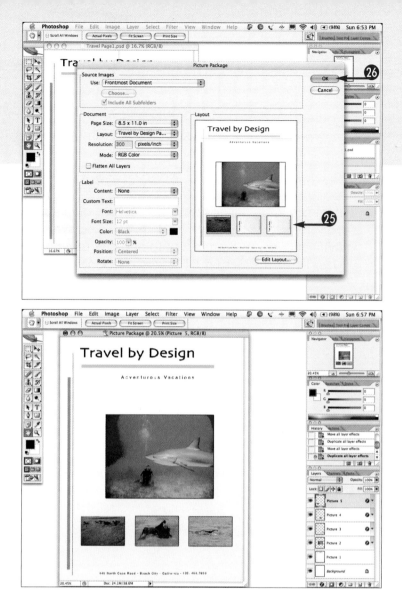

The Picture Package dialog reappears with the selected photo in the first zone.

㉕ Repeat Steps **22** to **24** to fill the other zones with images.

㉖ Click OK to apply the Picture Package.

90 CONTINUED

Photoshop builds the page.

TIPS

More Options!
Add a Layer Style to the photographs. Click a photo layer in the Layers palette. Click the Add a Layer Style icon and click Drop Shadow. Adjust the sliders to create the drop shadow. Click the word Stroke to open that style. Click the color thumbnail and set it to black. Click OK to apply the style.

Try This!
You can copy the Layer Style from one photo layer to the others to have them all match. Press and hold Option (Alt) as you click and drag the Layer Style icon from the first layer to the line just below the next photo layer. The Layer Style with all its attributes is added to the next photo.

Chapter 10

Plugging In to Photoshop CS2

Photoshop CS2 includes a variety of different brushes and shapes, and comes with the Bridge application for organizing and viewing images. You can make color adjustments, add edges, reduce noise, and sharpen all with the built-in filters. However, many third-party plug-ins can make improving your images quick and easy. Some have features and functionality that can make digital enhancements even better than you can do with Photoshop alone.

Plug-ins exist for nearly every project and for every user level. With the imaginative brush sets and edges from Graphicxtras and Graphic Authority you can easily make backgrounds, add edges, and even digitally age a photograph. Andromeda's many filters allow you to change a photograph into an engraving while visually controlling every line and direction. Eye Candy from Alien Skin allows you to quickly create realistic glass, chrome, perspective shadows, and more. Use AutoFX filters to easily add a little magic to your colors. Whether you are a professional or a hobbyist, using nik multimedia's Sharpener Pro and Dfine to sharpen and reduce noise removes the guesswork from Photoshop's filters. For the ultimate control over your colors, nik multimedia's Color Efex Pro 2 provides the optimal photographic enhancements and makes it easy to create professional-looking images. Portfolio 7 can help you organize, categorize, archive, and find your digital images from the time you first upload them to the computer through storing them on external media.

Third-party plug-ins can enhance the way everyone uses Photoshop.

CREATE MAGICAL BACKGROUNDS
with Graphicxtras brushes

The Graphicxtras brush collections from Abneil Software provide 10,000 brushes in native Photoshop form (ABR). The brushes are in separate themed sets with names like Stars, Wispy, Blurred, and Pencil Sketch, and can be used with any of Photoshop's brush tools in both 8- and 16-bit color modes. Copy the brush sets onto your hard drive and use them like any other brush, or use them at the large sizes for creating an inexhaustible variety of

original frames and backgrounds. You can click and drag small brushes to create everything from traditional-looking pencil marks to wild paintbrush strokes. On the other hand, you can use the brushes at the largest sizes and just click to create patterns and shapes.

You can find other plug-ins, including unique frames and gradients, at www.Graphicxtras.com.

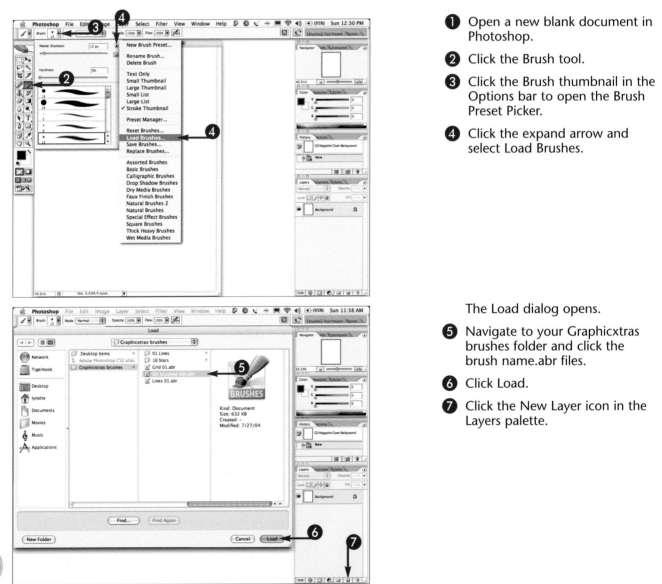

1. Open a new blank document in Photoshop.

2. Click the Brush tool.

3. Click the Brush thumbnail in the Options bar to open the Brush Preset Picker.

4. Click the expand arrow and select Load Brushes.

The Load dialog opens.

5. Navigate to your Graphicxtras brushes folder and click the brush name.abr files.

6. Click Load.

7. Click the New Layer icon in the Layers palette.

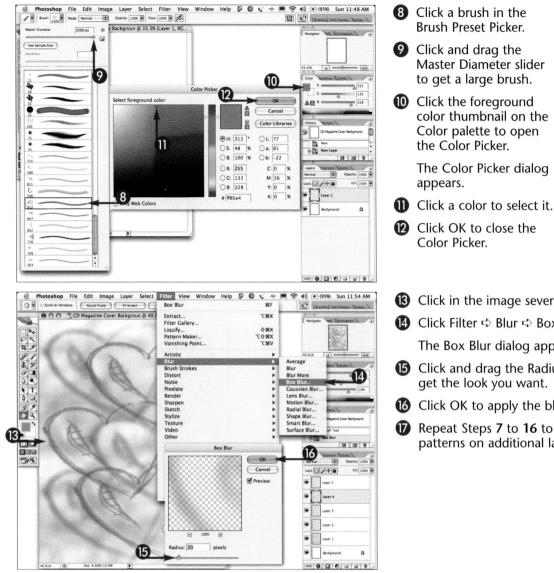

⑧ Click a brush in the Brush Preset Picker.

⑨ Click and drag the Master Diameter slider to get a large brush.

⑩ Click the foreground color thumbnail on the Color palette to open the Color Picker.

The Color Picker dialog appears.

⑪ Click a color to select it.

⑫ Click OK to close the Color Picker.

⑬ Click in the image several times.

⑭ Click Filter ➪ Blur ➪ Box Blur.

The Box Blur dialog appears.

⑮ Click and drag the Radius slider to get the look you want.

⑯ Click OK to apply the blur.

⑰ Repeat Steps 7 to 16 to create more patterns on additional layers.

TIPS

Important!

Copy the Graphicxtras brushes into a separate folder on your hard drive and load only the sets you want when you want to use them to reduce Photoshop's need for memory. In addition, by keeping the brushes in a separate folder out of the main brush folder, you will not have to reinstall the brushes if you have to reinstall Photoshop.

Try This!

Create and save your own brush set. Load the full sets you want. Press Option and click on a brush in the Brush Preset Picker to delete it. When you have only your particular favorites in the Preset menu, click the down-arrow and select Save Brushes. Save your set in a folder on your hard drive.

MAKE A DIGITAL ENGRAVING
with Andromeda's Cutline Filter

Andromeda Software makes a number of Photoshop plug-ins, including the Cutline filter, which applies high-quality engraved or woodcut effects to an image quickly and easily. The Cutline filter does all the work and allows you to select one of four different screening styles, from straight to wavy elliptical cutlines. You can set the position, curvature, and angle of the lines, and you can apply the effects selectively to the highlights, midtones, or shadows in the image. You can use a color or grayscale image and apply the effects to the entire image or just to a

selection. By applying the filter to a duplicated Background layer of a colored image, the filter changes that layer into a black-and-white engraving. You can use the traditional engraving or get a very different result by setting the layer blend mode to Overlay. The color from the original image in the layer underneath shows through for a unique effect.

You can find more plug-ins that can help you create a myriad of varied photographic, graphic design, and screening effects at Andromeda.com.

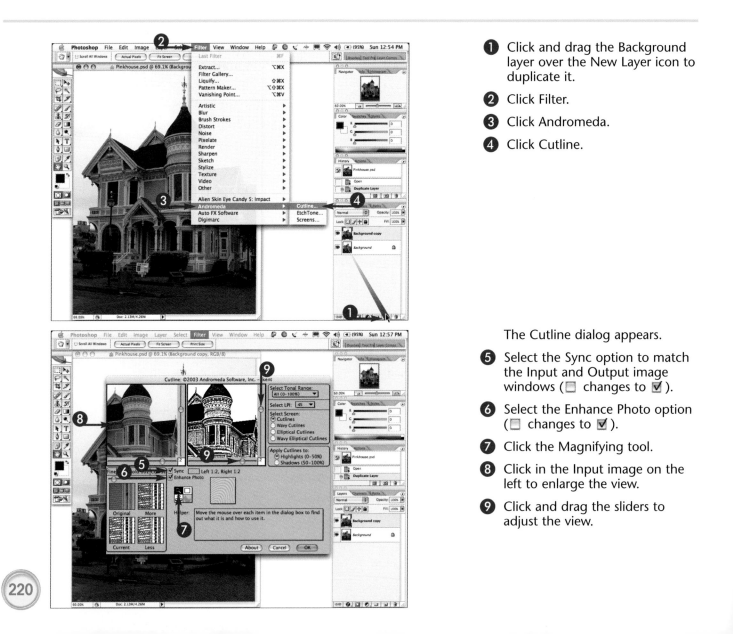

1 Click and drag the Background layer over the New Layer icon to duplicate it.

2 Click Filter.

3 Click Andromeda.

4 Click Cutline.

The Cutline dialog appears.

5 Select the Sync option to match the Input and Output image windows (☐ changes to ☑).

6 Select the Enhance Photo option (☐ changes to ☑).

7 Click the Magnifying tool.

8 Click in the Input image on the left to enlarge the view.

9 Click and drag the sliders to adjust the view.

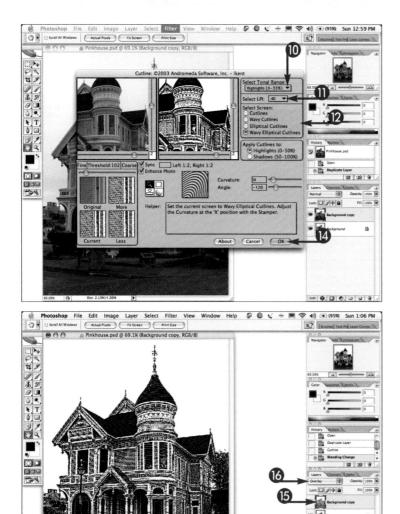

#92

DIFFICULTY LEVEL

⑩ Click the Select Tonal Range down-arrow and select the range for the first filter.

⑪ Click the Select LPI down-arrow to change the number of lines per inch.

⑫ Select one of the Screen style options (○ changes to ●).

⑬ Repeat Steps **10** to **12** for the other tonal ranges, if desired.

⑭ Click OK.

The Cutline filter applies an engraved look to the image.

⑮ Click the Background copy layer.

⑯ Click the blending mode up-down arrow and click Overlay.

TIPS

Did You Know?

When you select the Enhance Photo option (☐ changes to ☑), the Cutline Filter applies an Unsharp Mask to the image before it applies the screening filter and produces a sharper engraved look. Selecting the Sync option (☐ changes to ☑) allows you to preview the same areas in the thumbnails of the Input and Output images as you zoom.

Try This!

Click the More or Less thumbnails for the Threshold in the filter to increase or reduce the darkness of the lines. If the Threshold slider is set to Fine, clicking on the thumbnails changes the threshold by lower amounts each time you click. Setting the Threshold slider to Coarse causes the changes to vary by greater numbers with each click.

EXPLORE COLORS VISUALLY
with AutoFX software

The colors in your images can express moods and messages that transcend the subject matter. You can change how an image is perceived by varying the colors in Photoshop. However, using software plug-in filters such as Mystical Tint, Tone, and Color from AutoFX Software can help you explore color tones and enhance your images visually and easily. Mystical Tint Tone and Color is actually a package of 38 editing effects. You can apply these effects as global changes or you can brush over the specific areas of colors and tones you want to change. You can try the

Layer Presets from a visual gallery or try any number of the individual Special Effects, experiment with various settings, and watch the results in a large display. You can also combine multiple effects and still control the settings for each one until you see the results you want before applying the filters to the image. The following task uses only two of the effects to enhance the photograph.

On the gallery pages at AutoFx.com you can find other visual imaging solutions for creative effects.

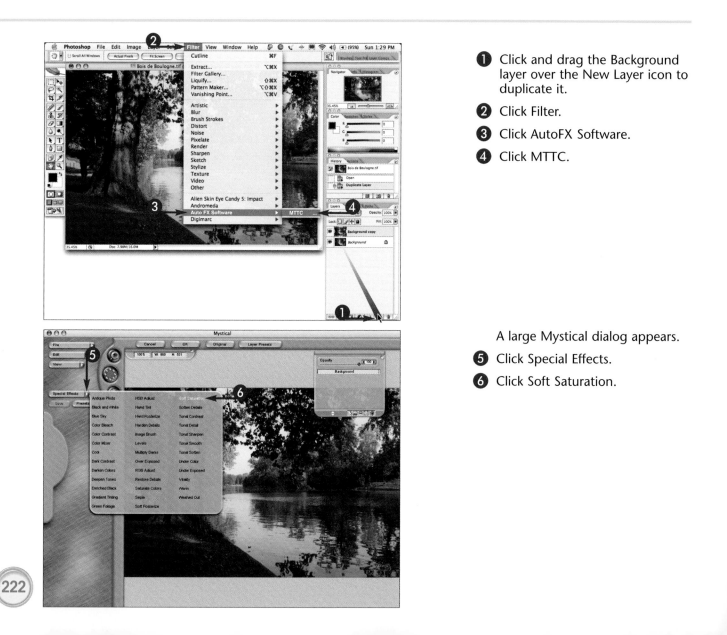

① Click and drag the Background layer over the New Layer icon to duplicate it.

② Click Filter.

③ Click AutoFX Software.

④ Click MTTC.

A large Mystical dialog appears.

⑤ Click Special Effects.

⑥ Click Soft Saturation.

The Soft Saturation controls appear.

⑦ Click and drag the Saturation slider to the right to increase the saturation.

⑧ Click Special Effects again.

⑨ Click Over Exposed.

 # 93

DIFFICULTY LEVEL

The Over Exposed controls appear.

⑩ Click and drag the Exposure slider to lighten the overall image.

⑪ Click Mode and select Brush On.

The overall effect reverts to the previous look.

⑫ Click the Brush icon.

⑬ Click the Brush Size Controls and drag the bottom slider to increase the brush size.

⑭ Click and drag in the image drawing over dark areas to lighten them.

⑮ Click OK to apply the filters and return to the Photoshop environment.

Did You Know?
You can add multiple effects on various layers by clicking Special Effects and selecting different filters each time. You can use the floating layers palette in the Mystical dialog to delete effect layers or even to add others.

Try This!
Apply an effect in the Global mode. Click the Eraser icon in the dialog. Change the Size, Feathering, and Opacity using the sliders in the thumbnail below the Eraser. Click and drag in the image to remove the effect in specific areas.

More Options!
Click the View down-arrow in the Mystical dialog and select Fit in Window. You can also use the Zoom tool to view specific areas as you add the effects. Press Option (Alt) and click the Zoom tool to zoom out.

CREATE INSTANT CHROME AND GLASS
with Alien Skin's Eye Candy

Adding the look of chrome to text or other objects on a page can illuminate any design. Creating gel-styled buttons or glassy text adds a modern look to Web pages and other projects. You can create these effects with Photoshop. However, using the third-party plug-ins from Alien Skin Software allows you to click a button to get the look you want quickly and easily. You can start with the factory settings and apply variations, or start completely from scratch to create your own effects. You can type the text or you

can use any tools to create a shape. When you select Alien Skin Eye Candy 5 from the Filter menu, you can choose any type of effect listed in the next menu. The Alien Skin dialog appears with another myriad of different choices for each effect. You can visually try any setting to see the result until you find the one you want. You can even customize an effect and save it for future applications. You will find many other filters at www.Alienskin.com.

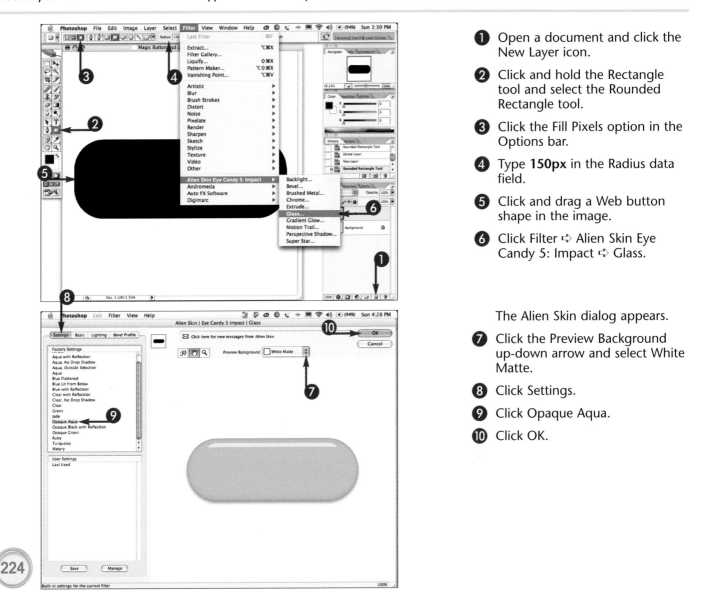

① Open a document and click the New Layer icon.

② Click and hold the Rectangle tool and select the Rounded Rectangle tool.

③ Click the Fill Pixels option in the Options bar.

④ Type **150px** in the Radius data field.

⑤ Click and drag a Web button shape in the image.

⑥ Click Filter ➪ Alien Skin Eye Candy 5: Impact ➪ Glass.

The Alien Skin dialog appears.

⑦ Click the Preview Background up-down arrow and select White Matte.

⑧ Click Settings.

⑨ Click Opaque Aqua.

⑩ Click OK.

The filter is applied to the layer.

⑪ Click the Type tool.

⑫ Click to select the Font family and size in the Options bar.

⑬ Type the text on the button and click the Commit button.

⑭ Click Filter ➪ Alien Skin Eye Candy 5: Impact ➪ Chrome.

A dialog appears to Rasterize the Type layer.

⑮ Click OK.

The Alien Skin dialog reappears.

⑯ Click Settings.

⑰ Click Rippled Edge.

⑱ Click OK to apply the filter.

![TIPS]

Did You Know?
Alien Skin filters ask you to Rasterize any Type layer or vector shape. The filter then places a layer above the rasterized layer. You can delete the original layer after the filter is finished or leave it for contrast.

Try This!
By default, Alien Skin's Preview Background is transparent showing a gray and white checkerboard. Click the Preview Background up-down arrow and select a solid-colored matte before you select settings, so you can clearly see how the effect will look.

More Options!
Apply different effects to different layers. Drag one layer over the other in the image. You can also add a layer style such as a drop shadow by clicking the Add a Layer Style icon in the Layers palette.

ADD A CUSTOM EDGE EFFORTLESSLY
with Graphic Authority's Extreme Edges

You can easily add a custom edge to give any photograph a professional or artistic style using Graphic Authority's Extreme Edges collections. You can make your photographs look like filmstrips and old transfers with the Film Effects Edges or you can make your image appear to be painted onto the page with the Artistic Brush Strokes Edges. Graphic Authority's Extreme Edges are a quick solution to add a custom look to any image. You can also scale, skew, twist, and rotate the high-resolution edges to create infinite possibilities. You can paste a photo into the edge or, for a very different look, create a clipping mask with the photo above it. The edge appears as part of the photograph itself.

You can open any of the edges and customize them with the Free Transform command to fit your image. You can also add layer styles, creating a unique and artistic piece. GraphicAuthority.com also offers imaginative Aging Brushes as well as Photoshop training CDs.

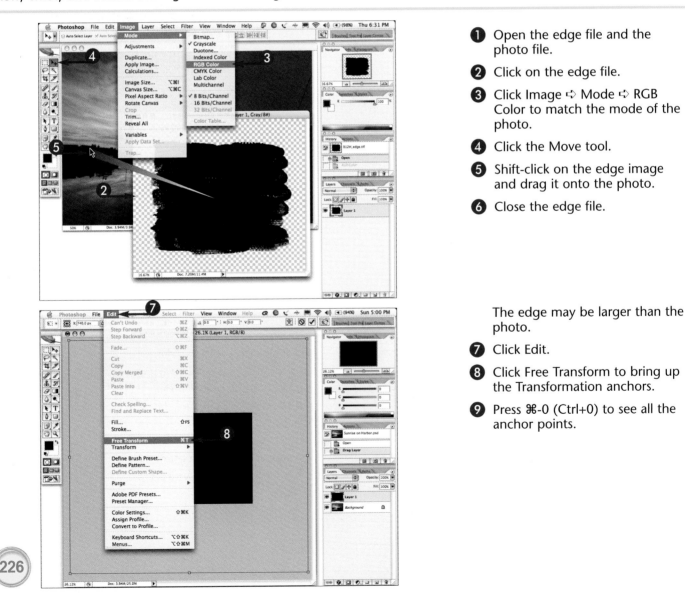

① Open the edge file and the photo file.

② Click on the edge file.

③ Click Image ➪ Mode ➪ RGB Color to match the mode of the photo.

④ Click the Move tool.

⑤ Shift-click on the edge image and drag it onto the photo.

⑥ Close the edge file.

The edge may be larger than the photo.

⑦ Click Edit.

⑧ Click Free Transform to bring up the Transformation anchors.

⑨ Press ⌘-0 (Ctrl+0) to see all the anchor points.

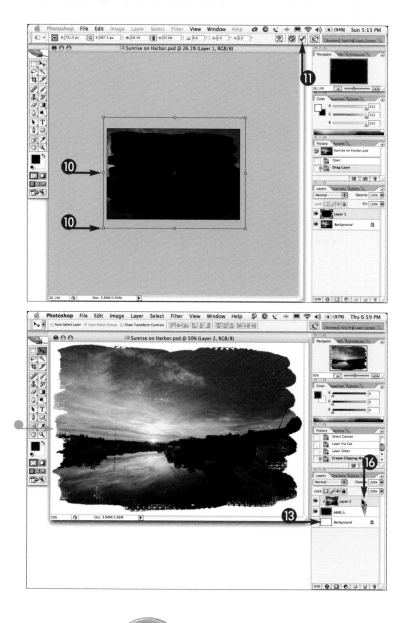

⑩ Click and drag on the anchors to make the edge fit on the photo.

⑪ Click the Commit button to commit the transformation.

⑫ Press ⌘-0 (Ctrl+0) to make the image fit the screen.

⑬ Click the Background layer.

⑭ Press ⌘-A (Ctrl+A) to select the photo.

⑮ Press ⌘-Shift-J (Ctrl+Shift+J) to jump the photo to its own layer.

⑯ Click and drag the photo layer above the edge layer in the Layers palette.

⑰ Press ⌘-Option-G (Ctrl+Alt+G) to create the clipping mask.

● The photo now has a custom edge.

TIPS

Did You Know?
You can adjust the edges layer even with the clipping mask applied. Click on the edge layer and press ⌘-T (Ctrl+T) to bring up the Transformation anchors. Press ⌘-0 (Ctrl+0) to see the anchors if necessary. Click and drag on the anchor points until the edges look the way you want.

Try This!
Add a layer style such as a drop shadow to the edge layer to make it stand out more. Click on the edge layer to target it. Click the Add a Layer Style icon in the Layers palette. Click Drop Shadow. Click and drag the various sliders to get the look you want. Click OK to apply the style.

CONTROL DIGITAL NOISE
with nik Dfine

Digital noise is inherent in digital photographs and appears as details that should not be in the image. Digital noise in an image can be seen as bright, colored specks called chrominance noise, while small, dark spots that often look like film grain are called luminance noise. Various factors can affect or create noise, including the light, length of exposure, and temperature when the photo is taken, as well as the peculiarities of individual cameras and sensors. Although you can reduce digital noise in a general manner with the built-in filter in Photoshop CS2, using nik Dfine enables you to control how you

reduce the noise and optimize the detail. Dfine reduces luminance noise, chrominance noise, and JPG artifacts; improves contrast; and adjusts colorcasts while taking into account the effects of the noise reduction. You can even apply the very effective presets. The multiple preview screens and histograms enable you to see the improvements as you try them. nik multimedia, Inc, also makes optional custom camera profiles for various digital camera models, making noise reduction even more simple and effective. You will find these products at www.nikmultimedia.com.

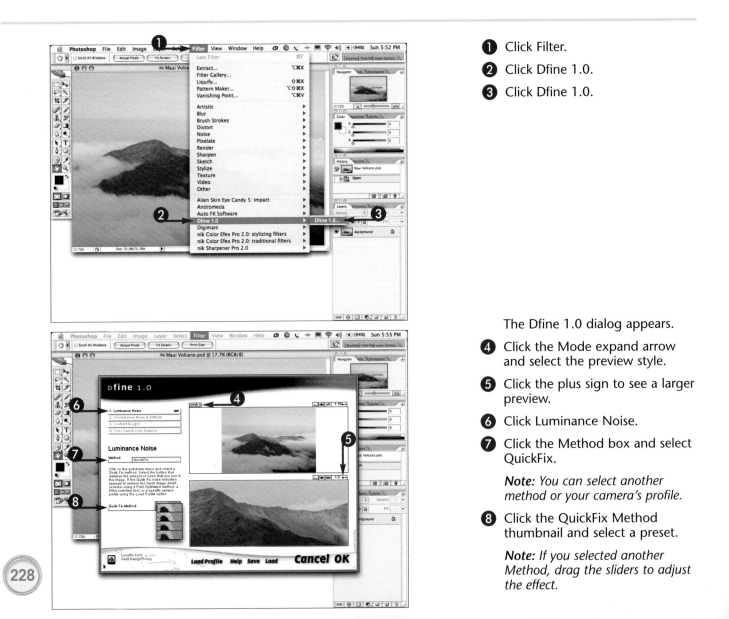

❶ Click Filter.

❷ Click Dfine 1.0.

❸ Click Dfine 1.0.

The Dfine 1.0 dialog appears.

❹ Click the Mode expand arrow and select the preview style.

❺ Click the plus sign to see a larger preview.

❻ Click Luminance Noise.

❼ Click the Method box and select QuickFix.

Note: You can select another method or your camera's profile.

❽ Click the QuickFix Method thumbnail and select a preset.

Note: If you selected another Method, drag the sliders to adjust the effect.

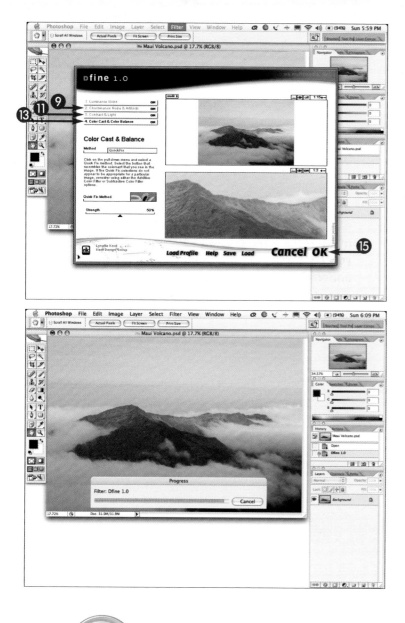

9 Click Chrominance Noise & Artifacts.

10 Repeat Steps 7 to 8.

11 Click Contrast & Light.

12 Repeat Steps 7 to 8.

13 Click Color Cast & Color Balance.

14 Repeat Steps 7 to 8.

15 Click OK.

DIFFICULTY LEVEL

nik Dfine applies the specific noise reduction to the image.

TIPS

Did You Know?

You can use Dfine Selective to reduce noise in specific areas. Click File ⇨ Automate ⇨ Dfine Selective. Click the style of noise reduction you want from the ten choices. Click Paint and click in the image where the noise reduction is needed. Click Apply. Use a pressure-sensitive tablet and stylus such as a Wacom Intuos or Cintiq for even more control.

Try This!

You can purchase and load specific camera profiles electronically through the Internet by clicking the Load Profile button and clicking Get Profile from Web. Once a profile is integrated into Dfine, it can be loaded by clicking the Load Profile button and clicking Load From Disk. The camera profile becomes an option under the Luminance Noise feature.

SHARPEN PHOTOS
with finesse using nik Sharpener Pro 2

Sharpening is an essential step in digital imaging. Photoshop's built-in filters base the sharpening on the screen image. To get optimal image sharpening, use Sharpener Pro 2.0 from nik multimedia, Inc. Sharpener Pro analyzes the image and sharpens according to the type of detail in the image, the type and resolution of the printer, the planned media for the print, as well as the intended viewing distance of the final print. You can compare the before and after images in the large preview in the dialog before applying the filter. nik Sharpener Pro 2.0 includes

specific sharpening settings for many of the inkjet printers on the market.

Sharpening should be the final step in the editing process to avoid introducing unwanted details in the image. Because most digital photos need some sharpening, it may be difficult to judge the quality of the image until sharpening is applied. Sharpener Pro 2.0 includes a Raw Presharpening filter to slightly sharpen Raw image files at the beginning of the editing process without introducing sharpening artifacts.

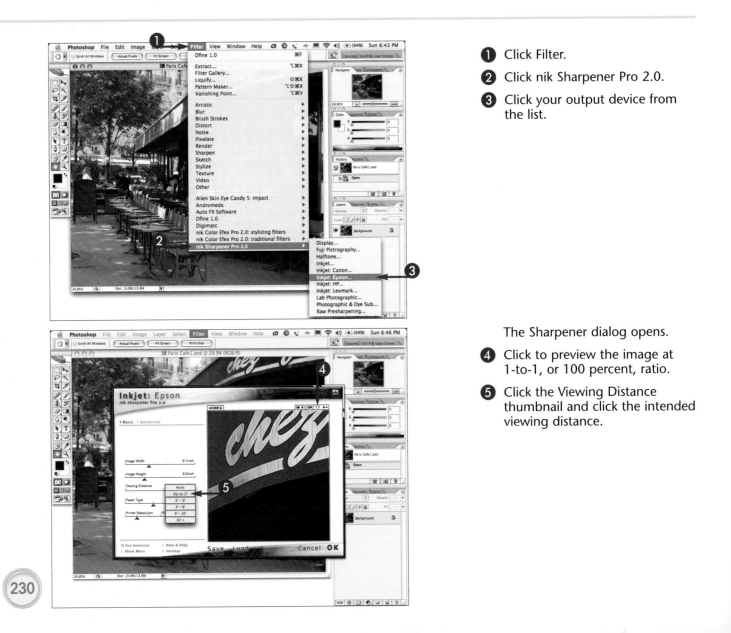

① Click Filter.

② Click nik Sharpener Pro 2.0.

③ Click your output device from the list.

The Sharpener dialog opens.

④ Click to preview the image at 1-to-1, or 100 percent, ratio.

⑤ Click the Viewing Distance thumbnail and click the intended viewing distance.

6 Click and drag the Paper Type slider to select the media.

7 Click and drag the Printer Resolution to match your printer's resolution.

8 Click Use Autoscan to enable Sharpener Pro to automatically adapt to the specific image.

9 Click OK.

Sharpener Pro 2.0 applies the correct amount of sharpening according to the settings.

TIPS

Important!

The order in which you apply image enhancements affects the quality of the final print. Apply noise reduction first, if necessary. Then apply the nik Raw Presharpening filter. Adjust the image for tone and color, and resize the image. Save the image. Apply nik Sharpener Pro 2.0 just before printing, based upon the printer, media, and intended viewing distance.

More Options!

You can apply sharpening to selected areas using the Sharpener Pro 2.0 Selective tool. Click ➪ Automate ➪ nik Sharpener Pro 2.0 selective. Click the filter in the nik Sharpener Pro 2.0 Selective palette that matches the intended output, adjust the settings, and click OK. Click Paint and click and drag in the image. Click Apply to apply the selective sharpening.

APPLY TRADITIONAL PHOTO FILTERS
to a digital image

Professional photographers often carry a selection of lens filters and light reflectors to take advantage of every lighting condition they might encounter. You can achieve similar effects using Color Efex Pro 2.0 from nik multimedia. nik filters can help you enhance images better than using Photoshop alone. Based on photographic filter technology, these filters consider the existing color and light in an image and adapt the effect accordingly. The filters can adapt to any previous adjustments in the photo so you can apply

multiple filters in a different order and get more natural photographic enhancements. You can use any of the Color Efex Pro filters and customize the settings to control the light and color in your digital images. You can even save your settings to apply them to a range of photos for a consistent workflow and increased productivity. The Sunshine filter is just one of the many traditional styled filters. It transforms the grayed colors from a photo shot on an overcast day into a bright colorful scene, yet in a very natural way.

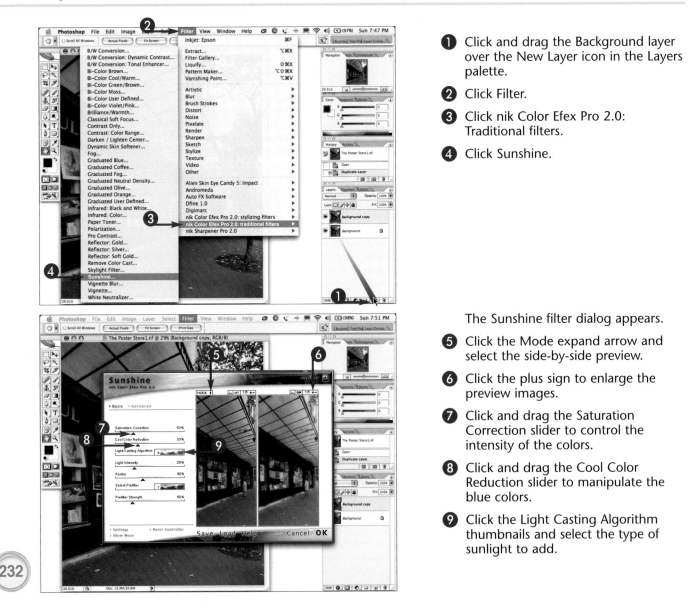

① Click and drag the Background layer over the New Layer icon in the Layers palette.

② Click Filter.

③ Click nik Color Efex Pro 2.0: Traditional filters.

④ Click Sunshine.

The Sunshine filter dialog appears.

⑤ Click the Mode expand arrow and select the side-by-side preview.

⑥ Click the plus sign to enlarge the preview images.

⑦ Click and drag the Saturation Correction slider to control the intensity of the colors.

⑧ Click and drag the Cool Color Reduction slider to manipulate the blue colors.

⑨ Click the Light Casting Algorithm thumbnails and select the type of sunlight to add.

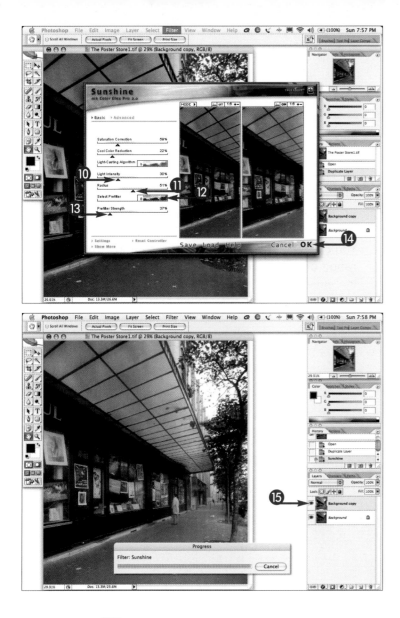

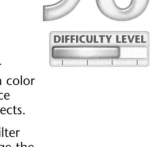

98

DIFFICULTY LEVEL

⓾ Click and drag the Light Intensity slider to control the amount of added light.

⓫ Click and drag the Radius slider to control the increased detail smoothing.

⓬ Click the Select Prefilter thumbnails and select a color contrast filter to enhance different colors and objects.

⓭ Click and drag the Prefilter Strength slider to change the amount of the prefilter added to the image.

⓮ Click OK.

Color Efex Pro applies the filter to the image.

⓯ Click the Visibility icon for the Background copy layer on and off to see the changes.

TIPS

Did You Know?

Color Efex Pro 2.0 includes traditional Reflector filters, Infrared conversions, and Cross Processing filters, as well as a Selective tool with the filters on a separate floating palette. Use the Selective palette to apply any of the filters with a paintbrush to control the location and amount of the effect. Use a pressure-sensitive tablet and stylus for even greater control.

Try This!

For black-and-white conversions, use the B/W Conversion: Tonal Enhancer instead of the B/W conversion filter. Select the Contrast Method by clicking one of the three thumbnails to change the tonality in the final black-and-white image. Adjust the Brightness and Contrast sliders. Then move the Spectrum slider to select the colors to be lightened in the conversion.

ADD ARTISTIC FLAIR
with stylizing filters

You can use nik multimedia's Color Efex Pro 2.0 filters to enhance the colors and style of your photographs and create artistic or abstract effects.

The Color Efex Pro filter collections include both traditional and stylizing filters. The traditional filters help you reproduce traditional lens effects from within Photoshop, while the stylizing filters help you add artistic interpretations to any image. The various collections of nik Color Efex Pro 2.0 include both types of filters. Stylizing filters such as Monday Morning or Midnight Sepia, which is shown in the task, allow you to change the mood of the photograph. Other filters such as Solarize and Pop Art help you transform your image into an abstract painting. After duplicating the Background layer, you can select from any of the Color Efex Pro Stylizing filters and use the sliders in the dialog to control the changes. You can see before and after results in the preview by selecting a different view mode or simply by clicking in the preview image to see the original and releasing the mouse to view the resulting image.

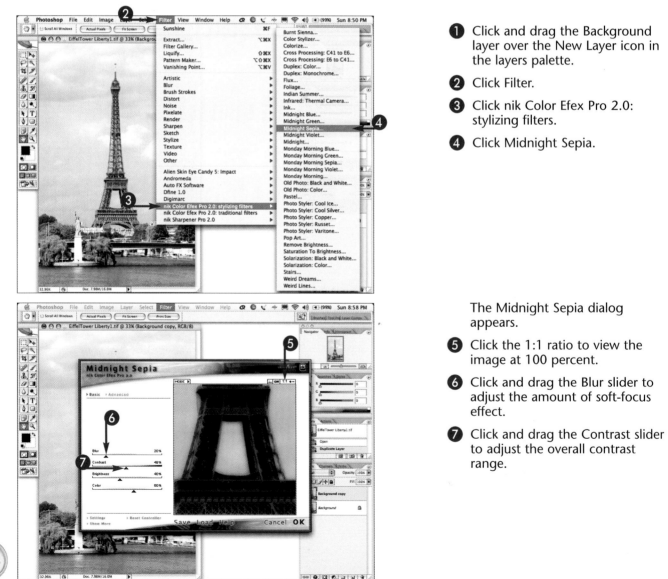

1 Click and drag the Background layer over the New Layer icon in the layers palette.

2 Click Filter.

3 Click nik Color Efex Pro 2.0: stylizing filters.

4 Click Midnight Sepia.

The Midnight Sepia dialog appears.

5 Click the 1:1 ratio to view the image at 100 percent.

6 Click and drag the Blur slider to adjust the amount of soft-focus effect.

7 Click and drag the Contrast slider to adjust the overall contrast range.

8 Click the minus sign to see more of the image.

9 Click and drag the Brightness slider to adjust the overall lightness.

10 Click and drag the Color slider to adjust the saturation of the original colors and the amount of colorcast that is applied.

11 Click OK.

99

DIFFICULTY LEVEL

The Midnight Sepia filter is applied to the image.

12 Click the Visibility icon for the Background copy layer on and off to compare the images.

TIPS

Customize It!

You can fade the filter effect with the Opacity slider for the layer. On the other hand, if you apply the filter to the Background layer, you can fade the effect immediately after applying it by clicking Edit ⇨ Fade Midnight Sepia. Use the Opacity slider in the dialog to reduce the effect. Use the Mode up-down arrow to change the blend mode of the filter.

Try This!

If Photoshop does not display all of your third-party plug-ins, install them into a separate folder you create and name inside the Photoshop application folder or even elsewhere on the hard drive. Launch Photoshop, click Photoshop (Edit) ⇨ Preferences ⇨ Plug-Ins & Scratch Disks. Click the Additional Plug-Ins Folder (☐ changes to ☑). Click Choose and navigate to select your new separate folder.

TRAVEL BEYOND THE BRIDGE
with Extensis Portfolio 7

Extensis Portfolio 7 is a unique tool that allows you to organize your files, share them in a variety of ways with clients or friends, and find them quickly whether they are stored on your computer or on any external drive, CD, or DVD. Because of its added functionality, Portfolio goes beyond the capabilities of the Bridge application included with Photoshop CS2, acting like a central hub for cataloging, archiving, tracking, sharing, and locating files. It can systemize your workflow or just help you archive and find your images. Use Portfolio to download your photos to

your computer, rename the files, and include any Exif or catalog data you want. Portfolio can even add thumbnails and screen previews to the database. Portfolio offers the option to burn a CD or DVD of the original images creating an archival copy from within the catalog dialog. Portfolio keeps track of your files in its powerful database and gives you a visual preview of the image wherever it is stored.

Portfolio offers many more advantages that you can find on the Extensis.com Web site.

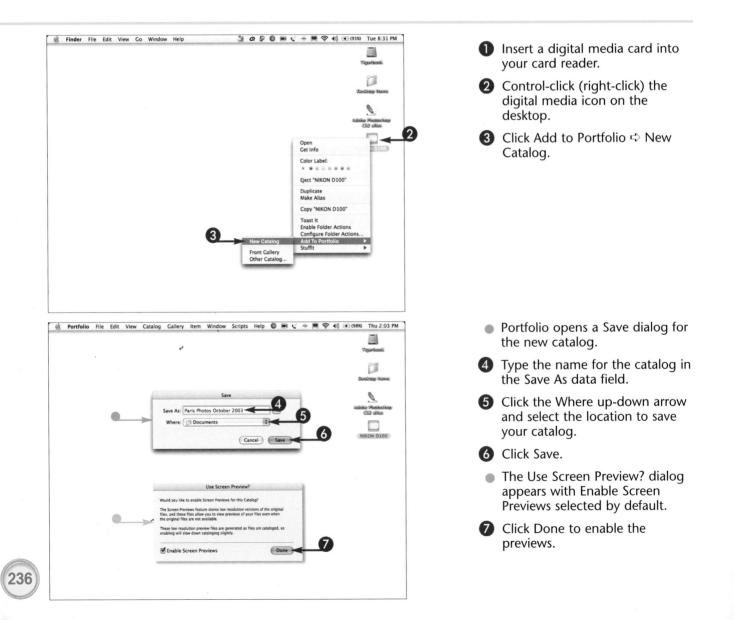

① Insert a digital media card into your card reader.

② Control-click (right-click) the digital media icon on the desktop.

③ Click Add to Portfolio ⇨ New Catalog.

● Portfolio opens a Save dialog for the new catalog.

④ Type the name for the catalog in the Save As data field.

⑤ Click the Where up-down arrow and select the location to save your catalog.

⑥ Click Save.

● The Use Screen Preview? dialog appears with Enable Screen Previews selected by default.

⑦ Click Done to enable the previews.

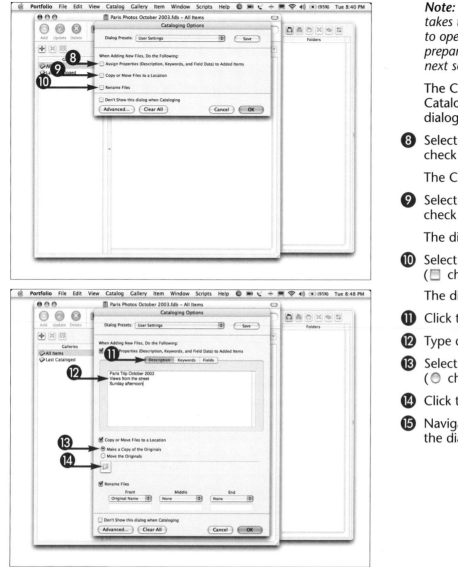

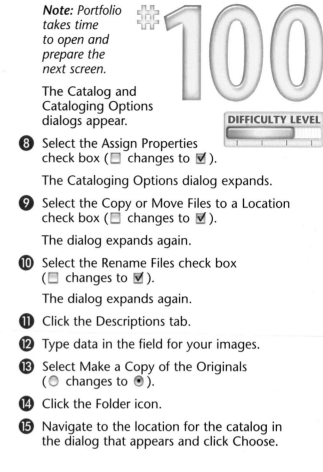

#100

DIFFICULTY LEVEL

Note: *Portfolio takes time to open and prepare the next screen.*

The Catalog and Cataloging Options dialogs appear.

⑧ Select the Assign Properties check box (☐ changes to ☑).

The Cataloging Options dialog expands.

⑨ Select the Copy or Move Files to a Location check box (☐ changes to ☑).

The dialog expands again.

⑩ Select the Rename Files check box (☐ changes to ☑).

The dialog expands again.

⑪ Click the Descriptions tab.

⑫ Type data in the field for your images.

⑬ Select Make a Copy of the Originals (○ changes to ◉).

⑭ Click the Folder icon.

⑮ Navigate to the location for the catalog in the dialog that appears and click Choose.

TIPS

Try This!

Burn a CD of the original images. Click Gallery and Burn to Disc. Click Original files, and Link Paths in Catalog to Files Burned to Disc (○ changes to ◉). Type a folder name. Click Create a Catalog and type the catalog name. Click the other empty check boxes (☐ changes to ☑) to include the Portfolio Browser applications on the CD, and click Burn.

More Options!

You can rotate JPEG images from portrait to landscape orientation or vice versa from within Portfolio without having to launch another program. Click on an image, or ⌘-click (Ctrl+click) any number of JPEG images to select them. Then Control-click (Right-click) to open the menu. Select the type of rotation to use. Portfolio rotates the image for you.

TRAVEL BEYOND THE BRIDGE
with Extensis Portfolio 7

The first step in using Portfolio is to catalog all your files. Portfolio can catalog almost any type of digital file. You can add individual file folders or complete volumes such as a CD or a hard drive by simply dragging the file, folder, or disk icon into an open catalog window. However, using the Instant Cataloging feature described in this task offers more options and control over the way Portfolio stores the information. By entering descriptions, keywords, or information in the custom fields, you can organize

your files more easily. You can then customize Portfolio to display images in galleries and to view images as thumbnails, lists, or individual items with all the stored data. To find a particular file, you can search with Portfolio's QuickFind, located on the Toolbar, using any words or phrase you entered when cataloging the file. You can also search using the Find command, and search for specific criteria associated with the file.

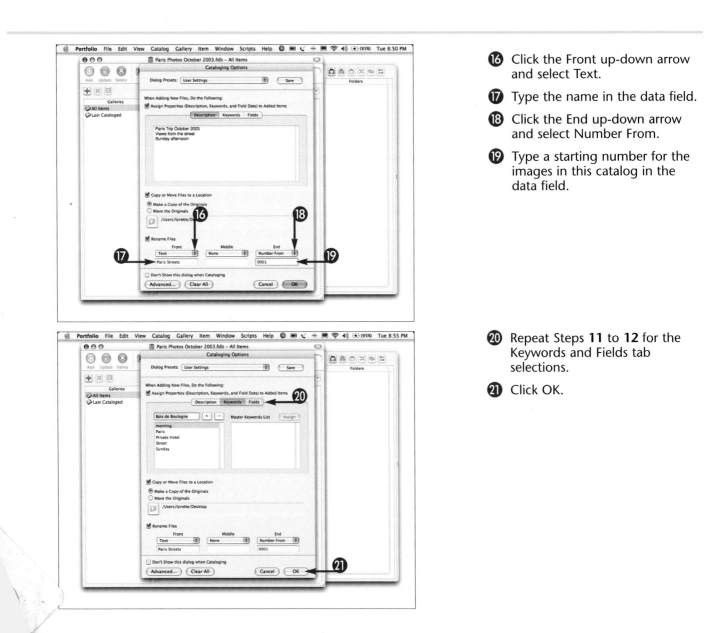

⑯ Click the Front up-down arrow and select Text.

⑰ Type the name in the data field.

⑱ Click the End up-down arrow and select Number From.

⑲ Type a starting number for the images in this catalog in the data field.

⑳ Repeat Steps **11** to **12** for the Keywords and Fields tab selections.

㉑ Click OK.

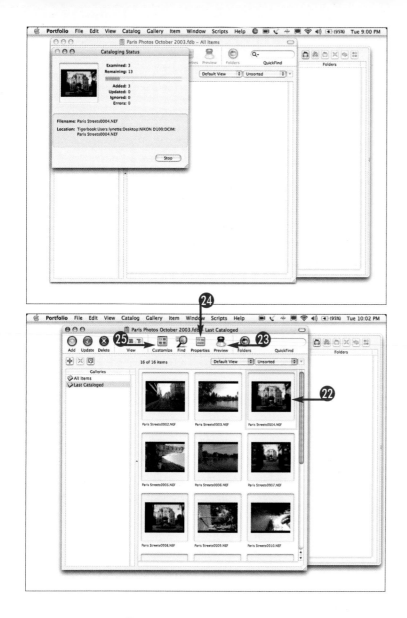

Portfolio opens a Cataloging Status dialog and a progress bar.

When the progress bar is complete, the Cataloging Status shows a thumbnail of each image as it is renamed and added to the new catalog.

Portfolio displays the new catalog on the screen.

㉒ Click one image thumbnail.

㉓ Click the Preview button to see it larger.

㉔ Click the Properties button to see the image data.

㉕ Click the Customize button to make changes to the catalog.

TIP

Did You Know?

Portfolio 7 includes a separate application called Portfolio Express that allows you to find cataloged files without launching the complete application. Once you launch Portfolio Express you can keep it running in the background and hide or show the palette using a Hot Key. The compact Portfolio Express palette floats above other document windows. Use the QuickFind feature from the palette to find a particular image and double click a thumbnail in the Portfolio Express palette to edit the original image. You can also drag and drop the thumbnail onto an alias (shortcut) of Photoshop to open it. You can even drag a thumbnail directly into an e-mail message to send a copy of the original file as an attachment.

Index

Index

Index

Index